THE TERRITORIAL DIMENSION IN GOVERNMENT

Also by Richard Rose
United Kingdom Facts, with Ian McAllister
Do Parties Make a Difference?
Can Government Go Bankrupt? with Guy Peters
What Is Governing? Purpose and Policy in Washington
Managing Presidential Objectives
Northern Ireland: A Time of Choice
The Problem of Party Government
International Almanac of Electoral History, with T.T. Mackie
Governing without Consensus: An Irish Perspective
People in Politics
Influencing Voters
Politics in England
Must Labour Lose? with Mark Abrams
The British General Election of 1959, with D.E. Butler

Edited by Richard Rose
The Territorial Dimension in United Kingdom Politics,
        with Peter Madgwick
Fiscal Stress in Cities, with Edward C. Page
Presidents and Prime Ministers, with Ezra Suleiman
Electoral Participation
Britain: Progress and Decline, with William B. Gwyn
Challenge to Governance
Elections without Choice, with Guy Hermet and Alain Rouquié
New Trends in British Politics, with Dennis Kavanagh
The Dynamics of Public Policy
Comparing Public Policies, with Jerzy Wiatr
The Management of Urban Change in Britain and Germany
Electoral Behavior: A Comparative Handbook
Lessons from America
European Politics, with Mattei Dogan
Policy-Making in Britain
Studies in British Politics

The Territorial
Dimension in Government

UNDERSTANDING THE
UNITED KINGDOM

RICHARD ROSE

Centre for the Study of Public Policy
University of Strathclyde

CHATHAM HOUSE PUBLISHERS, INC.
Chatham, New Jersey

THE TERRITORIAL DIMENSION IN GOVERNMENT
Understanding the United Kingdom

CHATHAM HOUSE PUBLISHERS, INC.
Post Office Box One
Chatham, New Jersey 07928

Simultaneously published as *Understanding the United Kingdom*
in the United Kingdom by Longman Group Limited

PUBLISHER: Edward Artinian
DESIGNER: Quentin Fiore
COMPOSITION: Chatham Composer
PRINTING AND BINDING: Hamilton Printing Company

LIBRARY OF CONGRESS CATALOGING IN PUBLICATION DATA

Rose, Richard, 1933-
    The Territorial Dimension in Government.

    Includes bibliographical references and index.
    1. Regionalism—Great Britain. 2. Great Britain—
Politics and government—1964-   . I. Title.
JN297.R44R67   1982   320.1'2'0941   82-9680
ISBN 0-934540-16-0 (pbk.)

MANUFACTURED IN THE UNITED STATES OF AMERICA

10   9   8   7   6   5   4   3   2   1

Acknowledgments

This book is short, but it has been a long time in the making. It started in 1953 with research about *Politics in England*. Seeking a fresh stimulus in 1965, I turned to researching Northern Ireland, writing two books about the least united part of the United Kingdom: *Governing without Consensus: An Irish Perspective* and *Northern Ireland: A Time of Choice*. This study also draws upon research about Scotland since moving there in 1966, and about Wales, conducted intermittently since 1968. It thus differs from many other books nominally dealing with the same subject because the author has consciously adopted a United Kingdom rather than a single-nation perspective on the government of the Crown.

In writing about a subject as vast and complex as the United Kingdom, any author must draw heavily upon the research of individuals who have specialized in the study of one of its multiple aspects. Laurence Pollock and Ian McAllister's *Bibliography of United Kingdom Politics* (1980) lists more than 2000 items, published and unpublished, of relevance to understanding the contemporary United Kingdom. In thinking through the ideas brought together here, I have benefited particularly from papers and discussions at the annual conferences of the Work Group on United Kingdom Politics, initiated in 1976 under the auspices of the Political Studies Association of the United Kingdom. Its aim has been to "deparochialize" the study of politics in all parts of the United Kingdom, including England. Within the group, Peter Madgwick has served with me as a congenial and knowledgeable co-convenor, and Jim Bulpitt has acted as a spokesman for England and the Imperial tradition. Major conclusions from the group's deliberations are set forth in Peter Madgwick and Richard Rose, eds., *The Territorial Dimension in United Kingdom Politics*.

The research reported here was supported by Social Science Research Council Grant HR 4689/1 for a study of the Political Structure of the United Kingdom. When the SSRC originally received my request for research support in 1976, there was some question whether there was need for research on the United Kingdom. I hope it finds this book a satisfactory answer. The Social Science Research Council also supported my initial research on Northern Ireland. It is sad to think how much the people of Northern Ireland have contributed by their travail to my understanding of the difficulties of exercising political authority.

During the years of preparing this study, the Centre for the Study of Public Policy at the University of Strathclyde has provided a congenial environment in which to develop a vocabulary to understand what we see each day — the territorial dimension in government. Upwards of one hundred *Studies in Public Policy* published by the Centre provide tangible evidence of the breadth and depth of this subject. Dr. Ian McAllister and Richard Parry served as research officers for the project. Each was ready to work hard, and has contributed significantly as an author or co-author of monographs cited here, as well as by finding information scattered across all parts of a Kingdom that is neither united nor consistent in its recordkeeping. The result of many searches is presented in a companion compendium, *United Kingdom Facts,* by Richard Rose and Ian McAllister.

Helpful comments were received about the manuscript, in whole or part, from John Archer, Vernon Bogdanor, Jim Bulpitt, Bernard Crick, Lord Fraser of Kilmorack, J.E.S. Hayward, David Heald, D. Hubback, J.G. Kellas, W.R. McKay, Peter Madgwick, E.C. Page, Phillip M. Rawkins, W. Reid, J.M. Ross, and Ian Thomas. Given the variety of views there are about the United Kingdom, it should be particularly emphasized that none of the persons or institutions named above necessarily endorses and certainly is not responsible for what follows. This book is solely my responsibility.

Once again, two Scots, Mrs. M. McGlone and Mrs. R. West, have made the task of thinking through this book much easier by taking in hand the burdens of keeping up with me, and June Roberts did a good job under pressure in typing the final draft of this manuscript.

RICHARD ROSE
University of Strathclyde

Contents

List of Tables

*Dedicated to my colleagues
in the Work Group on United Kingdom Politics*

THE TERRITORIAL DIMENSION IN GOVERNMENT

What know they of England
Who only England know?

Rudyard Kipling, *The English Flag*

Introduction:
In Search of the United Kingdom

The territorial dimension is inevitably important in any government larger than a postage stamp mini-state such as Liechtenstein or San Marino. To govern, rulers must make their authority felt throughout their domains. Historically, the first problem facing a king was the lack of means to preserve the peace or administer the kingdom's affairs. The king's household was the government as far as that extended, but it did not extend far. Feudalism evolved in order to extend the face-to-face authority of a monarch far beyond a royal court. In a democratic era federalism has given explicit constitutional recognition to the territorial dimension of government, as in the United States. In nonfederal countries such as the United Kingdom, there is no constitutional differentiation of territorial parts.

The territorial boundaries of a country pose a double challenge. First, a government wishes to defend these boundaries against foreign invasion. Equally, it wishes to provide effective government within its boundaries. The military balance between America and the Soviet Union has meant no change for years in the international boundaries of major Western nations. But a government can also face a challenge to its authority from within. In the 1970s the United Kingdom changed from a steady state to a fluid state in its territorial institutions of governance. Now it is best described as in an uncertain state, for governors and governed are of more than one mind about how the different parts of the United Kingdom can or should be governed.

Insofar as the United Kingdom is regarded as a single, homogeneous country, then the territorial dimension in government is of little or no political interest; it is a technical question of administration. Geography is often unthinkingly advanced as an argument demonstrating the presumed political homogeneity of Britain. In fact, geography argues against a homogeneous United Kingdom. The United Kingdom is not confined to a single island, nor is its principal island the home of only one nation. England shares its home island with Scotland and Wales. Nor does the United Kingdom any longer conform to the boundaries asserted as natural by Unionists prior to 1921, namely, a single Crown governing two offshore islands of Europe linked together by cross-channel traffic.[1] The present territory of the United Kingdom occupies one and one-sixth islands, an arrangement that cannot be easily explained by insular geography.

The spread of the mass media and standardized consumer products are also advanced as reasons why the people of all parts of the United Kingdom should be alike. Even if this were true, it would not make the people of the United Kingdom British. Given the transatlantic origins of so many contemporary consumer and media products, it would produce a "mid-Atlantic" identity. Few would claim that English people have lost their distinctive sense of national identity by breakfasting on Corn Flakes, driving a German or Italian car to work, and watching the Eurovision song contest on a Japanese-manufactured television set. If modern commercial forces have not made Englishmen into Americans or Europeans, there is no reason to assume that these influences should eliminate national identity among Scots, Welsh or Ulster people.

The national identities of the people of the United Kingdom are multiple, not singular. Most English people do not think that there is any difference between being English and being British. But most Scots, Welsh and Ulster people feel a difference between their land and the United Kingdom; they are proud of both their national identity *and* being British. Everyone resident in the United Kingdom will know intimately one part of it. Few people will feel equally at home in London, Edinburgh, Cardiff and Belfast. Anyone who did so would seem rootless rather than rooted in a British identity. Nor could such a person claim to be cosmopolitan, for some of these cities are considered provincial centres. A cosmopolitan politician would be expected to know Washington, Paris and Brussels, not the chief cities of government around the United Kingdom. A cosmopolitan Englishman is thus saved the shock of confronting a country that is British in a sense that cannot possibly be reduced to a copy of life beside the Thames.

In international law there is no government of England; there is only a government of the United Kingdom of Great Britain and Northern Ireland. To understand the United Kingdom we must understand its government as well as know its territory. Political institutions make the United Kingdom what it is. The United Kingdom was not created as the reflection of a single national identity. Instead, a sense of British identity is derived from common institutions of government that cut across the boundaries of communities that populate what is called the British Isles on one side of the Irish Sea and "these islands" on the other side, where the Republic of Ireland challenges the present boundaries of the United Kingdom.

To understand the United Kingdom as a whole, we must understand how its diverse territorial parts—England, Scotland, Wales and Northern Ireland

—are governed. To understand the parts, we must also understand the government of the whole. Parliament is more than the sum of representatives from diverse constituencies. It is, as it were, the fifth nation of the United Kingdom; it is the first loyalty of some and the last loyalty of others.

Most people do not need to understand the United Kingdom; government is immediately evident in local settings such as schools, hospitals, libraries or traffic signs. But the governors of the United Kingdom do need to understand the whole of their responsibilities. In the 1970s Westminster spectacularly demonstrated its *mis*understanding of the United Kingdom. In Northern Ireland it tried and abandoned policy after policy in a vain effort to assert authority. In response to electoral pressures from Scottish and Welsh Nationalists, Parliament debated devolution, and in 1978 endorsed Devolution Acts that authorized representative Assemblies for Scotland and Wales. But at the referendums in 1979 the Welsh electorate unambiguously rejected the devolution proposed, and the Scottish electorate failed to give it a clear endorsement. The Devolution Acts were then repealed. The continued existence of the United Kingdom cannot be accepted as evidence that its governors necessarily understand all of the territory that they are meant to govern.

The fact that devolution did not come does not make the United Kingdom secure against challenge. The history of nineteenth-century Europe and twentieth-century Third World countries offers ample evidence that disunion can be the fate of multinational governments. Institutions can institutionalize division rather than harmony, as the party system of Northern Ireland shows. Ardent proponents of the Welsh language movement claim that the electoral weakness of Plaid Cymru may justify extraconstitutional action to advance the Welsh language. Changes in values have meant that Scots showed more interest in nationalism in the 1970s than in any previous decade in the century.

Like most studies of British government, this book is much concerned with government at Westminster. But its emphasis is very different; it devotes most attention to what Westminster thinks about least: the territorial dimension in government. In countries such as Canada or Belgium, territory *is* of supreme political importance; Nationalist demands threaten to disrupt the very authority of government. Nor is the United Kingdom immune to Nationalist parties. Just as books are written about the governments of smaller European democracies, so too a book can be justified that emphasizes the smaller parts of a larger European democracy.

The Crown in Parliament symbolizes what all parts of the United Kingdom have in common, namely, allegiance and subordination to a common authority. But the manifestations of the government of the United Kingdom are multiple. Just as the Foreign and Commonwealth Office is one manifestation, a "tartan quango" such as the Red Deer Commission is equally an example of government in the United Kingdom. London is the home of the British Museum, but there is also a National Library of Scotland in Edinburgh, a National Library of Wales in Aberystwyth and a "national" library for Northern Ireland in Dublin. A thirsty traveller trying to buy a drink on Sunday in different parts of the United Kingdom will immediately become aware that laws can differ from place to place within it. Nor should such variations be surprising, in view of centuries of separate history in England, Scotland, Wales and Northern Ireland, and the continuance today of distinctive political institutions in each nation.

A search for the United Kingdom must start by looking for common factors. The first object of this book is to identify the Union that holds together the diverse nations of the United Kingdom. Defence of a Union can be the first priority of government, as it was with Abraham Lincoln, who defended the American Union by a bloody civil war.[2] It should not require the murder of a Member of Parliament within the Palace of Westminster by an Irish Republican bomb, as happened in 1979, to create a consciousness that each part of the United Kingdom is implicated in the Union. If the Union were to be broken up, whether by Scotland, Wales or Northern Ireland or by actions taken at Westminster, the government of the United Kingdom would be organically altered. Westminster cannot carry out a consistent and informed defence of the Union if it does not understand what it is. The use of the term *Unionist* in partisan settings (as in the Conservative and Unionist Party) should not detract from the importance of the principle of Union in a Kingdom that is not a natural entity.

The past decade has produced too many books and theories explaining events that have not happened in the United Kingdom.[3] Theories accounting for the rise of nationalism in Britain failed to note that in Wales electoral support for the Plaid Cymru actually *fell* from 1970 to 1974, and *fell again* in 1979. The up-*and*-down popular support for the Scottish National Party defies explanation by extrapolation from linear trends of economic conditions.[4] Northern Ireland was treated with neglect, being totally ignored by virtually every student of British politics until violence gained it international attention. It then suffered the fate of being "overexplained" by too many students of politics.[5] Guidebooks to the would-be government of a devolved Scotland and Wales were no sooner in print than devolution failed of support by those who were meant to be devolved.[6] A writer trying to explain four centuries of the political history of the British Isles will find it easy enough to select facts to fit his theory, but selective authors are often vulnerable to criticism on many sides.[7]

Like the *Report* of the Royal Commission on the Constitution, this study is concerned with the government of all parts of the United Kingdom.[8] But the purpose of the Royal Commission's *Report,* published in 1973, was very different: It was to prescribe, whereas this book's aim is to understand. The Commission's limited understanding can be inferred from the inability of individuals safe enough to be appointed to it to agree among themselves about how the United Kingdom should be governed. There was only a negative consensus — the dismissal of nationalism.

The approach of this book differs fundamentally from the outpouring of writings stimulated by troubles in Northern Ireland and sporadic Scottish and Welsh Nationalist electoral successes. It is a book about what *is,* a Union that has endured for centuries and not about what might be, or what might have been, such as hypothetically devolved Parliaments in Scotland or Wales, an independent Scotland or Wales, or a united Ireland. The political opponents of the United Kingdom, as much as its defenders, need to understand why England, Scotland, Wales and Northern Ireland have remained so long together in a Union under the Crown.

The second object of this book is to explain how and why the United Kingdom works as it does. Notwithstanding the existence of a single Crown, the institutions that collectively constitute government in the United Kingdom are multiple. For this reason, the United Kingdom cannot be explained by a single theory, for the things that require explanation are multiple and disparate.[9] There is no reason to expect a single theory to explain the very different positions under the Crown of Wales, Scotland and Northern Ireland, not to mention the position of the Republic of Ireland, established by secession from the United Kingdom. The authority of the United Kingdom today is best explained by three different yet complementary factors: by history, by the workings of contemporary political institutions and by the values that give consent to these institutions. For purposes of exposition, subsequent chapters emphasize particular influences one at a time. It is important to remember that historical determinants, contemporary institutions and consensual values have normally combined to maintain the United Kingdom.

The United Kingdom is initially best approached as the product of a multiplicity of historical events. It is certainly not the product of a logical plan, nor is it the product of a particular ideology. To refer to the making of the United Kingdom is to oversimplify. It treats the Union in its present form as if it were consciously made — and as if it had a purposeful maker. It did not; the United Kingdom today is the resultant of very disparate events and processes during more than four centuries. There is neither space nor need to relate here the history of the United Kingdom, but it is necessary to understand the present meaning of past history. The United Kingdom today is a multinational Crown. The Queen presides over a multinational kingdom as the Habsburg monarchs once did in Vienna, the czar in St. Petersburg, and the Ottoman sultan in Constantinople. Chapter 1 shows how each of the four parts of the United Kingdom retains a distinctive national identity, rooted in historically determined cultural differences. The historical causes of a multinational kingdom are expanded in chapter 2, which explains why authority in the United Kingdom is best represented by a stateless Crown of indefinite domain without a uniform set of institutions for governing the United Kingdom as a whole. The institutions for governing Scotland, Wales and Northern Ireland have each developed historically; they differ from each other, and incidentally make government in England unique as well.

The authority of the United Kingdom rests upon consent by the parties to Union. Chapter 3 demonstrates how competition between parties organized around functional economic issues strengthens the integration of England, Scotland and Wales. In all parts of the United Kingdom, each nation again and again votes for parties that concur in upholding Union, although disagreeing about much else. This is significant in Scotland and Wales, where Nationalist parties challenge the Union. It is even more important in Northern Ireland, where the challenge to the Union is expressed in bullets as well as in the ballots of the majority in favour of Unionist parties. The effect of party competition is to encourage parties to recognize the authority of Westminster, and Nationalist parties are forced to face the importance of winning broad popular support at free elections.[10]

To explain how the Union works today requires an understanding of the political institutions that collectively constitute the government of the United Kingdom. Institutions institutionalize history; the inertia of institutions embodies decisions taken through the centuries. For example, the Welsh Office reflects both the joining of Wales with England under one Parliament in 1536 and the creation of a separate Cabinet ministry more than four centuries later in 1964. Institutions also socialize individuals, both governors and governed, to accept particular forms of government. The abstract doctrine of the supremacy of the Crown in Parliament is authoritative because people have been socialized to think it so. The inertia of institutions can lead to the maintenance of Union by unthinking tradition. Few subjects of the Crown think it odd that the United Kingdom has two different established churches, one Episcopal and one Presbyterian. Most people are socialized to take for granted this distinctive relic of the historical past.

The institutions of the Mace, which symbolizes the Crown in Parliament, are the subject of chapter 4. Parliament brings together representatives of all parts of the United Kingdom to choose and sustain government. The Cabinet is the effective custodian of the Mace. When we examine what government does, that is, how institutions are organized to carry out public policies, then government appears as a maze. Chapter 5 shows how institutional responsibilities for providing public policies differ by territory; policies applied uniformly throughout the United Kingdom by a single Whitehall ministry are very much the exception. Most Whitehall ministries exercise some powers on a national basis, and some on a Great Britain or United Kingdom-wide basis. There is no consistency in the allocation of functional responsibilities by territory, or territorial responsibilities by organizations. From the perspective of the ordinary person, the distribution of public policies is of most importance. Chapter 6 examines how government distributes its chief resources — laws, money and public personnel — throughout the territory of the United Kingdom. The maze of distinctive administrative institutions for Scotland, Wales and Northern Ireland has an identifiable but very limited effect upon the distribution of the benefits of public policies. Chapter 7 resolves the puzzling relationship between the Mace and a maze of institutions by reviewing a variety of models of governing. It concludes that policy making is best described as an oligopoly in which organizations are few, unequal and interdependent.

The stability of the Union is contingent, not inevitable; it reflects an equilibrium of disparate forces within nations as well as between national parts. Chapter 8 demonstrates how a challenge to the steady-state United Kingdom can arise from the interaction of events within nations and actions at Westminster. The outbreak of troubles in Northern Ireland in 1968, followed by the suspension of Stormont in 1972, is one illustration. Westminster's adoption of Devolution Acts for Scotland and Wales in 1978, after the rise in Nationalist parliamentary strength in 1974, is another. The concluding chapter emphasizes the contingent nature of the authority of Parliament; it is strong yet vulnerable. The bulk of Westminster politicians ignore Union. Yet taking Union for granted at Westminster can work only when it is taken for granted elsewhere too. This is no longer the case. Today, there is an asymmetry of commitment. To maintain the United Kingdom, the proponents of Union in Scotland, Wales and Northern Ireland must actively support a multinational Crown, and this allegiance must not be undermined.

A reader familiar only with politics in England may be surprised at the frequent references to the Union and to nationalism. This will not surprise anyone familiar with politics in Northern Ireland, Scotland or Wales, where the maintenance of the United Kingdom as a Union under the Crown is under challenge from Nationalists and Republicans. Ironically, *the greatest importance is attributed to the Union by those who wish to break it up.* This book must therefore reflect the importance attached to the United Kingdom by such people. Irish Republicans will go to extreme and violent lengths to refuse recognition of the Crown and the United Kingdom it symbolizes. Scottish and Welsh Nationalists usually affirm that they are as loyal to the Crown as Australians and New Zealanders—and equally desirous of being independent members of the Commonwealth and the United Nations.

Only in Northern Ireland are there articulate and organized political parties explicitly proclaiming themselves as Unionists in opposition to Nationalists and Republicans. Inarticulateness on this issue does not mean that the Conservative, Labour or Liberal parties are not Unionist parties; it is a task of this book to draw out the content and significance of Unionist parties' attitudes towards the United Kingdom.

Since Unionist values and institutions dominate the government of the United Kingdom today, they are topics well suited to intensive analysis. To do this is not to say that Unionist values are necessarily the only or the most important values, any more than writing about Nationalism implies that the nation is the supreme justification for all political actions. There are other important values—such as free speech and representative government—which this author would put first, regarding both Unionism and Nationalism as subordinate to these ends. To write about the Union is simply to do what Nationalists and committed Unionists do, which is to take the United Kingdom seriously.

NOTES

1. For a sophisticated analysis of the role of geography in linking parts of the British Isles historically along an east-west water route, see M.W. Heslinga, *The Irish Border as a Cultural Divide* (Assen, Netherlands: Van Gorcum, 1962). Cf. comments in J. Blondel, *Voters, Parties and Leaders* (Harmondsworth: Penguin, 1963), p. 21; and A.H. Birch, *The British System of Government* (London: Allen & Unwin, 1967), p. 16.
2. Lincoln regarded the preservation of Union as more important than measures against slavery, writing to Horace Greeley on 22 August 1861: "My paramount object in this struggle is to save the Union, and is not either to save or to destroy slavery. If I could save the Union without freeing any slave, I would do it; and if I could do it by freeing all the slaves, I would do it; and if I could save it by freeing some and leaving others alone, I would also do that."
3. And much writing of value. On published and unpublished materials, see Laurence Pollock and Ian McAllister, *A Bibliography of United Kingdom Politics* (Glasgow: University of Strathclyde Studies in Public Policy, 1980).
4. On Scotland, see, e.g., Keith Webb, *The Growth of Nationalism in Scotland* (Harmondsworth: Penguin, 1978).

5. For useful reviews of the vast literature on Northern Ireland, see, e.g., J. Bowyer Bell's articles in the *Review of Politics* 34, no. 2 (1972): 147-57; 36, no. 4 (1974): 521-43; 38, no. 4 (1976): 510-33; and Arend Lijphart, "The Northern Ireland Problem," *British Journal of Political Science* 5, no. 1 (1974): 83-106.

6. A study of durable interest is Vernon Bogdanor's *Devolution* (London: Oxford University Press, 1979), which contains a critical historical survey, albeit presented as a prologue to Scottish and Welsh Assemblies.

7. Cf., e.g., Michael Hechter, *Internal Colonialism: The Celtic Fringe in British National Development, 1537-1966* (London: Allen & Unwin, 1975); Edward C. Page, "Michael Hechter's Internal Colonial Thesis: Some Theoretical and Methodological Problems," *European Journal of Political Research* 6, no. 3 (1978): 295-317; and A.W. Orridge, "Uneven Development and Nationalism," *Political Studies* 29, nos. 1-2 (1981): 1-15, 181-90.

    Tom Nairn's *The Break-Up of Britain* (London: New Left Books, 1977) is best regarded as a cultural polemic among Scots, among Marxists, and an "East Britain" dialogue on Edinburgh-London lines. For its omissions about Scotland, as well as about Wales and Northern Ireland, see the review by Richard Rose, "State or Nation," *New Society,* 4 August 1977. Notwithstanding their weaknesses, the popularity of Nairn and Hechter indicates what some people would like to believe about the United Kingdom.

8. Royal Commission on the Constitution, *1969-1973 Report* (hereinafter cited as *Report*)(London: HMSO, Cmnd. 5460, 1973), initially chaired by Lord Crowther and subsequent to his death by Lord Kilbrandon. All citations to the Commission are to Volume 1 of the *Report,* unless otherwise noted.

9. In social science terms, there is no "it" to explain. Instead there is a plurality of dependent variables, requiring explanation by a variety of different independent variables.

10. See Ian McAllister, "Party Organization and Minority Nationalism: A Comparative Study in the United Kingdom," *European Journal of Political Research* 9, no. 3 (1981): 237-55.

1. A Multinational Crown

The conventional view of government and society is today simple: A government expresses the political will of a nation, and each country should therefore be a nation-state. But until the great disruption of the First World War, the major states of Europe were normally multinational states — the Czarist, the Ottoman and the Habsburg empires notoriously so. Nationalism, the idea that each nation should become a separate state, became important politically only in the mid-nineteenth century, reaching its zenith at the Versailles peace conference. Kedourie defines nationalism as the belief that ". . . humanity is naturally divided into nations, that nations are known by certain characteristics that can be ascertained, and that the only legitimate type of government is national self-government."[1]

Theories that assume that the boundaries of a government are meant to match the boundaries of a nation can differ about whether society or government comes first.[2] From a sociological perspective, a nation can be said to make a state; for example, the idea of an Irish, German, Polish or Italian nation antedated the creation of a territorial state by centuries. From a political perspective, a state can be said to make a nation. For example, the government of the United States was prior in time to the creation of a national identity among scattered immigrants and their descendants. As long as the match between national identity and political institutions is well understood — as in unitary France or the federal United States — the relation between the whole and the parts of government is clear.

To see the United Kingdom as a single nation is to impose an *a priori* theory on the facts of history. Whatever the United Kingdom is, it cannot be considered a conventional nation-state. The normal term for the state — the Crown — has no territorial adjective to describe it. Nor has the government of the United Kingdom ever tried to make its subjects into a single nation, as Irish Nationalists did by reviving a dying Gaelic language, or as many states have done, whether starting with a very heterogeneous society, like America, or a society emphasizing homogeneity, as in the case of France. As subsequent pages will make evident, the Crown has tolerated a substantial degree of cultural diversity. To have tried to make the United Kingdom into an English nation would have required Anglicizing Scots, Welsh and Ulstermen — a difficult task given the resistance of English people to assimilating others as well as resistance from those to be assimilated. Alternatively, making a common British nation would involve an even more difficult task, "denationalizing" English people in order to make them Britons.

Trying to name the nation associated with the government of the United Kingdom displays the confusion about national identity. One thing is certain: No one speaks of the "Ukes" as a nation. For example, Harold Wilson fought a battle with the Foreign and Commonwealth Office to prevent the government being seated at a Commonwealth Conference behind a placard describing it as the United Kingdom. The Prime Minister insisted that he represented Britain.[3] International organizations are less easily intimidated; Westminster's representatives can even be placed alphabetically at the letter R — for *Royaume Uni*. A description of the United Kingdom as the nation of Britain leaves unclear whether Ulstermen are included. Most Catholics in Ulster — and many residents of the British "mainland" as well — would wish to exclude Northern Ireland from the definition of Britain. To speak of Britain as one nation not only denies a politically significant identity to Scots and Welsh; it also denies that England is a nation.

Authors of standard texts about the government of the United Kingdom consistently *avoid* describing it by this term, albeit differing about what the Crown's government should be called. The official term — Her Majesty's Government — is territorially opaque. Writers employing precise geographical terms often misuse them. For example, Walter Bagehot's classic analysis of *The English Constitution* was accurate in describing his viewpoint, inasmuch as Bagehot confined himself to a society very remote from Scotland, Wales or Ireland — and from much of industrial England as well. Yet the Constitution cannot be confined, as Bagehot's outlook was, to the agrarian South of England.

The charge to the 1969 Royal Commission on the Constitution reflected this confusion. It started from the identification of a singular but ill-defined group: "Our people under the Crown." It identified this community of allegiants as persons living in the "several countries, nations and regions of the United Kingdom." In intent, the Commission took a Unionist position, making its primary concern the maintenance of an undefined "essential unity" of the United Kingdom. But it was ready to accept that "unity does not necessarily mean uniformity." It went so far in recognizing diversity as to refer to Wales as a "country" and to the Scots as a "race of intelligent and hard-working people." It did not apply a racial epithet in Ulster, even though this is frequently and pejoratively done in England. The Commission accepted that Wales and Scotland were "nations" — and was prepared to consider that the United Kingdom could be a "multinational state." The first and second Chairmen of the Commission (Lord Crowther, a Yorkshireman, and Lord Kilbrandon, a Scot) differed publicly about whether Scotland was a nation.[4] The Commission studiously avoided saying whether Northern Ireland was one or two nations or part of another nation; it did recognize that within that area there were two "communities." At one point it accepted its own inconsistencies, noting, "We use the term United Kingdom mainly with Great Britain in mind, though most of what we say will be equally applicable to Northern Ireland."[5]

Sociologists have sought to identify a difference between Whitehall and "the rest" of the United Kingdom by writing about centre-periphery relations. The intention appears to be to contrast those who hold power at the centre of government with those who do not. But the term is usually used without definition, and certainly without any regard for consistency in definition. It may refer to geographical or nongeographical groups. If peripheral people are those who are socially and politically marginal, then the traditional "periphery" of the United Kingdom is the East End of London. Today, Brixton, a short bus ride form Westminster, may be considered peripheral because of its cluster of coloured Commonwealth immigrants. If the centre is defined geographically, it is either too small or too large. If it is restricted to London, then more than nine-tenths of the population of the United Kingdom is consigned to the periphery. To do this is to carry a fixation with elite politics to an indefensible extreme in a mixed-economy welfare state. Even if the centre is said to be the South East of England, this still unwarrantedly consigns nearly three-quarters of the population to the periphery. To equate England with the centre is to stretch the term too far. Why should Durham, Lincolnshire and Cumbria be considered the same as London and the Home Counties, given their distance from Whitehall in so many senses? Equally, why should Edinburgh and Cardiff, cities with good communication to London, be thought more peripheral than Workington, Wallsend or Minehead? A village in Merioneth or Fermanagh or a sheiling in the Scottish Highlands may appear peripheral from London, but equally, London can be over the horizon of people who live in these remote parts of the United Kingdom.

This chapter resolves this confusion by demonstrating that the United Kingdom is multinational rather than a nation-state. The first section demonstrates the existence of a multiplicity of national identities in the United Kingdom. The second section examines the extent of socioeconomic and cultural similarities and differences between and within the nations of the United Kingdom. The peculiar position of England — which lacks distinctive political institutions although it has a clear identity — is the subject of the concluding section. To show the multinational character of the United Kingdom is not to endorse the Nationalist case for breaking up the United Kingdom into a set of separate nation-states. The history of Europe shows that it is possible to have multinational states, as well as nations without states.

Territorial Communities and Political Nations

The number of groups into which society can be divided is virtually endless. A common identity and sense of community can be based upon a great variety of shared attitudes or characteristics. For example, the residents of the United Kingdom can be differentiated by such criteria as blood group, favourite sports or taste in soups, but these differences do not tell us anything about United Kingdom politics, even when the differences are related to territorial parts of the United Kingdom.[6] For most individuals for most purposes the most important community is the face-to-face community. Territorially, the face-to-face community, the place in which people feel most at home, is likely to be an area within ten minutes walking or driving distance of their residence.[7] It is a community very much smaller than a nation, and also smaller than the typical local government unit.

A nation is a distinctive kind of community, defined by a combination of social psychological and political characteristics. The first test of a nation is that a group of people share a common *collective identity;* it is this sense of community that gives nationalism a distinctive emotional quality. The second test is that this community makes political demands related to its distinctive identity (and not, for example, to an economic interest). A nation is a special kind of community; it is particularly concerned with distinctive *institutions of governance.* Demands can vary from requests for minor or symbolic variations of specific policies to a claim for independence as a separate nation-state. Third, a nation demands distinctive political institutions for a particular *territory* that it regards as its homeland. A territorial focus makes it possible for government to institutionalize distinctive treatment, whether in special regions or a separate independent state. The territorial concern of Nationalists differentiates them from conventional interest groups.

The first test is to ascertain the national identification of people within the United Kingdom. The thesis of British nationhood posits that people in all parts of the United Kingdom share a single national identity. Theories of modernization offer many reasons why the people of the United Kingdom should share a common identity. They argue that industrialization creates structural imperatives in the economy and society that lead to standard patterns of behaviour in both work and leisure activities. Class differences then become the only social difference of any political consequence. The industrial revolution began in the United Kingdom—in addition to Manchester and Birmingham, Glasgow, Belfast and Cardiff are among the earliest industrial cities of the world. The theory of national homogenization by industrialization is therefore particularly relevant. In the contemporary world, the mass media—television, radio, and newspapers—are said to be additional forces for cultural homogenization, providing the same messages and vicarious experiences to an audience that thereby gains a common identity. The degree of centralization of the media in London, which is also the political capital of the United Kingdom, adds to the relevance of this theory.

The thesis that the United Kingdom is a multinational political system can be justified by the presumed political importance of cultural factors.[8] Cultural differences antedate economic differences in point of time; the peoples of Europe, including the territories now constituting the United Kingdom, were divided by communal identities, language and religion for centuries before the industrial revolution began in the late eighteenth century. These earlier influences upon political outlooks are hypothesized to persist through the centuries. Instead of cultural influences being superseded by economic differences, the greater age of cultural influences may give them greater strength.

Survey evidence rejects the theory that economic and social modernization has led to the creation of a single national identity for the United Kingdom. The United Kingdom is a multinational political system (see table 1.1). Surveys have found that 57 percent of people living in England identify themselves as English, 57 percent in Wales as Welsh, 52 percent of people in Scot-

TABLE 1.1. NATIONAL IDENTITY IN ENGLAND, SCOTLAND,
WALES AND NORTHERN IRELAND

	England	Scotland	Wales	Northern Ireland Protestant	R. Catholic
Thinks of Self as	%	%	%	%	%
British	38	35	33	67	15
Scottish	2	52	—	—	—
Welsh	1	—	57	—	—
English	57	2	8	—	—
Ulster	n.a.	—	—	20	6
Irish	1	1	—	8	69
Other, mixed; don't know	1	10	2	5	10
	100	100	100	100	100

SOURCES: For Scotland and Wales, data supplied by survey directors from their respective machine readable files: J. A. Brand and W. L. Miller, *Scottish Election Survey 1979* (Glasgow: University of Strathclyde); and Denis Balsom and P. J. Madgwick, *Welsh Election Survey 1979* (Aberystwyth: University of Wales). For Northern Ireland, see E. Moxon-Browne, "Northern Ireland Attitude Survey: an Initial Report" (Belfast: Queen's University, duplicated, 1979), p. 9. For England, data supplied by the Gallup poll, London.

land as Scots, and in Northern Ireland 69 percent of Catholics identify themselves as Irish. Ulster Protestants are the only group that shows a majority
identifying as British (67 percent); they are also the group most likely to be
treated as "alien" by English people.[9]

The United Kingdom is unambiguously multinational. At least six different national identities can be found within the United Kingdom: English,
Scottish, Welsh, Ulster, Irish and British. The very quantity of identities is politically important because it means that the United Kingdom is not polarized
into two and only two communities, as is the case, for example, in Belgium,
divided between French-speaking Walloons and Dutch-speaking Flemings.
The non-English people of the United Kingdom are divided from one another
by history as well as geography. To describe Scots, Welsh and Ulster people as
Celtic, as is sometimes done, is to make a major error: The Celtic language
spoken in parts of Wales differs more from the Celtic language spoken in parts
of Scotland and Ireland than English does from German or French. Moreover,
a large portion of the Scots and Ulster population is Anglo-Saxon or Norse by
descent and is unconnected with the Gaels of Ireland and the Western part of
the Scottish Highlands.[10]

Each nation of the United Kingdom is internally divided in its identity.
The division is most evident in Northern Ireland, where at least 69 percent of
Catholics think of themselves as Irish, as against 67 percent of Protestants
thinking of themselves as British. But it is also noteworthy that one-third of
people in England, Scotland and Wales consider their primary identity as British, albeit without the distinctive meaning given by the majority community in
Northern Ireland. Overall, it is simplest to regard the United Kingdom as consisting of four national communities — England, Scotland, Wales and Ulster,[11]
with a minority of Ulster people identifying with a nation outside the United
Kingdom, the Republic of Ireland.[12]

National identities are not necessarily exclusive identities.[13] A person
who thinks of himself as English, Scottish, Welsh or Ulster does not deny the
possibility of also being British. The two are logically compatible. A person
may think of himself as Scottish in a discussion of football, but as British in
politics. English people certainly see no incompatibility between being English
and being British; the two identities are used more or less interchangeably. Indeed, if Scots or Welsh are said to have a problem of dual loyalties, English
people may have a problem of confused loyalties, not knowing what it means
to be British.

In Northern Ireland the Protestant majority see their British identity and
Ulster loyalty as compatible. Only those who identify themselves as Irish exclude a British identity by doing so. Furthermore, holders of national identi-

ties do not see differences as a cause of antagonism. A major survey of Scottish attitudes, for example, found that only 5 percent of respondents disliked English people. The research concluded: "Although Scots may be able to identify an Englishman it is much rarer that they will identify a difference of interests between them."[14]

Distinctive national identities can be explained by cultural differences that reflect very different historical experiences. National identities are reinforced by contemporary experiences often overlooked in simple class models of society. For example, national identities are reinforced by the low level of immigration into each of these nations. According to the 1971 census, 91 percent of the population of Scotland, 91 percent of the population of England, 90 percent of the population of Northern Ireland and 81 percent of the population of Wales were born in the nation in which they reside.

Modern media of communications reinforce ties within national communities. Of all telephone calls, 83 percent are local telephone calls. Postal deliveries too are disproportionately concentrated within a nation; for example, 71 percent of all postings in Northern Ireland are delivered in Northern Ireland.[15] The London-based press is "national" in circulation, but the nation it dominates is England, not the United Kingdom. The preeminence of papers printed within the nations of Scotland, Wales and Northern Ireland is even greater when account is taken of evening newspapers and numerous local weeklies, which are never circulated on a British-wide basis. Television has distinctive regional elements. The Independent Broadcasting Authority programme companies are regional companies, and the British Broadcasting Corporation maintains "national regions" for Scotland, Wales and Northern Ireland.[16]

Since nations are differentiated from other social groups by their political concerns, a second test is whether political demands are made for distinctive institutions of government. Nations are differentiated from the units composing a federal system because the treatment they demand is exceptional for their own nation. In a federal system of government, *all* subfederal units are treated alike. What the Americans call "states' rights" groups are not lobbying for distinctive national status for California or Mississippi; they demand more power for all fifty states in the Union. In Switzerland, the weakness of the federal government is complemented by the strong powers of all the cantons. In Canada, demands for more power for the provinces against Ottawa do not threaten the existence of the federal government. This occurs only when there is a demand from the Parti Quebecois, a Nationalist party, for distinctive treatment for Quebec alone, sovereignty plus association.

Distinctive political treatment for nations does not necessarily mean a demand for independence. Ironically, the Crown itself has shown the most consistent recognition of the United Kingdom as a multinational political system because it provides distinctive political institutions for governing Scotland, Wales and Northern Ireland. The Scottish Office, the Welsh Office and the Northern Ireland Office are the most prominent among many institutions of government affecting nations differently within the United Kingdom (cf. chapter 5). The devolution debate of 1974-79 and recurring attempts to create new institutions for governing Northern Ireland demonstrate Westminster's readiness to endorse distinctive national treatment for nations within the United Kingdom and simultaneously to reject independence.

Nor does a distinctive national identity necessarily lead to voting for Nationalist* parties. If that were the case, then the Scottish National and Welsh Nationalist parties would win a majority of votes in Scotland and Wales. But this does not happen. At the 1979 general election in Scotland, only 21 percent of those identifying themselves as Scots voted for the Scottish National Party (SNP). In Wales, only 10 percent of those identifying themselves as Welsh voted for the Welsh Nationalist Party. And in England, no one who identifies as English can have voted for an English Nationalist Party because none contests elections. Only among Catholics in Northern Ireland is there a direct link between national identity and voting for a Nationalist party: 60 percent of Catholics describing themselves as Irish vote for the Social Democratic and Labour Party (SDLP), which has as its goal the withdrawal of Northern Ireland from the United Kingdom and the creation of a 32-county united Ireland.[17]

The United Kingdom is a multinational political system in spite of, not because of, its Nationalist parties. The United Kingdom has an unusually large number of Nationalist parties. The Scottish National Party, Plaid Cymru (literally, the Welsh Party), and the Social Democratic and Labour Party are all unambiguously Nationalist parties. The proclaimed constitutional aim of the Scottish National Party is "self-government for Scotland—that is, the restoration of Scottish national sovereignty by the establishment of a democratic Scottish Parliament within the Commonwealth." The proclaimed constitutional aim of Plaid Cymru is "to secure self-government for Wales and the right to become a member of the United Nations Organisation." The constitutional aim of the Northern Ireland Social Democratic and Labour Party is "to promote the cause of Irish unity." Most representatives of the Ulster Protestant community at Westminster, whether calling themselves Unionists, Democratic Unionists or by some other name, also demand distinctive political institutions for their Province.

---

*The capitalisation of the word Nationalist indicates reference to Nationalist political parties and their claim to independence.

By comparison with other Nationalist parties in Europe, the Nationalist parties of the United Kingdom do relatively well, or, put more accurately, are *less unsuccessful.*[18] But by comparison with Unionist parties, the three principal Nationalist parties — the SNP, Plaid Cymru and the SDLP — are relatively weak in the votes they poll within the nation they claim to represent. The United Kingdom persists because parties supporting the Union have invariably won a majority of parliamentary seats in all the nations of the Kingdom.

A third distinctive feature of nations is that their political demands have a territorial focus. The existence of a "land" of Scots, Welsh and Ulstermen or Irishmen makes it easy to identify a nation institutionally as well as culturally. Given the high level of emigration from Scotland, Wales and Northern Ireland, it is particularly noteworthy that Nationalist parties define their nation primarily in terms of the people living there. Nationalist parties appeal to the electorate within their nation and not, like Zionists, to an ingathering of dispersed exiles. The territorial definition of nationality is particularly important. People can become Scots, Welsh or Ulstermen by living in a place and expressing an emotional identification with it. (It may also be suggested that emigrants such as Irish-Americans or London Scots would not now feel at home in the nation their ancestors left, insofar as they hark back to an outdated romantic vision from the past.) A territorial definition of identity is also consistent with a multiplicity of identities, for the United Kingdom's boundaries encompass four nations.

A territorial focus makes it easy for Nationalist parties to organize electorally; they concentrate resources upon a small proportion of the United Kingdom. The Scottish National Party could win 11 seats at the October 1974 general election with 839,000 votes, whereas the Liberals could win only 2 more seats with 4,507,000 more votes, because the SNP concentrated its appeal upon 71 Scottish constituencies, whereas the Liberals fought 619 of the 635 parliamentary constituencies of the United Kingdom. Equally important, a territorial focus makes it possible for government to provide distinctive political institutions for a given area, if only for purposes of administration. Making Edinburgh, Cardiff and Belfast administrative headquarters for delivering major public policies can be administratively convenient, and as long as policies do not detract from principles laid down by Parliament, it is entirely consistent with maintaining Westminster's unique authority.

A territorial focus is also important in distinguishing territorial nations from ethnic groups making demands for distinctive political treatment in the name of a common identity. In the United Kingdom today, the chief ethnic groups lacking a territorial base are coloured Commonwealth immigrants from the West Indies, Pakistan, India and Africa and their offspring. They voice demands for distinctive political treatment, and may assert a common identity as "coloured," or "black," Britons.

Coloured immigrants are scattered among more than a dozen major cities of Britain. Territorial dispersion makes it difficult to organize for political action, especially when immigrants are divided internally. Coloured immigrants and their British-born offspring are not sufficiently concentrated to dominate a single parliamentary constituency or the population of a single city. It would not be politically realistic for a group of coloured immigrants to demand "national" independence for a few wards of Bradford, Birmingham or London where the coloured population is a majority.

Because ethnic groups are territorially dispersed, many of their primary political demands concern intergroup relations. In the case of coloured Britons, there is a particular concern with the prevention of discrimination by whites in housing, employment and accommodation in public places. Whereas Nationalist politics is about mobilizing solidary demands on behalf of a single group that wishes to separate itself from others, coloured Britons are principally concerned with demands for integration in a multiracial community. Ethnic politics therefore presents demands that are potentially more likely to create conflict than separatist demands of Nationalists, for ethnic demands immediately affect the majority community as well as minorities. Whereas the claims of a Nationalist party can be ended by allowing a nation to secede, the claims of ethnic groups to "fair" or "distinctive" treatment can be met only by continuing cooperation within the United Kingdom. Whereas Westminster has shown a readiness to create distinctive national institutions, the institutions it creates for ethnic groups (e.g., the Commission for Racial Equality) are much more limited in their powers.

The multiple political orientations of Jews provide a second illustration of the political difference between territorial nations and nonterritorial ethnic pressure groups. Jews are dispersed among a number of major cities in the United Kingdom and are not numerically dominant in any city. Some Jews in Britain reject the idea that they are or should act as a distinct political group. Others consider that on a limited number of issues Jews should act as a pressure group. A few Jewish organizations want legislative protection for Jews against discrimination on the grounds of religion or ethnic status.[19] Although Zionists are Jewish Nationalists, their concern is a territorial homeland for Jews in the state of Israel, not the status of Jews within the United Kingdom.

To describe the United Kingdom as a multinational state (with additional ethnic differences derived from race and religion) is to adopt language not frequently heard at Westminster or, for that matter, in the most populous (but least clear about being British) nation of the United Kingdom. The Royal

Commission on the Constitution noted, "Most Englishmen would probably be surprised to hear the United Kingdom spoken of as a multinational state."[20] Yet no historian would be surprised by such a term, for most governments for most of history have ruled over what would today be called multinational states.

Similarities and Differences Within and Between Nations of the United Kingdom

The geographical boundaries of the United Kingdom differentiate people into national groups but do not, ipso facto, make people different. The very fact of being under a common government may encourage common patterns of behaviour. A visitor from a Third World nation might be struck by what the nations of the United Kingdom have in common: Nearly all are white, speak English, live in urbanized areas and by Third World standards have a high standard of living.

Any search for differences between nations will also identify similarities. Nationalist writings often imply that a nation is both internally homogeneous (everyone is alike because of a common national identity) and completely different from its neighbours. But nature and man have each set limits to the extent of cross-national differences. For example, we would not expect one nation of the United Kingdom to be all male or all working class and another to be all female or completely middle class. Paradoxically, one way in which nations are likely to resemble each other is in the pattern of their internal differences; for example, every nation is internally divided along lines of age, sex, social class, and the like.

In comparing the nations of the United Kingdom, it is particularly important to be precise about the kind and degree of difference. For example, wage levels can differ considerably within a nation—yet a comparison of average national wage levels might find cross-national differences too. Contrasts that may appear significant when stated verbally can appear trivial when stated numerically. For example, the statement that Scotland has a Gaelic-speaking population and England has none, a seeming difference, conceals a basic similarity: 98.5 percent of Scottish people have no knowledge of Gaelic, and the same is true of virtually 100 percent of people in England. The greater the hypothesized political significance of national differences, the greater should be the arithmetic degree of difference. It would be foolish to expect Nationalist groups to take up arms against government, say, because of a 10 percent difference in average weekly earnings and live in peace if differences fell below 10 percent. From a Unionist perspective, a 10 percent difference between nations can be interpreted as 90 percent similarity.

The existence of social differences need not cause political differences and certainly not the political disruption of the United Kingdom. Many differences can be a basis for cooperation—for example, the exchange of goods and services between town and country or the redistribution of revenue to finance public expenditure throughout the United Kingdom (cf. chapter 6). Internal differences can also create cross-national links—for example, manual workers in Scotland and England may have more in common politically than working-class and middle-class voters within Scotland. Cross-cutting cleavages may strengthen political union.

A variety of social science theories predict that economic differences should lead to major political differences or even territorial conflict. Within the United Kingdom, differences in living standards cannot be expected to approach those differentiating the United Kingdom from such new Commonwealth countries as India, Pakistan or Nigeria. But theories of relative deprivation hypothesize that differences in the degree of prosperity can lead to political grievances: A perception of relative differences in living standards between nations is said to create a sense of relative deprivation. Just as cross-class economic differences are predicted to lead to class conflict, a cross-national sense of relative deprivation is predicted to cause Nationalist conflicts.[21] Both Unionist and Nationalist politicians are quick to score political points—for Union or against—by invoking comparative standards of living within the United Kingdom.

To argue that relative economic deprivation is likely to encourage Nationalists to demand independence also implies that the absence of relative deprivation will maintain the United Kingdom. This implication is usually overlooked by proponents of relative deprivation theories, who assume the inevitability, rather than the contingency, of conflict. Yet some explanation must be found for what is an undoubted historical fact, namely the continuance of the United Kingdom on a multinational basis for centuries.

Insofar as relative economic deprivation is meant to create political conflict among the nations of the United Kingdom, then the degree of difference between nations should be great to justify the prediction of great political disturbances. The extent of economic differences can be tested thoroughly by using seven varied indicators of economic well-being: weekly industrial earnings, gross domestic product per capita, car ownership, employment, occupational class, subjectively perceived class, and trade union membership.

A systematic comparison of economic characteristics of the four nations of the United Kingdom today emphasizes their similarities (see table 1.2., page 22) The relationship of each nation to the United Kingdom standard can be measured precisely by setting that standard to equal 100. England will inevita-

TABLE 1.2. SIMILARITIES IN NATIONAL ECONOMIC CONDITIONS WITHIN THE UNITED KINGDOM

Indicator	England	Scotland	Wales	Northern Ireland	UK average (1979)
	(UK = 100)				
1. Weekly industrial earnings	100	98	99	93	£97.27
2. Gross domestic product, per capita	102	97	88	78	£2,866
3. Employment level	102	97	97	93	92.6% employed; 7.4 % unemployed
4. Car ownership	101	89	106	89	58% households at least one car
5. Occupationally middle class	107	87	89	101	34% middle class by occupation
6. Subjective middle class	102	89	95	123	49% subjectively middle class
7. No union members in family	101	98	98	87	58% nonunion
AVERAGE	102	93	96	95	100

All data for 1979 unless otherwise indicated.

SOURCES: (1) *Regional Trends 1981* (London: HMSO) table 13.5.
(2) Ibid., table 15.1.
(3) *Employment Gazette* 89, no. 2 (February 1981), table 2.3.
(4) *Regional Trends, 1981*, table 3.5.
(5) *1971 Census: Economic Activity Tables* (HMSO).
(6) Calculated from 1979 Gallup poll election surveys, plus Rose, *Governing without Consensus* (London: Faber, 1971), p. 286.
(7) Calculated from 1979 Gallup poll election surveys, plus Rose, *Governing without Consensus*, p. 504.

bly vary least from this standard because it contributes by far the largest part to the standard. This also means that other nations will find it relatively easy to depart from the standard. In fact, Scotland, Wales and Northern Ireland are normally close to the United Kingdom standard on a very wide variety of measures of socioeconomic conditions. Weekly differences in industrial earnings, perhaps the most straightforward measure of individual economic well-being, differ by only 1 or 2 percent within Great Britain, and by 7 percent between Northern Ireland and the United Kingdom average. Employment levels (i.e., the proportion in work) differ by 7 percent. In car ownership, Wales ranks above England. In the proportion of the population thinking of themselves as middle class, Northern Ireland ranks above England. English people are slightly more likely to be middle class by occupation, and non-English are more likely to belong to trade unions. The greatest difference is in gross domestic product per capita, with Northern Ireland one-quarter below England on this measure.

Overall, an analysis of economic conditions emphasizes the socioeconomic homogeneity of the nations of the United Kingdom. All seven measures have been scored to make a higher number an indicator of a nation being more middle class. On this basis, England has an average score of 102, Wales 96, Northern Ireland 95 and Scotland 93. The differences among the four nations within the United Kingdom are less than differences between the United Kingdom as a whole and other member countries of the European Community, such as more prosperous France and Germany or less prosperous and more agricultural Ireland and Italy. The 95 percent degree of socioeconomic similarity thus refutes speculative theories postulating that relative deprivation encourages Nationalist politics. The absence of a large measure of relative social and economic deprivation should strengthen Union.

An additional test of relative economic deprivation can be made by comparing the *direction* of economic change in recent decades. The neo-Marxist orientation of many relative deprivation theories implies that "the rich get richer and the poor get poorer," that is, that economic differences should be increasing within the United Kingdom. It would therefore follow that Nationalist political activity should also increase, as the hypothesized divergence in national economic conditions leads to greater relative deprivation.

In fact, economic conditions among the four nations of the United Kingdom are tending to converge. The convergence is most striking in Northern Ireland, which has been "catching up" with the United Kingdom standard in weekly industrial earnings and gross domestic product since the 1960s. Whereas Ulster was on average 21 percent below the United Kingdom standard for the first three indicators in table 1.2 in the 1960s, it is now only 12 percent below the standard. Scotland and Wales have also become more prosperous and more middle class in this period. On average, each nation has moved 4 percent closer to the United Kingdom standard since the 1960s. England, too, has contributed to convergence by reducing its relative lead in economic conditions, especially in employment, as recession has pushed unemployment in the London area and the West Midlands towards the average elsewhere in the United Kingdom. If relative deprivation theories were correct, then Nationalist parties should have done better in the 1950s and '60s and declined in the '70s as the nations converged. The exact opposite happened.[22]

Cultural characteristics such as race, religion and language offer an alternative explanation for the differences between multinational states *and* nation-states. A given political society can be united by having the same religion, language and skin colour; if cultural differences do exist, these can constitute a basis for a multinational political system. The fact that religious and linguistic diversities have been more important in the past suggests that cultural differences can create national differences. National identities are not the product of contemporary events, but reflect instead influences from many centuries.

Race, in the sense of skin colour, has historically been a ground for cultural unity throughout the United Kingdom. It also differentiated the people of the United Kingdom from the nonwhite people constituting nearly nine-tenths of the population of the British Empire. In everyday English parlance, race can also be used to draw ascriptive barriers between the people of Britain and other nations of white people, whether found on the other side of the Irish Sea, or across the English Channel beginning at Calais.[23] It is an open question whether race will be a unifying or divisive force in the United Kingdom in the year 2000, when the bulk of the country's significant nonwhite population will be British-born.

Language is also a unifying force within the United Kingdom. Virtually the whole of the population of England, Scotland and Northern Ireland habitually speak English at home, as well as using it in everyday social contacts. This is also true of the great majority in Wales, for 79 percent of the population speak only English, a proportion that has grown steadily from census to census. A minority (21 percent) of Welsh are bilingual. Even among persons for whom Welsh is the home language, English is likely to be used in public business, for all but 1 percent of Welsh-speakers also speak English.

Since the Reformation, religion has differentiated the nations of the United Kingdom. In England, an episcopal church is the religion of the majority, and is by law established. In Wales, the alien nature of the episcopal established church was a major political grievance to Protestant nonconformists until the Church in Wales was disestablished in 1920. In Scotland, the Presbyterian Church of Scotland is the established church. Since the seventeenth century, Northern Ireland has experienced continuing religious frictions between the episcopal Church of Ireland, the Presbyterian Church brought from Scotland, and the Roman Catholic Church. These differences have caused great political conflict by sustaining contrasting national identities and political loyalties.

Religious differences persist today between the nations of the United Kingdom. When surveys ask people to state their religion, a majority of English identify with the Church of England and a majority of Scots with the Church of Scotland. In Wales, there remain substantial divisions between the formerly established church and nonconformist chapels. In Northern Ireland, the Protestant majority faces an equally committed and well-organized Catholic minority.[24]

Given the tendency for people to exaggerate their religious attachments in interviews, a better test of religious adherence is the manner of celebrating marriage. The choice of a church or a civil ceremony for a major event in life is significant in itself; furthermore, marriage statistics are kept in all parts of the

United Kingdom on a consistent and comparable basis. These figures confirm survey evidence: Religion differs between the nations of the United Kingdom as well as dividing nations internally. Among those marrying in church, the bulk of people in England and Wales are married in the Church of England; in Scotland in the Church of Scotland; and in Northern Ireland, the most frequent site is a Roman Catholic Church because the larger number of Protestant marriages are divided among several Protestant churches (see table 1.3).

TABLE 1.3. DIFFERENCES IN RELIGION WITHIN THE UNITED KINGDOM

	England	Wales	Scotland	N. Ireland	United Kingdom
	(% form of marriage)				
Church of England[a]	33	32	1	17	29
Church of Scotland[b]	1	1	40	23	6
Other Protestant[c]	7	16	4	9	7
Roman Catholic	8	6	15	41	9
Civil	51	44	40	9	49

SOURCES: *Marriage Statistics 1977* (HMSO), table 3.11; *Annual Report of Registrar-General for Scotland 1978*, vol. 2, table Q2.2; *Annual Report of Registrar-General for Northern Ireland 1977*, table D1. All data for 1977, except Scotland, which is for 1978.

a. Under its different names in various parts of the United Kingdom.
b. Includes Presbyterian churches outside Scotland.
c. Includes a small number of Jewish and other non-Christian marriages.

Differences in civil marriages are greater than differences in economic conditions among the nations of the United Kingdom. When the proportion of civil marriages in the United Kingdom is set at 100, then England ranks at 105, Wales at 90, Scotland at 82 and Northern Ireland at 20. When each nation's distribution of forms of marriage is compared to the United Kingdom average, then the difference index is 6 percent for England, 12 percent for Wales, 40 percent for Scotland and 51 percent for Northern Ireland.[25]

While the whole of the Western world has experienced a decline in religious commitment in the postwar era, cultural differences established by religious differences continue to persist. In all parts of the United Kingdom, civil marriages have become more frequent, but not at the same rate. Since 1951, Scotland has moved closer to the United Kingdom standard for civil marriage, but Wales and Northern Ireland have moved farther away—and historic differences in patterns of church marriage persist.[26]

National averages mask within-nation differences. Anyone who has travelled around Scotland is immediately struck by the contrasts between Edinburgh and Glasgow and the Highlands; in Wales, between industrial Glamorganshire and rural West Wales; and in Northern Ireland, between the urban concentration of Belfast and the rural uplands of Fermanagh and Tyrone.

Equally important, the characteristics that divide each nation also create cross-national similarities. This is most evident in industry, for the histories of Belfast, Glasgow, Cardiff, Manchester, Liverpool and Birmingham are intertwined; all owe their eminence to the common phenomenon of industrialization.

Regional differences within nations of the United Kingdom are potentially important. As Sharpe notes, "The logic of regionalism is inimical to the logic of nationalism."[27] The greater the differences within a nation, the less likelihood that its residents can unite to challenge Westminster's authority in the name of a common identification. All four parts of the United Kingdom are subdivided into regions by government, albeit for different purposes. In Scotland and Wales, nine regions and eight counties are respectively primary units of local government. In England, eight regions are denominated for economic planning purposes. In Northern Ireland, there is a recognized distinction between the wholly rural area West of the River Bann, the area East of the Bann just within reach of United Kingdom industry, and Belfast. In Northern Ireland, counties are no longer meaningful units of local government.

If only by a statistical artifact, dividing the nations of the United Kingdom will reveal differences masked by comparing national averages. National statistics are in a sense population-weighted averages of regional characteristics within each nation. For example, the region with the least unemployment in the United Kingdom (the Scottish Borders) will be well below the Scottish national averge, just as the region with the most unemployment (West of the Bann) will be well above the Northern Ireland average.

Inevitably, regional economic and cultural differences exist within the United Kingdom. But the regions of the United Kingdom also show cross-national similarities, most obviously between the very rural regions, such as the Scottish Highlands, Powys in Wales and Northern Ireland West of the Bann, and between industrial regions, such as Strathclyde region, the North of England and mid-Glamorganshire. Within-nation disparities are particularly extreme in agricultural employment: Powys and Mid Glamorgan in Wales respectively rank 1st and 27th among the 28 regions of the United Kingdom; Northern Ireland West of the Bann and Belfast rank 2nd and 28th respectively, and Dumfries & Galloway and the Strathclyde regions of Scotland rank 3rd and 23rd respectively.[28]

Within nations, cultural differences are much less evident. The only significant division along territorial lines is found in Wales, where Welsh speakers tend to be concentrated in rural West and North Wales. In consequence, the proportion of Welsh speakers runs as high as 65 percent in rural Gwynedd and 52 percent in Dyfed; it is down to 5 percent in South Glamorganshire and 2 percent in Gwent. Cultural differences in Scotland and Northern Ireland are not strictly regionalized. This is particularly important in Northern Ireland, for the intermixture of Protestants and Catholics in all parts of Ulster means that there is no way in which boundaries can be redrawn to reduce religious-based political conflict.[29]

Interregional differences do not deny national communities. One reason for this is that patterns of regional differences tend to vary from nation to nation of the United Kingdom. A complex statistical analysis of the social characteristics of all local authorities within Great Britain found that significant differences between areas within Scotland were not the same as those subdividing Wales, which in turn differed from England. For example, Scotland has far more areas with large numbers of council houses, Wales is unusually high in its proportion of traditional industry areas, and England in its proportion of suburban growth areas. But within each nationally distinctive pattern, Scottish and Welsh local authority areas tend to be relatively homogeneous, especially by comparison with England.[30]

A second reason for the relative unimportance of interregional differences within nations is that they tend to be found in the least populous regions. For example, the region with the lowest unemployment in the United Kingdom, the Scottish Borders, is also the smallest in population; and the region with the highest proportion in agriculture, Powys in Wales, is second smallest in population. The largest regions in each nation tend to conform to their national pattern. Since Strathclyde contains nearly half of Scotland's population, generalizations about Strathclyde tend to be true of Scotland. Generalizations about Glamorganshire tend to be true about Wales, since its three parts contain nearly half the population of Wales. Similarly, Belfast and its environs contain about half the population of Northern Ireland.

Within each of the four nations of the United Kingdom, interregional differences are diminishing.[31] This reflects a very long-term historical process. Industrialization helped create national communities within Scotland, Wales and Northern Ireland, instead of denationalizing or homogenizing them in a single community of the United Kingdom. Before industrialization, the population of all the nations of the United Kingdom was scattered among farms and villages. Industrialization concentrated people in a central belt of Scotland, in Glamorgan and Monmouthshire in South Wales, and in Belfast and environs. Only in England did industrialization create a national concentration of population (the North of England) that could act as a counterweight to the dominant South of England. By comparison with 1801, the population of Scotland, Wales and Northern Ireland today is far more concentrated in one area, an important condition for creating or sustaining a sense of common identity. Moreover, these concentrations are greater than within England itself.[32]

Systematically comparing national characteristics on both economic and cultural criteria leads to important negative as well as positive conclusions. First, it rejects the idea that economic conditions constitute a major source of difference among the nations of the United Kingdom. All four are old industrial nations by the standards of almost any part of the Western world, including the United States, Germany, Sweden and Japan. In the 1980s all four nations of the United Kingdom share economic difficulties. Second, cultural differences, as symbolized by national identity and religion, differentiate the four nations of the United Kingdom from one another. Whereas economic differences create common group identifications that cut across the boundaries of England, Scotland, Wales and Northern Ireland, cultural differences create divisions parallel with the national boundaries of the United Kingdom.

How Does England Fit In?

In specific situations it is usually not difficult to identify English people or England. But the national identity of England is not clearly articulated, conceptually or institutionally. There is no agreed use of the term *England* differentiating it from *Britain*. It is not thought odd that an intergovernmental organization should be known as the Anglo-German Foundation in English and in German as the Deutsche-Britische Stiftung. Often the problem of nomenclature is resolved by omitting the name of the country, as with postage stamps and coins. This is also a token of the security of an unspecified national identity. At least six different usages are common:

1. *England to refer to England:*	England's football team hopes for World Cup win.
2. *England to refer to Britain:*	England expects that every man will do his duty (Nelson at Trafalgar).
3. *England and Britain used interchangeably:*	*Alas, Alas for England: What Went Wrong for Britain,* a book by Louis Heren.
4. *Britain to refer to Britain:*	British Rail.
5. *Britain to refer to the United Kingdom:*	British Broadcasting Corporation.
6. *Britain to refer to more than the United Kingdom:*	The British Empire, British nationality.

At general elections, English people are not asked to support an English National Party demanding secession from the United Kingdom, as a counterpart to Nationalist parties elsewhere in the United Kingdom. To assert an exclusively English identity would be a disruptive claim in a multinational United Kingdom. Major parties do not do this. Historically, the Conservative Party was an expansive Imperial party. Insofar as it is today the party of the status quo, the Conservative Party is a party of Union. The Labour Party is even more committed to campaigning on a Union basis because it is disproportionately dependent upon winning seats in Scotland and Wales to secure a parliamentary majority.

The nearest equivalent to a Nationalist party in England is a very inadequate approximation, the National Front. At the 1979 United Kingdom election, 297 of the 303 constituencies that the National Front fought were in England. The principal characteristic of the National Front is that it has a racialist rather than a Nationalist appeal. It is against nonwhite immigrants, but it does not claim that England is a separate race deserving its own government independent of Scotland, Wales and Northern Ireland. Moreover, the weakness of the National Front—it won only 0.6 percent of the vote in 1979 and much less in the two 1974 elections—emphasizes the weakness of its racialist or pseudo-Nationalist appeal.

England is a state of mind, not a consciously organized political institution. The strength of communal identity in England is such that there is no need to organize St. George's Day feasts as a counterpart to the Welsh St. David's day or to organize "Shakespeare Night" banquets as Scots have "Burns Night" suppers. The origins of nationhood in England are buried so far back in time that there is no founding date to celebrate, as Ulster Protestants celebrate the Twelfth of July 1690 or Americans celebrate the Fourth of July.

From an English point of view, the simplest thing to do is to treat the United Kingdom as if it were a single homogeneous nation. As the Royal Commission on the Constitution noted, "What many Scots and Welshmen consider a partnership of nations, the average Englishman tends to regard as one nation comprising different kinds of people." Doing this avoids the problem of thinking specially about Scotland, Wales or Northern Ireland. But it can also cause offence elsewhere in the United Kingdom, for, as the Royal Commission Report also noted, "The English tend to use the terms England and English when they mean Britain and British, often to the annoyance of the Scots and the Welsh."[33] From an English point of view, the distinctions are of no importance, but they are significant in a multinational state. Non-English parts view being British as a significant and different identification from their national identity. The failure of English people to see the difference leads a Welsh critic, John Osmond, to argue that there is a "refusal of the English to participate in the idea of Britishness."[34]

Failing to distinguish between England and Britain is a great handicap for English politicians if they wish to speak about distinctively English political cocerns. The upsurge of Scottish and Welsh Nationalism has challenged some English politicians to think in such terms. But parliamentary debates about devolution — which could be perceived from an English perspective as giving favoured treatment to Scotland and Wales at the expense of England — demonstrate the fundamental confusion of national identity among MPs sitting for English constituencies. Some MPs sought to deny the existence of a multinational United Kingdom; for example, Sir William Elliott, representing Newcastle-upon-Tyne North, proclaimed, "People are British whether or not they live in Wales, North East England, in Scotland or in Northern Ireland." Other MPs, such as Eric Moonman, representing Basildon in Essex, articulated a demand "for England's voice to be heard." Yet a third group contradict themselves; for example, Sir Bernard Braine of South East Essex could assert that ordinary people "consider themselves British" and then, a few minutes later, could add, "I am trying to speak for the ordinary people of England." Gerry Fowler, briefly a minister concerned with devolution, was unusual in asking the House of Commons to recognize a "sense of nationhood" throughout the United Kingdom, asserting, "I am proud to be both English and British."[35]

Population provides the key to understanding England's role as the inarticulate yet preeminent nation of the United Kingdom. As long as England constitutes 81 percent of the constituencies in Parliament, there is no need for English people to organize to advance distinctive demands. English views will never be overlooked at Westminster as long as representation is related to population and England is preeminent in population. The division of the non-English parts of the United Kingdom into three different nations further increases the preeminence of England. The population of England outnumbers Scotland by a ratio of 9 to 1, Wales by 16 to 1 and Northern Ireland by 30 to 1. Nor is there great cause for friction from cross-national mobility, for the English-born population is only 2 percent of the population of the non-English parts of the United Kingdom, and internal migration from these parts to England accounts for only a small proportion of the population of England. The United Kingdom is analogous to the proverbial "horse and rabbit" stew; there is no doubt which nation contributes the largest animal to this potpourri.

The population of the United Kingdom has changed greatly since the creation of the United Kingdom in 1801. At that time, England contributed but 53 percent of the 16 million people of the United Kingdom, and Ireland 33 percent. Politically, England was dominant, returning 74 percent of members of the unreformed House of Commons. England remained preeminent even after reform related parliamentary representation to population, because of the relative and absolute decline of the population of Ireland. Scotland and Wales have maintained a relatively static share of the population of Great Britain.[36] Famine and mass emigration on a scale unknown elsewhere in Europe caused the population of Ireland to contract between 1801 and 1901 when every other nation, especially England, was growing greatly in size. The secession of the 26 counties of Southern Ireland further enhanced England's parliamentary dominance. Had Ireland maintained its population share and its position in the United Kingdom, then by 1901 it would have had 223 rather than 101 Members of Parliament. Northern Ireland could have claimed 42 MPs rather than 12 (the number it has today), had its share of the United Kingdom population remained constant at 6.6 percent.

Today the United Kingdom is politically asymmetrical: Three of the four nations of the United Kingdom are self-consciously nations, demanding and receiving distinctive political treatment within the United Kingdom, with at least one party promoting national independence from Westminster. By contrast, the largest nation in the United Kingdom, England, claims no distinctive institutions of governance, though it acquires these, if only by default, when Scotland, Wales and Northern Ireland opt out on specific policies. Yet England, for all its inarticulateness, is no less distinctly a nation and part of a multinational United Kingdom.

The Union Jack symbolizes the complex unity of the nations of the United Kingdom. It is a single flag, representing the authority of the Mace—but it is also composite in composition. A Union flag was first flown in 1606 after England and Scotland gained a common monarch in James VI and I. It combined the crosses of St. George for England and St. Andrew for Scotland. Wales was deemed to be represented by the Cross of St. George. Following the creation of the United Kingdom in 1801, a cross for St. Patrick of Ireland was added. The asymmetry of national consciousness within the United Kingdom is shown by the fact that an Englishman will normally identify England with the Union Jack rather than the Cross of St. George. Elsewhere the Union Jack is identified with the United Kingdom. National identity is symbolized in Scotland by the blue on white saltire and in Wales by a dragon pennant. In Northern Ireland, the Protestants take as their emblem the Red Hand of Ulster, and Ulster Catholics the tricolour flag of the Republic of Ireland. Given the indefinite domain of the Crown, the Union Jack has also been used as a part of the flags of Canada, Australia and New Zealand to assert their "Britishness."[37]

NOTES

1. E. Kedourie, *Nationalism* (3rd ed.; London: Hutchinson, 1966), p. 9.
2. See, e.g., S.N. Eisenstadt and Stein Rokkan, eds. *Building States and Nations,* 2 vols. (London: Sage Publications, 1973); and Charles Tilly, ed., *The Formation of National States in Western Europe* (Princeton: Princeton University Press, 1975).
3. See Sir Harold Wilson's letter published in the *Daily Telegraph* of 6 August 1979.
4. Royal Commission on the Constitution, *Minutes of Evidence II: Scotland* (London: HMSO, 1969), p. 75.
5. See Royal Commission on the Constitution, *Report,* pp. 111, 122, 128, 45, 2, 54, 121.
6. See D.E. Allen, *British Tastes* (London: Hutchinson, 1968).
7. See Royal Commission on Local Government in England, *Community Attitudes Survey: England* (London: HMSO, Research Studies 9, 1969), pp. 11ff; and Richard Rose, "Ordinary People in Extraordinary Economic Circumstances," in Rose, ed., *Challenge to Governance* (London: Sage, 1980), pp. 152-58.
8. See, e.g., S.M. Lipset and S. Rokkan, eds., "Introduction," in *Party Systems and Voter Alignments* (New York: Free Press, 1967); Richard Rose, *Governing without Consensus* (London: Faber & Faber, 1971), chap. 14; and Richard Rose and D.W. Urwin, *Regional Differentiation and Political Unity in Western Nations* (London: Sage Professional Paper in Contemporary Political Sociology No. 06-007, 1975), pp. 6ff.
9. See Richard Rose, Ian McAllister and Peter Mair, *Is There a Concurring Majority about Northern Ireland?* (Glasgow: University of Strathclyde Studies in Public Policy No. 22, 1978).
10. For a brief introduction to the plurality of Celtic peoples, see, e.g., Nora Chadwick, *The Celts* (Harmondsworth: Penguin, 1970); and Joseph Raftery, ed., *The Celts* (Cork: Mercier Press, 1964).
11. Historically, the term *Ulster* referred to a nine-county province in pre-1921 Ireland, which in turn was part of the United Kingdom. It is used here to refer to the population of the six counties of that historic province that now constitutes the Northern Ireland part of the United Kingdom.
12. Arguably, the United Kingdom could be said to consist of three nations and two part nations, that is, Northern Ireland Protestants forming only part of Ulster, and Northern Ireland Catholics a part of Ireland. Institutionally, the United Kingdom definitely has four territories—England, Wales, Scotland and Northern Ireland—and it is these "parts" that are referred to as nations here.
13. For a parallel example from Canada, see Maurice Pinard, "Self-Determination in Quebec," in *Resolving Nationality Conflicts,* ed. W.P. Davison and L. Gordenker (New York: Praeger, 1980), pp. 143-76.
14. See J. Brand, W. Miller and M. Jordan, "National Consciousness and Voting in Scotland" (paper to the 1981 Conference of the Political Studies Association, University of Hull), pp. 11, 30; and D. Balsom, P. Madgwick and D. van Mechelen, "The Red and the Green: Patterns of Partisan

Choice in Wales" (paper to the 1981 Conference of the Political Studies Association, University of Hull). On commonalities of outlooks within Northern Ireland, see Rose, *Governing without Consensus,* chap. 10.

15. See *Post Office Report and Accounts 1979-80* (London: HMSO) and *Report on the Delivery, Performance and Potential of the Post Office's Mail Services* (London: Post Office Users National Council Report No. 17, 1979), Annex 1.

16. For an outline and statistics, see Richard Rose and Ian McAllister, *United Kingdom Facts* (London: Macmillan, 1982), chap. 7.

17. Calculated from the sources reported in table 1.1.

18. Cf. Rose and Urwin, *Regional Differentiation and Political Unity in Western Nations.*

19. For an embarrassed political colloquy about the position of Jews in Britain, see a passage in a parliamentary debate on a race relations bill, House of Commons, *Debates,* vol. 711, cols. 932-33 (3 May 1965). On differences among Jews about their political status in Britain, see Geoffrey Alderman, *The Jewish Vote in Great Britain Since 1945* (Glasgow: University of Strathclyde Studies in Public Policy No. 72, 1980).

20. Royal Commission on the Constitution, *Report,* p. 102.

21. See, e.g., the citations in the Introduction, note 7.

22. Convergence figures calculated from sources in table 1.2 and Richard Rose, "The United Kingdom as a Multi-National State," as printed in Rose, ed., *Studies in British Politics* (3rd ed.; London: Macmillan, 1976), tables 11, 12. For further details, see Ian McAllister, Richard Parry and Richard Rose, *United Kingdom Rankings: the Territorial Dimension in Social Indicators* (Glasgow: University of Strathclyde Studies in Public Policy No. 44, 1979), esp. table 1.3.

23. See, e.g., R.M. White, "What's in a Name? Problems in Official and Legal Usages of Race" *New Community* 7, no. 3 (1979): 333-49; and on historical background, L.P. Curtis, Jr., *Anglo-Saxons and Celts* (New York: New York University Press, 1968).

24. See Rose, "The United Kingdom as a Multi-National State," table 6.

25. The difference index is calculated by taking the arithmetic difference from the United Kingdom figure of the proportion of each group within a nation, summing these differences, and dividing by two.

26. For further details, see Rose and McAllister, *United Kingdom Facts,* table 9.6.

27. See L.J. Sharpe, "British Politics and the Two Regionalisms," in *The Exploding City,* ed. W.D.C. Wright and D.H. Stewart (Edinburgh: Edinburgh University Press, 1972), p. 145.

28. For full details of regional rankings, see Rose and McAllister, *United Kingdom Facts,* chap. 9; for an analysis, see McAllister, Parry and Rose, *United Kingdom Rankings,* pp. 17-25.

29. See Richard Rose and Ian McAllister, "Repartition Not the Solution to Northern Ireland's Problems," *Irish Times* (Dublin), 16 September 1975.

30. See Richard Webber and John Craig, *Socio-Economic Classification of Local Authority Areas* (London: HMSO, Office of Population Censuses and

Surveys, Studies on Medical and Population Subjects No. 35, 1978), p. 16
and appendix. For an analysis of territorial similarities and dissimilarities
at a smaller scale, see Richard Webber, *Parliamentary Constituencies: a
Socio-Economic Classification* (London: Office of Population Censuses
and Surveys, Occasional Paper No. 13, 1978).

31. See McAllister, Parry and Rose, *United Kingdom Rankings,* tables 2.2 and
2.3.
32. See Rose, "The United Kingdom as a Multi-National State," table 2.
33. Royal Commission on the Constitution, *Report,* pp. 102, 58.
34. John Osmond, "Wales in the 1980s," in *Nations Without a State,* ed. C.R.
Foster (New York: Praeger, 1980), p. 50.
35. The quotations are from House of Commons *Debates* as follows: Elliott,
Moonman and Fowler, vol. 922 (13 December 1976), cols. 1011, 1027 and
1081 respectively; Braine, vol. 924, col. 470 (19 January 1977).
36. See Rose, "The United Kingdom as a Multi-National State," table 14.
37. After nearly a century, Canada adopted a maple leaf flag without the Union
Jack to emphasize its changing social composition.

2. Union Without Uniformity

Before we can explain how the United Kingdom works, we need to know what the United Kingdom is. Unfortunately, ordinary English lacks the vocabulary and grammar to talk about what we see around us. Because the United Kingdom is an abstract concept, it is far easier to see its manifestations than to identify the thing itself. The palpable evidence of government is everywhere about us: in schools and hospitals, in Cabinet deliberations covered by the Official Secrets Act and in well-publicized debates in Parliament. But its defining properties are elusive.

Conventionally, one way to identify a government is to identify the people subject to its authority. But Parliament has never been able to identify the citizens of the United Kingdom in clear or stable terms. Until 1948 a British subject was any resident of the Empire and Commonwealth "belonging to any country of the Commonwealth who is a subject of the King." The 1948 British Nationality Act created a new status of citizenship, dividing British subjects into two categories: those who were citizens of the United Kingdom or its still numerous colonies, and those who were citizens of an independent Commonwealth country. Both native-born United Kingdom residents and subjects from the most remote parts of the Commonwealth had a common right to enter the United Kingdom and vote in British elections. Popular resentment of the entry to Britain of coloured Commonwealth immigrants has led successive governments from 1962 to restrict the right of coloured British subjects to enter the United Kingdom, and in the case of East African Asians, to restrict entry by coloured British citizens. To allow entry by the right (i.e., white) people, 1971 legislation added a further complicating concept: patrial citizens of the United Kingdom and Colonies, i.e., Commonwealth citizens with a parent born in the United Kingdom. With customary English illogicality in matters Irish, "the status of citizens of the Irish Republic in United Kingdom law is that they are neither British subjects nor foreigners." The 1975 devolution proposals declared explicitly that anyone who was a citizen of the Republic of Ireland could be elected to national Assemblies proposed for Scotland and Wales.[1]

Today United Kingdom citizenship embraces British subjects who are also citizens of the United Kingdom; British subjects who are citizens of the few remaining colonies; and patrials, Commonwealth citizens who can claim one parent who was a British subject born within the United Kingdom. The uncertainty and instability of who is or is not British is illustrated by the attempts of the 1974 Labour government and the 1979 Conservative government to create what a white paper called "new citizenships" in the plural. Six categories of citizenship were proposed in the 1980 white paper *British Nationality Law:* British citizenship, citizenship of the British dependent territories, British overseas citizens, British subjects without citizenship, British protected persons, and Irish citizens who are neither British nor foreign. Only the first and last of these groups would have an unqualified right to reside in the United Kingdom.

Another way to come to grips with the government of the United Kingdom is to ask: What is the territory of the United Kingdom? A modern state must define its territory both in international law and in its institutions of domestic government. International law imposes a definition of territory upon the United Kingdom; geographically, it consists of the islands of Great Britain and ancillary islands (e.g., the Isle of Wight, the Hebrides, Orkney and Shetland) and the northeastern portion of the island of Ireland. But politically, the Crown has never confined its claims to this territory alone. It is a Crown of indefinite domain, and of global extent in Imperial days.

A third way to define government is in terms of its institutions. But the institutions for governing the United Kingdom are not uniform. Legislation can be and is enacted separately for Scotland, for Northern Ireland and for England and Wales. At the apex of government, the Cabinet combines functional and territorial ministries. The Treasury normally deals with the whole of the United Kingdom; whereas the Scottish, Welsh and Northern Ireland Offices deal only with one part. The functional ministries responsible for the major programmes of the contemporary welfare state are concerned with needs common to all the United Kingdom, but their territorial scope is often restricted to one part (see table 5.2).

The Crown is the most appropriate symbol of the United Kingdom. Like any symbol, it requires careful explication. The first section of this chapter examines the historical evolution of the Crown's indefinite domain as it expanded from being the government of less than half the island of Britain to claiming sway over one-fifth of the globe, only to contract in the past generation to its present post-Imperial limits. In the second section, the role of the Crown is elucidated as the source of the authority of government and also as the source of the Union of territories and peoples that makes the United Kingdom what it is today. The multiform character of the principal institutions of territorial governance is examined in the third section, which shows that the United Kingdom is a Union without uniformity.

A Crown of Indefinite Domain

The United Kingdom today is the product of accident rather than design. As its name implies, it is a Union of territories that were once subject to a multiplicity of lords and monarchs. The parts were joined in a variety of ways; force as well as consent were important. If wars centuries ago had gone differently, then the United Kingdom might be a Union of the Crowns of England and France, or at least Wessex and Normandy. The English Channel would then be described as a grand canal, facilitating movement between two parts of this Kingdom.

History is important for understanding the territorial extent of the United Kingdom today; it cannot be deduced from any constitutional principles. The United Kingdom was created by dynastic unions and military conquests; it was not intended as the result of a conscious, rational plan. The varied, even egregious institutions grouped together to form the United Kingdom today can be understood in terms of their historical origins. Historical explanation is not to be confused with justification. The reasons of history are different from the reasons of politicians, economists or social scientists.

The gradual evolution of the Crown stands in marked contrast to the histories of many major Western countries. The United Kingdom was not created as a positive act of nineteenth-century nation-building or re-created after the political devastation of a twentieth-century war. Through an accident of insular history, the United Kingdom has been spared the traumas of military occupation, and politicians have maintained continuity of political institutions. Hence, it is not the product of a compact, drafted and signed by its constituent partners, as is usually the case in a country with a written Constitution. It is an agglomeration created by the expansion and contraction of territorial power in the course of a thousand years.

A millennium ago, geography militated against the creation of any common government within the boundaries of the present-day United Kingdom. Water, not land, was the primary means of communication. The 4900 miles of coastline around the island of Great Britain, the 2200 miles of Irish coastline and the virtually unlimited coastline of the European continent made travel easy between these territories. Movement brought different people together, but by very different routes than land-based communication by rail and road. The East Coast of Britain was open to penetration from the European continent. Romans and Normans entered the South East of the island; Danish and Norse invaders penetrated the East Coast of what is now Scotland as well as England. The West Coast of the island of Britain was closer by water to Ireland than to its east coast; the West of Scotland is only 12 miles from Ireland by boat. Liverpool's proximity by water to Dublin gave it an orientation to

Ireland, just as Dover faced toward France, East Anglia toward the Netherlands, and Newcastle toward Scandinavia.

Uncertainties, ambiguities and controversies about the domains of the Crown have been a millennium in the making. Attempts to trace the origin and evolution of the terms *Britain* and *Great Britain* emphasize how contingent upon events are present-day labels of the United Kingdom. Prior to the Norman Conquest of 1066, the term *Britain* was applied to both sides of the English Channel, that is, to the Celtic area of Brittany as well as to its island neighbour. A scholar concludes, "From the twelfth century, though Britannia means Brittany and can mean Wales, it frequently also means Britain."[2] The terms *Greater* and *Lesser Britain* were developed to distinguish territories on facing sides of the Channel. By the later Middle Ages, Greater Britain could also mean England, or alternatively, as in the Crown's petition to the Council of Constance in 1414, the term could be used interchangeably to refer to England, Scotland and Wales, or to "the English or British nation."[3]

The passage from Tudor to Stuart kings is particularly revealing of differences of opinion about what monarchs thought they were the rulers of. Mary Stuart, known to history as Mary Queen of Scots, initially styled herself Queen of France, Scotland, England and Ireland, in that order.[4] By contrast, James Stuart, known as King James VI of Scotland and James I of England, was originally proclaimed in London as "King of the realms of England, France and Ireland," but then altered his style to "King of Great Britain, France and Ireland."[5] Attempts to describe the island by the pair of titles, South Britain and North Britain, failed.

The United Kingdom today demonstrates the importance of politics imposing institutions that cut across geographical links. London is the capital of the United Kingdom, notwithstanding its peripheral position at the extreme southeastern part of the island of Great Britain. In geographical terms, London would only be apt as the capital of the Kingdom of England, France and Ireland, for it is closer to France than it is to the non-English parts of the United Kingdom. In geographical terms, Liverpool would be the logical capital of the United Kingdom, given its central place in sea-based communications with Ireland and Scotland, as well as western England. But territorial tensions have never caused London to be abandoned as the capital, a fate that did occur to chief cities in America, Australia and Germany.

The Kingdom of England is the primary Kingdom to which other jurisdictions were joined, yet a millennium ago England itself was a disparate and uncertain number of petty kingdoms and jurisdictions, sometimes known as the Heptarchy (seven kingdoms), but at times with as many as twelve kingdoms. Whereas the sea created a clear geographical boundary between England and the Continent, England's land boundaries with Wales and Scotland created territorial disputes. The ruins of Border castles are silent reminders today of the contingent nature of the limits of the Kingdom of England.[6]

By contrast with continental Europe, the making of England has three noteworthy features. The first is that an effective nationwide authority was established relatively early, whether it is dated from the Norman Conquest or the Tudor revolution in the machinery of government. Second, institutions of government have continued for many centuries; they have been adapted rather then repudiated. Parliament, with origins in the thirteenth century, is a particularly important example of continuity. It has changed from an aristocratic to a democratic assembly, but is has always been a representative body. Third, the Crown has never confined its territorial claims to England, or for that matter, to Great Britain. Claims to the Continent were abandoned *de facto* with the withdrawal from Calais in 1558, but the Crown's claim to the Kingdom of France was abandoned *de jure* only with the Treaty of Amiens in 1802.

The steps required to create the United Kingdom, as distinct from a medieval holding company of separate kingdoms, began with the joining of Wales and England. While Wales had been occupied if not governed by Roman forces, the territory subsequently lapsed into diverse hands controlling isolated jurisdictions. William, the Norman conqueror, failed to subdue Wales at the end of the eleventh century and established lords along the Welsh Marches for protection against Welsh invaders. Wales was more or less brought under the Crown in 1282. The accession of Henry VII in 1485 brought a Welshman to the throne. In 1536 Wales was formally annexed and became *de jure* like England, having members of Parliament, an established church and using English as the language of the law. The framework of government for the principality was indistinguishable from that of English shires. From 1746 until 1967 the word England in an Act of Parliament was explicitly deemed to include Wales.

Political integration did not result in cultural assimilation. Language was the most obvious badge of differentiation in Wales. Prior to industrialization, the whole of Wales was overwhelmingly Welsh-speaking. Compulsory education was to become the means of compulsory Anglicization, for Welsh was not a language of classroom instruction, though it was the language of everyday life. Welsh was dismissed by the nineteenth-century education commissioners as "a language of old-fashioned agriculture, of theology and of simple rustic life" conducive to "the most unreasoning prejudices or impulses, and an utter want of method in thinking and acting." The first language census in Wales in 1891 found that 54 percent of the population was Welsh-speaking (but many were bilingual, speaking English as well).[7] Religion, too, divided Wales from England until the disestablishment of the episcopal Church in Wales in 1920.

Whereas the economic leadership was English-speaking or Anglocentric, religious and educational leaders remained Welsh oriented.

The territory that became known as Scotland was created in medieval times by amalgamating the lands of clans, petty rulers and kings. It was defined externally by wars and skirmishes with England and alliances further afield directed against the English Crown. By 1603 Scotland was a Kingdom that had maintained its independence and effective authority for centuries, with a Parliament, legal system, religion and politics distinct from England. At that point James VI of Scotland fell heir to the English Crown, and moved to London. There he reigned as King of England, Scotland and Ireland and claimant to France, each with separate institutions of governance. In 1707 an Act of Union decreed the abolition of "the two Kingdoms of Scotland and England" and declared that they should "forever after be united into one Kingdom by the name of Great Britain." This language incidentally paid silent tribute to the integration of Wales within England.

Scotland's position within the United Kingdom has been anomalous since the Act of Union of 1707 merged the Scots and English parliaments in a British Parliament, yet simultaneously entrenched in the Act of Union separate and different Scottish institutions of law and religion. While these fields of public policy are of limited importance today, at the time they were of first importance, for government was concerned with little else. Presbyterians, denied many public posts in England because they were nonconformists, were the backbone of establishment in Scotland. Union allowed Scotland to trade directly with foreign nations; Scotland could thus participate fully in the industrial revolution and the expansion of international trade that followed. After the crushing of the 1745 rebellion raised in Scotland by Prince Charles Edward Stuart, Scottish regiments were raised to fight under the Union flag for the Hanoverian Crown. The creation of Great Britain led to the expansion of opportunities for Scots and, equally important, to the protection of the particular interests of major groups within Scottish society—the church, the law, education, landowning and the military.

Like Irish kings such as Brian Boru, the Crown failed to establish effective authority throughout Ireland. The late twelfth century conquest of Ireland by the Crown was followed by a settlement of territorial lords nominally owing allegiance to the Crown but often siding with the "mere Irishry," that is, native groups. Authority was best exercised within the Pale, the territory around Dublin, the capital and chief garrison. The Reformation was followed by a century of insurrection and battle. The authority of the Crown was much strengthened in Ulster by the plantation of Protestant settlers, beginning in 1607. It was made effective throughout the island by the army of King William in a series of battles against the forces of James II, still commemorated by Ulster Protestants on the Twelfth of July, the anniversary of the victory at the Boyne in 1690. The government of Ireland was in the hands of a viceroy (literally, in place of the king) and exercised principally from Dublin Castle.

The United Kingdom of Great Britain and Ireland was created in 1801 by the abolition of the Irish Parliament and the addition of Irish representation at Westminster. For most practical purposes, the administration of Ireland continued as before from Dublin Castle, but it was now directly linked to Parliament. The government of Ireland was subordinate to Westminster, but the governed were often insubordinate. In the nineteenth century, Irish politicians began demanding home rule or independence. Westminster sought relief from seemingly endless troubles with Ireland by alternating between policies of coercion and conciliation.

Many English writers have viewed the United Kingdom as simply "the extension of England into the world."[8] In advancing this proposition, the Oxford scholar Nevil Johnson describes the national *(sic)* identity of Britain as "always composite and in some degrees artificial." To say it is artificial is to imply that there is an artificer. England is seen as taking this role: "England cast its energies into the creation of an imperium, acquiring riches throughout the world and applying the political ideas of her own people." Johnson notes that both the idea of the United Kingdom and the Imperial idea involved a readiness of other nations to adapt to England's lead and an English tolerance of the customs of others. The civilization of England could be the motive of Imperial rule without assimilating or being assimilated by other cultures of Greater Britain.

Writing with all the authority of a world-famous English historian, A.J.P. Taylor denies that it is necessary to discuss anything but English history when telling the story of Westminster government. Taylor uses the term *England* to incorporate Wales, Scotland and Ireland and the Empire indiscriminately insofar as they have the same history as England or "made a stir in English politics or aroused English interests in other ways." Thus, Ireland enters into English history because of its rebellion against England's rule. Scotland does not, because it went along with the events of what Taylor calls English politics. The term *Britain* is dismissed as "the name of a Roman province which perished in the fifth century and which included none of Scotland, nor indeed, all of England."[9]

By contrast, the New Zealand historian J.G.A. Pocock argues that British history can no more be reduced to a study of England than the history of the German-speaking people can be reduced to the study of the German state of the moment. "Scotland is no more English than Britain is European." British history, Pocock argues, is a "*plural* history of a group of cultures situated along an Anglo-Celtic frontier."[10] In the fullness of centuries two things happened: England became the dominant area within the British Isles, and the British people moved outward from the "Atlantic archipelago" to populate domains aroun the world. From Pocock's perspective, British history is an account of the *interaction* between different societies originating in Britain but dispersed across three continents. If the American colonies had not successfully rebelled, then, Pocock speculates, the capital of the British Empire might have been Philadelphia, not London.

The Royal Commission on the Constitution adopted an Imperial conception of Britain. Like Pocock, it rejected Taylor's reductionist assertion that Britain was nothing more than England writ large: "The United Kingdom has been greater than the sum of its constituent parts." It treated Britain, "a vague consciousness" surviving from Roman times, as the primordial concept, the first identification of the home island. It praised the way in which Britain had prospered as the first industrial nation and spread across the world in the days of Empire. It saw these achievements as owing much to Union, which allowed "the energies and talents of all the British people to be directed to peaceful pursuits at home and to expansion abroad." In other words, the political stability of Union was a condition of economic prosperity.[11]

Concurrently with the creation of the United Kingdom, the Crown was confronted with problems of how to govern lands that were far from the British isles. The Plantation of Virginia occurred in 1607, the same year as the Plantation of Londonderry. In the two centuries following, the Crown acquired some form of suzerainty over a very heterogeneous group of territories on every inhabited continent of the earth. Diversity was the chief characteristic of the polyglot and multiracial people brought together under the Crown. Like the parts of the United Kingdom, each territory came under the Crown by a separate act, specific to particular historical circumstances and reflecting local conditions. Since diverse political arrangements predated the Crown's claim to rule, it followed that there was diversity in the instruments of Imperial authority.

The Crown was the linchpin of Imperial authority, but in no sense was the King-Emperor the actual ruler. Given the difficulties of communication with the farflung Empire, there was no way in which anyone in London could actually be the effective day-to-day governor of disparate and distant lands. Nor was there any wish at Westminster to become bogged down in the details of governing such distant lands. There was need to create institutions of everyday governance on the ground, reserving to Westminster decisions on matters of Imperial concern, such as war and peace, and trade.[12]

The adoption of anything but uniform institutions to rule the Empire did not detract from the supreme authority of the Crown in Parliament. Edmund Burke, an Irishman as well as a major figure at Westminster, argued during the American Revolution that maintaining the authority of Parliament did not require centralization at Westminster of responsibility for governing territories oceans distant from it. It required the opposite, the grant of substantial measures of autonomy to local assemblies, to administrators appointed by the Crown or to resident political advisers sustaining indirect rule through native leaders. Burke argued that dual institutions of government were "the most reconcilable things in the world."

> The Parliament of Great Britain sits at the head of her extensive empire in two capacities: one as the local legislature of this island, providing for all things at home, immediately, and by no other instrument than the executive power; the other, and I think her nobler capacity, is what I call her *imperial character,* in which, as from the throne of heaven, she superintends all the several inferior legislatures, and guides and controls them, without annihilating any.[13]

The Imperial idea gave institutional form and territorial substance to the Crown. Nothing more remote from the political and economic unity of the United Kingdom could be imagined than the British Empire at its multicontinental and multigovernmental zenith. Any attempt to draw the lines of institutional authority under the Crown, say, in 1901, the year of Queen Victoria's death, would have produced a maze of entanglements. Yet the authority of the Crown was unchallenged. Westminster was the home of an Imperial Parliament with limited but real responsibilities for lands outside as well as within the United Kingdom. Westminster saw no challenge to this Imperial authority in granting Dominion status to governments in Canada, Australia, New Zealand and South Africa.

Ironically, Westminster itself proved a weak point, having the double task of maintaining Imperial authority and simultaneously acting as a "local" government for the British isles. Imperialists wondered whether it was necessary or desirable for the Westminster Parliament to be concerned with problems of municipal sanitation as well as Imperial affairs. Leading Imperialists such as Joseph Chamberlain began to promote the idea of separating the domestic government of the United Kingdom from Westminster's Imperial concerns. This was to be done by making the United Kingdom a federation, with separate Parliaments for Ireland, Scotland, Wales and England, and a federal Parliament in London also responsible for Imperial concerns.[14] The promotion of devolution from above reached its high point in a 1919 House of Commons resolution declaring the need to "devote more attention to the general interests of the United Kingdom . . . and matters of common Imperial concern." It called for "federal devolution of government to England, Scotland and Ireland," with Wales subsumed under England. The next year a Speaker's Conference presented to the Commons a scheme for federal devolution, but no action was taken by the government. Interest quickly lapsed with the resolution of the Irish conflict that had also done much to stimulate interest in home rule.[15]

The challenge that Ireland presented to the authority of the United Kingdom was great, but also ambiguous. The claim of Ireland to be a nation was commonly accepted by both Protestants and Catholics. Nor could Ireland be exempted from the reform of its distinctive institutions at a time of great reform in England as well. The Irish Parliamentary Party demanded "home rule" for the Irish nation. The difficulty was in determining whether home rule was or was not consistent with the authority of the Crown. Mr. Gladstone argued that it was, telling the House of Commons that home rule would allow "self-government in Irish not in Imperial affairs. . . . The Irishman is more profoundly Irish, but it does not follow that because his local patriotism is keen he is incapable of Imperial patriotism."[16] The Irish Parliamentary Party was called Nationalist, but many were ready to accept an Imperial loyalty as well. For example, Arthur Griffith, founder of Sinn Fein, in 1904 published a tract entitled *The Resurrection of Hungary: A Parallel for Ireland,* recommending a dual monarchy along Habsburg lines for Britain and Ireland—and an Irish share in the Imperial government of those races that were neither British nor Irish. The opponents of home rule, such as A.V. Dicey, argued for a much stricter definition of the authority of Parliament, citing the practical difficulties that would arise in Westminster with a home rule Parliament in Dublin as well.[17]

Like the succession states created at the Versailles peace conference following the First World War, the United Kingdom as currently constituted (i.e., the government of Great Britain and Northern Ireland) dates only from 1921. The settlement of the Irish troubles by the 1921 Anglo-Irish Treaty was within the Imperial tradition: Westminster recognized the Irish Free State as a Dominion, and a Dominion subject to special restrictions and special privileges. The acceptance of Dominion status by Ireland triggered a bloody civil war there; the full and unequivocal achievement of its status as the Republic of Ireland did not come until 1949. The creation of a separate Northern Ireland Parliament at Stormont was equally within the Imperial tradition.[18]

The House of Commons gave supreme expression to its confidence in the indivisible integrity of the United Kingdom: it hardly discussed the subject. A search of *Hansard* from 1921 reveals very few debates about the Union for half a century. Where the problem was greatest, in Northern Ireland, Westminster followed a practice of letting sleeping dogs lie, a metaphor that was as apt as it was tactless. MPs who were veterans of pre-1914 debates, such as Winston Churchill, had no wish to see Parliament once again disrupted by Ireland.

From time to time Welsh and Scottish MPs made incidental reference to their national distinctiveness, but this was done only to reassert the compatibility of dual loyalties. For example, Arthur Woodburn, Secretary of State for Scotland from 1947 to 1950, described the existence of Great Britain as "one of the greatest domestic partnerships the world has ever seen." Welsh Labour MPs such as George Thomas (subsequently Secretary of State for Wales and Speaker of the House of Commons) could dismiss devolution on these grounds: "It interests nobody except a few clergymen and university dons."[19]

The justifications offered by MPs for the United Kingdom were multiple and reinforcing. Staunch Conservatives such as Sir Robert Boothby praised it as having given Scots the opportunity to "run the British Empire for over 300 years from London."[20] A Labour minister, Aneurin Bevan, could reject the idea of devolving powers to Wales, then perceived as no more conceivable than national independence would be today, as "a constitutional impossibility." Bevan attacked Welsh Nationalists as a divisive force within Wales, who could create "a vast majority tyrannised over by a few Welsh-speaking people." Characteristic of British Socialists, Bevan favoured using Westminster to change the economy of the whole of the United Kingdom.

> Is it not rather cruel to give the impression to the 50,000 unemployed men and women in Wales that their plight would be relieved and their distress removed by this constitutional change? It is not socialism. It is escapism. This is exactly the way in which nation after nation has been ruined in the last 25 to 50 years, trying to pretend that deep-seated economic difficulties can be removed by constitutional changes.[21]

The territories of the Crown have contracted greatly in the past half century, and particularly rapidly since the end of the Second World War. In 1945 the newly elected Labour government had Cabinet ministers for the Dominions, the Colonies, and for India & Burma. Imperial matters were also a major concern of the Prime Minister, the Foreign Secretary, the Chancellor of the Exchequer and Economic and Trade ministers. Imperial concerns are now gone. The partition of India and the creation of India and Pakistan as Dominions led to the demise of the India Office. The Colonial Office continued in being until 1967, after winds of change had altered much in Africa. The last great act in the long saga of colonial independence occurred in 1980: the resolution of the Southern Rhodesian problem by the grant of independence to Zimbabwe. Today only a few colonies remain, such as Bermuda and Gibraltar. The expansion and the contraction of the Crown are reminders that the territorial jurisdiction of Westminster is a variable, not a constant.

The entry of the United Kingdom into the European Community has not expanded the political community of those loyal to the Crown. It has only confirmed the remark of the American diplomatist, Dean Acheson: "Great Britain has lost an Empire and has not yet found a role."[22] The United Kingdom is a full member of the European Community, with all the rights and responsibilities of the treaty. But whereas many of the six original members saw the association as a major step toward the creation of a supranational political community, in the United Kingdom the principal meaning of membership is economic, the costs and benefits of a Common Market. This aversion to Europe as a community is consistent with Pocock's argument that British history should be conceived outside the limits of Europe, as part of the history of people stretching to the Antipodes. England is involved with other nations that are not European but still British.[23] Yet entry to the European Community was also a sign that the United Kingdom was reducing its obligations to an Empire-turned-Commonwealth, in favour of a new network deemed more suitable for the interests of the United Kingdom itself.

Today Westminster is no more and no less than the government of the United Kingdom. Occasionally a politician may still refer to Westminster as the "Imperial Parliament," as Harold Wilson did in 1976 when arguing that devolution would not detract from the overriding authority of Parliament.[24] In Northern Ireland, as long as Stormont was in existence, it was customary to refer to Westminster as the Imperial Parliament, to differentiate it from the Northern Ireland Parliament. But Her Majesty's Government today can no longer claim to be the Parliament of an empire at its zenith.

The indefinite domain of the Crown is today defined by representation in Parliament at Westminster. In the words of the Royal Commission on the Constitution, "What distinguishes the people of the United Kingdom from others who pay homage to the Crown is their representation in the Parliament at Westminster."[25] All parts of the United Kingdom are represented in Parliament and are equally subject to its authority. Around the coast of Great Britain there are islands offshore this offshore island, such as the Isle of Man and the Channel Islands. But they are not considered part of the United Kingdom because they do not send representatives to the Westminster Parliament. Their more or less autonomous governments were described by the Royal Commission on the Constitution as "full of anomalies, peculiarities and anachronisms," that should be "accepted so long as they are cherished by those most directly affected, and do no harm to others."[26]

The contingent nature of the United Kingdom's boundaries was strikingly evidenced in a 1955 official proposal to extend the United Kingdom into the
Mediterranean, incorporating Malta. By no stretch of the imagination could
Malta, an island between Sicily and Africa, be considered geographically, culturally or historically part of what is normally defined as Britain. But the
Westminster government faced a problem: Malta wished self-government,
and at that time Westminster thought the island's strategic importance was
too great to grant it independence. Hence, an all-party committee of senior
British MPs proposed a Northern Ireland-type legislature for Malta, three
MPs at Westminster and giving this Mediterranean island more representatives in Parliament than the average English industrial town.[27]

A Stateless Crown

In international law the United Kingdom is a state, that is, a Kingdom that
claims sovereign authority within given territorial boundaries. Other countries are meant to respect the integrity of these boundaries, and Westminster is
expected to act effectively within them. But the term *state* is rarely used to describe the contemporary United Kingdom. In the judgement of the constitutional historian F.W. Maitland, the state is "a person whose personality our
law does not formally or explicitly recognize."[28] So careful a scholar of modern English history as G. Kitson Clark can casually assert that defining the
state is "relatively easy," but the definition he gives—"the State is the Community organized for the purposes of government"—begs more questions than it
answers.[29] It implies that the United Kingdom is a single community, embracing both Northern Ireland Protestants and Catholics, or else that the United
Kingdom is not a state. Contemporary Marxists often use the term state to refer to the sum of political power in society; however, so broad a definition refers to everything—and nothing in particular.[30]

To describe the United Kingdom as a state is to import a continental European term to political discourse in Britain. The idea of the state as a thing in
itself, an institution independent of and superior to members of society, can be
found in most parts of Europe for most of the modern era. But it is alien to
British political thinking. France, Germany, Italy or the Soviet Union may call
themselves states, but to describe the United Kingdom thus would require the
translation of a continental idea into English, a translation in which something important and distinctive is lost. A polycultural review of the idea of the
state in Europe rightly concludes that the idea is a variable, not a constant.
Britain and America have governments that are relatively "stateless," being
without an idea of the state.[31]

Nor can a Constitution be invoked to define the United Kingdom. In most countries of the world, a Constitution sets out the fundamentals of governance. If we wanted to know what constituted government in the United States, France or the Federal Republic of Germany, we could first look at a Constitution. It establishes, positively and negatively, the principal rules for the exercise of political authority. No lasting Constitution can describe everything that government consists of; even less can it describe or determine everyday activities of policy making. But when fundamentals are in question, a Constitution is important because it is what Germans call the *Grundgesetz* (basic law).

The United Kingdom, however, has no written Constitution. Alone among major countries of the world, there is no single written document that sets out the major institutions, powers and procedures of government. At no time in the past was there a complete break with tradition, forcing politicians to sit down to think about basic forms of government, as American politicians were forced to do at Philadelphia in 1787, consequent to winning a revolution against the Crown. The United Kingdom is also distinctive in Europe, for Germany and Italy have written their constitutions since the Second World War, and France has written two.

From time to time an ambitious scholar seeks to compile a Constitution for the United Kingdom from seven centuries of documents concerning topics dealt with in other countries by a Constitution approved at a single point in time. But one author who has done just this concludes, "It would be foolish to suppose that this mode of systematising the material gives a complete picture of the British Constitution."[32] Alternatively, a scholar can try to elucidate what appears to him to be the principal rules of government in the United Kingdom. But one person's catalogue of customs and conventions is not necessarily acceptable to another, especially when political controversy is an incentive to depart from customs or act unconventionally, and there are no formal legal constraints against doing so. S.E. Finer rightly concludes that as far as the United Kingdom is concerned, "what is or is not 'the Constitution' is a matter for the scholar's individual judgment."[33]

The stateless and nonconstitutional nature of government in the United Kingdom means that questions about its institutions and territorial extent are neither confronted nor resolved. The amalgamation of separate territories into the present-day United Kingdom may be discussed by constitutional authorities — but under such headings as Commonwealth Affairs.[34] As much attention can be devoted to considering such deviant territories as the Channel Islands or the Isle of Man as is given to defining the Kingdom to which they are exceptions.[35] The absence of a written Constitution means that there has been no need to answer such awkward questions as: Could the 1707 Act of Union between England and Scotland be amended, and if so, how?

If we ask what is the primordial idea on which government in the United Kingdom rests, the answer is the Crown, in its impersonal legal sense. The government of the United Kingdom does not, like the United States, act in the name of "We, the people," nor is it like the Fifth French Republic founded on "the French people." The Republic of Ireland proclaims its 1937 Constitution on behalf of "the Irish nation," while acknowledging also "the Most Holy Trinity from whom is all authority." The Soviet Union rests upon "workers and peasants." Yugoslavia, both socialist and federal, emphasizes its federalism, basing authority on "voluntarily united and equal peoples."[36]

The Crown is the formal representation of government in the United Kingdom.[37] Members of Parliament take an oath to "be faithful and bear true Allegiance to Her Majesty Queen Elizabeth, Her Heirs and Successors, according to Law." They do not swear allegiance to any particular constitutional form, to any particular territory, or to any particular political ideal. The governors of the United Kingdom swear simply that they will act as Her Majesty's Government. The fact that the monarch has not been a ruler in the personal sense for centuries makes the doctrine a flexible basis of government. It also means that to understand the United Kingdom today we must go beyond the legal fiction of government by the Crown.

The Crown is an idea, not a territory. The Crown is without an identifying place name; it is a Crown of indefinite domain. Given the German roots of so much of their family tree, monarchs can hardly claim to be the patriachs of an English or a British race. Unlike Parliament, each of whose members is tied to a territorial constituency, the Crown can be everywhere—yet no place in particular. The Crown is infinitely portable and flexible. The creation of the Commonwealth showed its adaptability as a unifying symbol for Republics as well as for countries formally allegiant to the Crown, without any identification as British. In parliamentary debate about the conversion of the British Empire into the Commonwealth, Prime Minister Clement Attlee said it was a matter of indifference whether or not the Commonwealth was called British; it was "better to allow people to use the expression they liked best."[38] The infinite extensibility of this landless concept is also indicated by the increasing vagueness of the Queen's title, which embraces "Great Britain and Northern Ireland and her other Realms and Territories."

Like the unwritten Constitution, the Crown can sometimes be useful *because* it is a nebulous concept. Like a sultan in seclusion, the Crown is always out of sight. Political authority resides in those who act in the name of the Crown. The authority of government in the United Kingdom has not depend-

ed upon personal ties to the Crown for centuries. This has facilitated continuity in the passage from predemocratic rule to the contemporary world, in
which the monarch lacks any effective authority. The monarchy survives because it is politically weak. It is above the everyday battles of politics, thus
avoiding becoming a party to controversy.[39]

The Crown can substitute for the idea of the state because it is both sovereign and singular, incorporating in it the "sum total of governmental powers."[40]
There is only one Crown. Like the Queen's own person, the Crown has the
unity of a single body. But this formulation is limited in value for it substitutes
mysticism for meaning, and the impact of political mystery is very slight in a
contemporary secular culture. It is more likely to cause confusion than allegiance.

The Crown has political effect only insofar as action can be taken in its
name. In the United Kingdom today, government acts on behalf of the Crown
in Parliament. Actions taken in the name of the Crown must be authorized by
a popularly elected assembly representing all parts of the United Kingdom.
The concept of the Crown in Parliament thus joins executive actions with representative approval. While the term is compound, the symbol of its authority
is singular: the Mace.

The Crown in Parliament gives authority to government, but it does not
give it territorial boundaries. These are fixed by the terms of a political Union.
The United Kingdom today is a political Union bringing together territories
with separate previous histories. The parts joined together today are two old
Kingdoms (England and Scotland), one Principality (Wales) and two-thirds of
a Province (Ulster) of an inchoate Kingdom that is now a Republic. The authority of the Crown in Parliament is meant to be supreme within the boundaries of this Union. If this authority cannot be sustained, then the boundaries
will change, as happened in 1921 at the conclusion of the Irish war for independence.

The Union of territories that constitutes the United Kingdom today is
more than the sum of its parts. It is the fundamental allegiance of all parts to
the authority of the Crown in Parliament. Without this, the Union would have
less authority than the Confederation that preceded the act of Union creating
the United States of America. Just as the United States is a Union, different
from and above its fifty states or its most populous state, California, so too the
United Kingdom is something different from and above its four nations, or its
largest nation, England.

The Union can be identified by the voices of people upholding and attacking Union. Unionists can be grouped under three broad headings. First there
are *traditional* Unionists, who uphold the status quo form of territorial gov-

ernment of the United Kingdom. For half a century after the resolution of the Irish question in 1921, traditional Unionists did not need to say anything to uphold the Union. It was taken for granted. Their voices have been raised since in defence of the Union as it is. The challenge to the status quo brought forward two other groups, devolutionary Unionists and federal Unionists. *Devolutionary* Unionists advocate significant changes in the territorial government of some or all parts of the United Kingdom, but they do not wish to challenge the unique and comprehensive authority of Parliament. It was on this premise that the 1974 Labour government promoted devolution to Scotland and Wales, and it was even more evident in attempts to modify political institutions in Northern Ireland in accord with Westminster's wishes. *Federal* Unionists, a small group with no weight at Westminster, preach a fundamental change of relations between nations of the United Kingdom, but do not wish any part to secede from it. Federalism (also known by the vaguer term *home rule*) has more supporters in the smaller nations of the United Kingdom than in England, which has shown no desire for a separate English Parliament, as a counterpart to home rule Parliaments demanded elsewhere. A minority of devolutionary Unionists have hoped that devolution would lead to a federal Britain—and traditional Unionists have opposed them fearing that this would be the case.

Nationalists reject the validity and desirability of the political Union that constitutes the United Kingdom today. They recognize its existence—but only with the intent of seceding from it. Nationalists argue that their nation has the unilateral right to self-determination, whereas Unionists declare that changes in territorial boundaries can be decided only by the Crown in Parliament. Nationalists believe that they should be governed by a nation-state. Unionists reject this claim in the name of a multinational United Kingdom.

A political Union is a complex concept. On the one hand, it emphasizes government by a singular entity. Yet it also implies the existence of a number of constituent parts brought together in the Union. (Cf. the American motto *E pluribus unum:* "from many, one.") The problem of bringing many different parts of a territory under a single government is a classic problem of "statemaking." There are two major alternative forms of political Union: unitary and federal states.

A unitary state recognizes the territorial dimension in government by delegating responsibility for action to numerous subordinate institutions. It remains a *unitary state as long as the power to delegate or revoke delegated power remains in the hands of the central authority.* (By contrast, in a federal system of government the *federal compact* establishing the state sets out an *irrevocable* division of powers among the different constituent units.) In a unitary state, the central authority determines the policies for which subordinate units are responsible, and it also determines the size and boundaries of these units. The central authority may even abolish a subordinate jurisdiction. Responsibilities for carrying out public policy are divided among a multiplicity of institutions, but authority is undivided in a unitary state.

The political institutions of unitary states take many different forms, and variations on this simple idea are endless.[41] France is at one extreme among Western nations, for it has a uniform structure of administration throughout its European territory. Italy is at the other extreme, for it has five special autonomous regions plus fifteen elected regional councils. Among the old Dominions, New Zealand is the only example of a unitary parliamentary government. Ireland is also a unitary state—except for the "lost" two-thirds of the Province of Ulster.

The United Kingdom meets the basic definitional criteria of a unitary state. The Crown in Parliament is the sole political authority, and its authority is formally unlimited. In Blackstone's words, "It can, in short, do everything that is not naturally impossible"[42]—and modern medical science has even removed the traditional inhibition that it lacks the power to make a man a woman! Under the authority of the Crown in Parliament, Westminster can establish institutions to which it devolves powers to act within specified statutory limits.

Like most unitary states, the United Kingdom has displayed some apparent departures from the doctrine of undivided authority. But these departures are more apparent than real. Kellas speaks of a "Scottish political system,"[43] but the phrase begs the question: What is its government? The answer is very clear: British government is the dominant force in the Scottish political system. The Scottish Office, like Her Majesty's Treasury, is a part of the British Cabinet, sustained by the Westminster Parliament. Scottish local authorities are established (and to a substantial extent funded) by a Westminster Parliament. Scottish politics is best conceived as a *subsystem* of United Kingdom politics and government. The Stormont Parliament of Northern Ireland was long an anomaly within a unitary state. But the fundamentally subordinate status of Stormont was dramatically demonstrated when Westminster revoked its powers in 1972, establishing direct rule from Westminster in its stead. The proposed devolution Assemblies for Scotland and Wales were completely consistent with the doctrine of the unitary state. Not only did Parliament delegate these Assemblies powers in the 1978 Scotland and Wales Acts, but also it repealed these acts less than twelve months later.

The chief constitutional alternative to unitary government is federalism. Both proponents and critics of federalism agree that the United Kingdom does *not* have a federal form of government. The Royal Commission on the Constitution argued that "such a strange and artificial system was not suited to the present stage of constitutional development in the United Kingdom," adding gratuitously that countries such as the United States suffered from its alleged drawbacks. By contrast, a number of politicians and academics have argued that federalism is desirable and that the United Kingdom *ought* to become a federal system. Notwithstanding the many different definitions of federalism —one author has identified 44 different meanings and another 267—the United Kingdom can readily be shown to differ from features common to most federal systems.[44]

Federalism is founded by a compact, that is, an irrevocable covenant. The United Kingdom, by contrast, was formed by an amalgamation of different jurisdictions, a Union that meant the abolition of prior bodies. For example, the Scots Parliament was ended by the Act of Union forming Great Britain in 1707, and the Irish Parliament by its Union with Great Britain in 1801.

Because the partners of a federal compact are juridically equal, disputes between them are normally resolved by a court independent of both signatories. The United States Supreme Court is the best-known example of such a court. A supreme court can overrule actions of the federal government, as well as actions by its partners. In the United Kingdom, by contrast, Parliament is judge, jury and often party to disputes about the powers of government. If Scots thought that Parliament had violated the terms of the 1707 Act of Union between Scotland and England, they would not find it easy to seek redress in court, as in a federal system. Instead, complaints are likely to be dismissed, in the curious words of a law lord, as concerning actions that are "unlawful but nonjusticiable."[45] An aggrieved local government cannot go to court to seek nullification of Westminster's measures. Even if a court were to rule in its favour, Parliament could pass an act retrospectively conferring the power to do what a court had said was outside its powers.

In a federal system there are two sets of representative bodies, each claiming the full legitimacy of popular election. One is elected for the country as a whole, and another elected for each of the provinces, states or *Länder* that are signatories to the federal compact. The lower-tier assembly can claim it is closer to its electorate, and the federal assembly can claim to represent the country as a whole. Responsibilities for major functions often may be assigned one of the two assemblies, but in practice, the two can be interdependent because policies often have interacting consequences, even if separate in constitutional law. In the United Kingdom, Parliament is the only constituent assembly. Local governments have elected councils, but their powers are derived from Acts of Parliament and are far inferior to the powers of lower-tier assemblies of federal states. Moreover, as local government reorganization demonstrated in the 1970s, Parliament can abolish established local government units and substitute new institutions in their place, a power denied the top tier of government in a federal system.

While the United Kingdom is stateless by comparison with continental countries, the Crown nonetheless has a clear and unlimited claim to political authority. The Union is not, as in federalism, a compact of juridical equals. It is a Union under a Crown in Parliament that is lawfully supreme over all its parts.

The Multiform Institutions of Union

The institutions of government cannot be confined to one place, even in the most formally centralized of governments. If Westminster is to govern the United Kingdom effectively, policies decided at the centre must be effective throughout the whole territory. If we take what Fesler[46] describes as "the under-all position of the ordinary citizen," the most important institutions of government are those that deliver, wherever people live, the goods and services of the contemporary welfare state — education, health services, housing, roads, police and fire protection. The reciprocal of government at Westminster is not local government, but United Kingdom-wide government.

In a state that was uniform as well as unitary, the central authority would consist of a series of functional ministries, each responsible for the uniform provision of a particular policy United Kingdom-wide. Many of the responsibilities for delivering services could be delegated to local government, but local government would also be uniformly organized. But this is not what we find in the United Kingdom today. The Cabinet contains a mixture of functional ministries, concerned with such things as education and health and industry, and territorial ministries, concerned with parts of the United Kingdom, the Scottish, Welsh and Northern Ireland Offices. Functional ministries are usually circumscribed in their territorial competence, being less than United Kingdom-wide ministries; territorial ministries are usually multifunctional, albeit within one nation only. The Crown is singular, but the institutions that exercise its authority are multiform. They are differentiated by both function (i.e., what they do) and territory (i.e., the area they serve).

The present maze of institutions appears untidy only if government is expected to conform to a contemporary standard of uniform rationality. But twentieth-century rationales could not influence the historical evolution of the Crown. The United Kingdom was created, as it were, by a merger of different properties. The passage of diverse pieces of real estate into single ownership does not make all the pieces identical or imply that all should be managed alike. Initially at least, transfer of ownership does not affect individual properties. And so it was with the amalgamation of Kingdoms that went to make up the United Kingdom.

When the different parts of the Crown were first joined, government did little. There was no need for Parliament to be concerned with the administration of public policies, for government was normally passive, and in wartime its principal actions were directed abroad. There was no need to disturb preexisting territorial arrangements — except insofar as rebellion led to military actions, as in seventeenth-century Ireland or the 1745 Jacobite rebellion in Scotland. Each part of the United Kingdom was governed according to customary arrangements. There was not even a uniform government within England. For example, until 1836 the Bishops of Durham exercised some palatine powers there, similar to those of the German Rhineland. Scotland was administered by a variety of traditional institutions, in which the Lord Advocate was the central figure, proferring advice to the Privy Council, and from 1782 to the Home Office. In Ireland administration was vested in the Viceroy or Lord Lieutenant, for whom a British minister acted as Chief Secretary. Wales was administered as part of England.

The work of eighteenth-century government was not great enough to require the differentiation of the Crown's advisers according to function, let alone territory. Individual Privy Councillors had a common responsibility for acts of government; they had no specific responsibility. A preliminary step to rationalize matters was taken in 1782 by identifying one Privy Councillor as Home Secretary, including special responsibilities for Scotland and Ireland, and another as Foreign Secretary.

The Victorian growth of government greatly multiplied the responsibilities of the Crown. The growth of government preeminently emphasized functional problems — public health, education, safety in factories and in public transport, and the relief of poverty. In the second half of the nineteenth century government claimed only one-tenth of the gross national product. In the twentieth century it has come to claim 40 to 50 percent of a much larger gross national product. From 1900 to 1960, public expenditure increased more than six times in real terms. The total number of public employees has increased greatly, too; from 1900 to 1979, public employment has increased by 7 million people, and more than five times as a proportion of the labour force; it now accounts for 30 percent of the total labour force.[47]

The growth of government has been United Kingdom-wide, but its territorial significance has been incidental to the primary functions of the mixed-economy welfare state. In managing the economy, the government is first and foremost concerned with macro-economic policy, that is, the total size of the gross national product, total employment, the aggregate level of inflation and the overall balance of payments. As long as macro-economic objectives can be achieved, then territorial variations between parts of the United Kingdom are of secondary importance. In providing major benefits of the welfare state—health, education and pensions for the elderly—government deals with individuals without regard to their place of residence. The same pension or unemployment benefit is paid to a person, wherever he or she may live. Residence in the United Kingdom, rather than residence in England, Scotland, Wales or Northern Ireland, is the primary requirement for a benefit. The growth of government emphasizes common welfare concerns of people in the United Kingdom, and a common dependence upon the United Kingdom economy as a whole.

The territorial implications of functional growth were slow to be felt at Westminster. The development of contemporary territorial ministries followed after the functional differentiation of Whitehall ministries. Major steps were taken at different times for different reasons in different parts of the United Kingdom: in 1885 in Scotland, in 1921 and 1972 in Northern Ireland, and in 1964 in Wales.

For all that is claimed about the distinctiveness of Scottish institutions, for nearly two centuries after the Act of Union government did without a Secretary for Scotland. The post was created in 1885; the holder has always been in Cabinet in peacetime since 1892. The appointment of a minister did not immediately affect administration. For upwards of half a century many administrative responsibilities of government in Scotland continued in the hands of boards concerned with such matters as agriculture, local government, prisons and health. The headquarters of the Scottish Office remained in London until the building of St. Andrews House in Edinburgh in 1939. The transfer of administrative headquarters to Edinburgh occurred in tandem with the vesting in the Secretary of State for Scotland of powers formerly held by separate boards. In the postwar era the Scottish Office has grown by the adoption of new policies by Westminster and by the transfer of responsibilities formerly held by other Whitehall departments. In 1962 a Scottish Development Department was created within the Scottish Office, and in 1973 a Scottish Economic Planning Department was created to demonstrate concern with economic problems. This has further differentiated administration in Scotland while continuing to secure administration in the hands of a Cabinet Minister directly accountable to the Westminster Parliament.

The span of Scottish Office responsibilities today covers programmes administered by eleven other Cabinet departments in England and Wales. It is equally important to note that thirteen Whitehall departments besides the Scottish Office administer some programmes in Scotland (see tables 5.2 and 5.3). The issue of chief contemporary concern in Scotland, namely, the management of the economy, is very much a collective Cabinet matter. The bulk of decisions affecting the economy in Scotland are made by the Treasury, the Department of Industry, the Department of Energy, the Department of Employment, Social Security and nationalized industries, and not by the Scottish Office. As a member of the Cabinet, the Secretary of State for Scotland does have the right to be consulted about other departments' measures affecting Scotland, but it is other Cabinet ministers who collectively have the biggest say in major decisions.[48]

The irony of government in Wales is that the circumstances that made Wales most distinctive — the widespread use of a different language and adherence to nonconformist Protestantism — were never met by separate political institutions. From incorporation with England in 1536 until the twentieth century, Wales was governed as if it were England. The growth of government in two world wars and under the 1945-51 Labour government was accomplished without recourse to a separate Welsh ministry. As a public relations exercise, the Conservatives in 1951 appointed a peer as a Home Office Under-Secretary with special responsibilities for Wales. The Prime Minister's Private Secretary privately dismissed the appointment as an "absurd idea."[49]

Arguments advanced for creating the Welsh Office in the 1950s and early '60s were multiple and confusing. Some economic arguments were effectively integrationist, holding that a Secretary of State for Wales would be better placed in Cabinet to influence the Treasury to direct economic benefits to Wales. This argument was particularly powerful among some Labour politicians; others feared that a Welsh Office would potentially limit their influence upon government (especially a Labour government) by confining them to a minor government department. There were also arguments for the Welsh Office from those who foresaw particularistic advantages in decisions being taken by a Cardiff-based, rather than a London-based, ministry. Arguments about the influence of a Welsh Secretary of State upon language and culture were chiefly important to supporters of the Welsh Nationalist Party, which favoured independence, not a change within the Westminster system. A bystander, R.H.S. Crossman, harshly described the motives for creating the Welsh Office in 1964 thus: "Another equally idiotic creation is the Department for Wales, a completely new office for Jim Griffiths and his two Parliamentary Secretaries, all the result of a silly election pledge."[50]

The Welsh Office has grown substantially since its creation in 1964. Responsibilities for government were not devolved to Wales but were gradually transferred from one Cabinet minister to another. The Welsh Office grew gradually, taking responsibility for policies in Wales formerly administered by other Whitehall ministries. After nearly two decades of expansion, the Welsh Office has nearly caught up with the Scottish Office in the scope of the programmes it administers.[51] The Welsh Office administers programmes that are the responsibility of eight Whitehall departments concerned with England. But it is equally important to emphasize that fifteen other Whitehall departments also administer programmes in Wales (see tables 5.2 and 5.3). The lack of a separate legal system means that legislation concerning the Welsh Office is normally embedded in an act introduced by a functional minister, whereas the Scottish Office has significant legislative responsibilities too.

Northern Ireland has been the extreme example of devolution within Union because of the establishment of a separate Stormont Parliament in 1921. Westminster kept to itself Imperial policies, such as defence and customs, while transferring powers for welfare services, the environment and security to the Northern Ireland Parliament. The creation of Stormont was not initially sought by Ulster Unionists; it was regarded as a derogation from the province's status as an integral part of the United Kingdom. It was accepted because, in the exceptional circumstances arising from the Anglo-Irish war of 1916-21, it provided a bulwark against Ulster being placed under rule by Dublin. From Westminster, Stormont was regarded as a means of distancing Ulster's difficulties. The Speaker of the House of Commons ruled that matters transferred to Stormont could not be debated in the Commons.[52]

The Stormont Parliament made defence of the Union its first aim: "Not an inch" was one of its mottos. The Royal Ulster Constabulary and the B Special Constabulary successfully defended Stormont against violent attack by the Irish Republican Army from 1956 to 1962. In social and economic policies, from 1945 Stormont gradually began to adopt the framework of a welfare state, following lines laid down and substantially financed by Westminster. In 1963 Terence O'Neill became Prime Minister of Northern Ireland. O'Neill promoted economic measures intended to accomplish what force of arms had not, namely, removing age-old economic differences between Protestants and Catholics in the common pursuit of material well-being, a policy that O'Neill described as encouraging Catholics to "live like Protestants."[53]

The eruption of civil rights demonstrations against Stormont in 1968 brought British troops and British political advisers into Northern Ireland in August 1969. Westminster's attempt to govern Northern Ireland through "indirect rule" failed in the face of a twin assault. First, the Irish Republican Army (IRA) launched an armed attack upon British soldiers in pursuit of its demand for a 32-county united Ireland. Second, the Unionist government at Stormont, representing an electoral majority in the province, viewed issues differently from Westminster. Unionist leaders who collaborated with Westminster (such as O'Neill and Brian Faulkner) were repudiated by their party. In 1972 Westminster exercised its Imperial authority by suspending Stormont, the last of the Parliaments it had created that it still had the power to suspend.

Superficially, the creation of the Northern Ireland Office as a Cabinet department to administer temporary direct rule in 1972 makes the government of the province analogous to Scotland and Wales.[54] The Northern Ireland Office is divided into functional departments that collectively parallel thirteen Whitehall departments administering programmes for England or Britain. Twelve Whitehall departments have some programmes affecting Northern Ireland (see tables 5.2 and 5.3). In political terms, however, the Secretary of State does not and is not meant to represent Northern Ireland's voters. Ministers are chosen to represent Westminster's view of how Northern Ireland ought to be governed, and British parties do not contest seats in the province.

The political and military challenge to Northern Ireland's constitutional status also raises issues of concern to other Westminster departments.[55] The Ministry of Defence has interests in Northern Ireland because it supplies the soldiers meant to prevent widespread disorder or, in the phrase of one minister, to maintain "an acceptable level of violence" in the province. Since the Ministry of Defence moved troops into Northern Ireland in 1969, more than 2200 people have been killed in political violence, as of June 1982. In proportion to population, this is equivalent to 75,000 killed in political violence in Great Britain, or 300,000 killed by political violence in the United States. The Foreign Office also maintains an interest; at one time it had staff *within* Northern Ireland, and at all times it deals with the Republic of Ireland, which also claims sovereignty over Northern Ireland.

All three territorial ministries have much in common with one another, and equally, much in common with the fifteen to twenty other ministries in Cabinet. The presence of Secretaries of State for Scotland, Wales and Northern Ireland in Cabinet gives each member the right to voice departmental interests; equally, it assures that territorial ministers will be bound by the collective decision of Cabinet, whether or not they are entirely in harmony with the views of an individual minister. In Cabinet, the territorial ministers are not the most important voices: They tend to be in the "second eleven" of Cabinet, by contrast with the Chancellor of the Exchequer, the Foreign Secretary and others of that ilk. The territorial ministers, like their Cabinet colleagues, immediately hold office at the choice of the Prime Minister, with the support of the dominant party in Parliament, and finally, by endorsement of their party at a United Kingdom general election. Their territorial title does not mean that they necessarily are the choice of a majority of Scots, Welsh or Ulstermen (cf. table 3.4) any more than a minister for Employment or Industry is necessarily the choice of a majority of trade unionists or industrialists. The territorial ministries are staffed by members of the home civil service,[56] particularly at their upper echelons, where advice is tendered to ministers and agreements are negotiated with other ministries. Promotion prospects may involve movement between ministries, thus reinforcing a loyalty to the civil service as a whole, as against narrow departmental interests.

The most obvious respect in which territorial ministries differ from other ministries is that their chief administrative offices are not in London but in Edinburgh, Cardiff and Belfast. Although the ministry is distant, the minister spends most of his working week in Whitehall. Wesminster is "where the action is"; it is where ministers can engage themselves with Cabinet colleagues and defend and advance policies in Parliament.

Within England, the most obvious example of the territorial dimension of government is the placement of responsibility for delivering major government services, such as education, housing and social services in the hands of local government. But local government today is no longer local. Councils are established by Act of Parliament, have duties laid down by Act of Parliament and receive half their funds from Parliament. Their territorial extent is determined less by history than it is by putative criteria of efficiency. L.J. Sharpe, Director of Research for the 1960s Redcliffe-Maude Royal Commission on English local government reform, has argued, "The essence of local government is that it is local; but almost all the reformist pressure over the past twenty years has been designed to transform it into something else."[57] The reorganization of local government was conceived and promoted primarily in functional terms, and the 1980 legislation by the Thatcher government to contain local government expenditure is a further development in advancing Westminster's functional priorities through local bodies.

Today there is a low level of interest in local government. A Gallup poll taken shortly before the 1981 municipal elections found that less than one-quarter know the names of the local authority areas in which they live, and less than half know the name of any local councillor or feel confident that they understand the system well enough to know whom to complain to.[58] Moreover, local government even lacks a clear focus of attention in Whitehall. Four different ministries—Environment, Education, Social Security and the Home Office—have oversight of major programmes of English local government, and the Treasury is inevitably interested in its spending.

Any attempt to create an English Office in Whitehall would collapse of its own weight. If an English Office were to incorporate all the programmes for which territorial ministries are usually responsible in Scotland, Wales or Northern Ireland, it would have to be about ten times the size of the average Whitehall ministry, and the responsibilities of a single Secretary of State would be impossibly broad. The creation of an English Office would collapse the Cabinet to about half its present size, or else leave some functional ministers virtually functionless. For example, a separate English Office would mean that the Department of Education and Science would have no responsibility for primary or secondary education anywhere in the United Kingdom.

Any attempt to create devolved assemblies for Scotland or Wales also stumbles over the problem, What to do about England? To offer England a separate devolved Assembly would be to create an English national voice that could swamp that of counterparts elsewhere in the United Kingdom; to deny this would also cause criticism. As some members of the Royal Commission on the Constitution argued: "The grant of a measure of self-government to Scotland or Wales alone, with nothing comparable in the English regions, would produce a situation of intolerable anomaly and injustice." As a counterpart for national assemblies for Scotland and Wales it recommended the subdivision of England into a series of regional assemblies. But, the Commission noted, there was "no public demand for English regional assemblies with legislative powers." It resolved the conundrum it faced by concluding, consistent with the history of the Crown, "The system of government that is best for one part of the country will not necessarily be best for another."[59]

The creation of a territorial ministry or assembly is not the only source of political influence. The absence of an English Office from the Cabinet does not mean that English voices are not heard in Cabinet or that English voters are unrepresented in the House of Commons. But they are not there to voice specific demands on behalf of a territorial constituency. Equally, there is no Cabinet minister who is specially concerned with maintaining the Union, or a Cabinet committee on United Kingdom affairs. Looking after the Union is a responsibility that falls to everyone in Cabinet and to no one in particular.

The great majority of Cabinet ministries have a functional focus. Most Cabinet ministers are responsible for such functional problems as foreign affairs, the treasury, defence, education, health and social security, housing, industry, agriculture, trade, and so forth. Functional ministers outnumber territorial ministers by six to one in Cabinet. The territorial scope of a functional minister's responsibilities is incidental to his primary concern. The expansion of the responsibilities of territorial ministries in the postwar era has incidentally subtracted from the territorial scope of functional ministries.

Policy unites what geography divides. Attempts to describe as "Scottish" policy measures of a Secretary of State for Scotland are misleading because it emphasizes only one-half of the responsibilities of the Secretary of State for Scotland, his departmental role. It ignores the more important fact that the policies of any territorial minister are valid if, and only if, they are collectively endorsed by Cabinet and also by Parliament.

An explanation of the multiform territorial and functional institutions of the Crown today rests in the annals of history. Only a "too clever by half" theorist would create a state with two separate legal systems (one Scots and the other for England, Wales and more or less for Northern Ireland), have two different state churches, or govern one of its parts by "temporary" direct rule. Historical anomalies do not deny constitutional fundamentals. Multiform institutions are consistent with the maintenance of Union as long as all partners to the Union continue to accept the authority of the Crown in Parliament.

NOTES

1. See *Our Changing Democracy: Devolution to Scotland and Wales* (London: HMSO, Cmnd. 6348, 1975), p. 61; and *British Nationality Law* (London: HMSO, Cmnd. 7987, 1980), pp. 2-5, 21.
2. See Denys Hay, "The Use of the Term 'Great Britain' in the Middle Ages," *Proceedings of the Society of Antiquaries of Scotland* 89 (1958): 56.
3. Ibid., pp. 58, 61.
4. S.T. Bindoff, "The Stuarts and Their Style," *English Historical Review* 60, no. 2 (1945): 201.
5. Ibid., p. 192; and Hay, "The Use of the Term 'Great Britain,'" p. 55.
6. H.P.R. Finberg, *The Formation of England, 530-1042* (London: Hart, Davis, MacGibbon, 1974).
7. See the Commissioners of Inquiry into the State of Education in Wales; *Report, Carmarthen, Glamorgan and Pembroke* (London: Reports from Commissioners, 1847) 27: 3, 6; *Digest of Welsh Statistics No. 20* (Cardiff: HMSO, 1974), p. 45; *Census: England and Wales 1891,* vol. 3 (London: HMSO), table 24; and comments on the reliability of the 1891 Census, in *General Report,* 3: 81-83.
8. Nevil Johnson, *In Search of the Constitution* (Oxford: Pergamon Press, 1977), p. 121.
9. A.J.P. Taylor, *English History, 1914-1945* (London: Oxford University Press, 1965), pp. 21-22.
10. J.G.A. Pocock, "British History: A Plea for a New Subject," *Journal of Modern History* 47, no. 4 (1975): 605; italics added.
11. Royal Commission on the Constitution, *Report,* pp. 16, 20.
12. See, e.g., W.R. Louis, ed. *Imperialism: the Robinson and Gallagher Controversy* (New York: Franklin Watts, 1975); Ronald Robinson, "Non-European Foundations of European Imperialism: Sketch for a Theory of Collaboration," in *Studies in the Theory of Imperialism,* ed. R. Owen and B. Sutcliffe (London: Longman, 1972), pp. 117-40; and Jim Bulpitt,

"The Making of the United Kingdom," *Parliamentary Affairs* 31, no. 2 (1978): 174-89.

13. Edmund Burke, *Speeches and Letters on American Affairs* (London: Dent, 1908), pp. 59-60. Speech of 19 April 1774; italics in the original.

14. Earl Grey, quoted in J.E. Kendle, "The Round Table Movement and 'Home Rule All Round,'" *Historical Journal* 11 (1968): 334. Incidentally, Grey was uncertain whether there should be one local legislature for England or two separate legislatures, North and South.

15. See the Chairman's letter of transmittal in *Speaker's Conference on Devolution* (London: HMSO, Cmnd. 692, 1920); H.J. Hanham, *Scottish Nationalism* (London: Faber & Faber, 1969), chap. 5; and J.D. Fair, *British Interparty Conferences* (Oxford: Clarendon Press, 1980), chap. 11.

16. Quoted in Vernon Bogdanor, *Devolution* (London: Oxford University Press, 1979), p. 13.

17. Cf. Arthur Griffith, *The Resurrection of Hungary: A Parallel for Ireland* (Dublin: James Duffy, 1904); and A.V. Dicey, *England's Case Against Home Rule* (London: Murray, 1886).

18. Cf. D.W. Harkness, *The Restless Dominion: The Irish Free State and the British Commonwealth of Nations, 1921-31* (London: Macmillan, 1969); and P. Buckland, *The Factory of Grievances: Devolved Government in Northern Ireland, 1921-1939* (Dublin : Gill & Macmillan, 1979).

19. See Woodburn, House of Commons *Debates,* vol. 469, col. 2098 (16 November 1949); and similarly, W. Ross, ibid., vol. 777, col. 391 (5 February 1969); Thomas, ibid., vol. 495, col. 680 (4 February 1952).

20. Ibid., vol. 472, col. 623 (10 March 1950).

21. Ibid., vol. 428, col. 405 (25 October 1946).

22. "Britain's Independent Role About Played Out," *The Times,* 6 December 1962.

23. See J.G.A. Pocock, *The Limits and Division of British History* (Glasgow: University of Strathclyde Studies in Public Policy No. 31, 1979).

24. House of Commons, *Debates,* vol. 903, col. 218 (13 January 1976).

25. Royal Commission on the Constitution, *Report,* p. 18.

26. Ibid., p. 441. See also D.G. Kermode, *Devolution at Work: A Case Study of the Isle of Man* (Farnborough, Hants: Saxon House, 1979).

27. See Malta Round Table Conference 1955, *Report* (London: HMSO, Cmnd. 9657, 1955).

28. Quoted in Geoffrey Marshall, *Constitutional Theory* (Oxford: Clarendon Press, 1971), p. 12.

29. G. Kitson Clark, "The Modern State and Modern Society," *Proceedings of the Royal Institution of Great Britain* 37 (1959): 551.

30. Cf. Bob Jessop, "Recent Theories of the Capitalist State," *Cambridge Journal of Economics* 1, no. 4 (1977): 353-73; and Richard Rose, "Is the United Kingdom a State?" in *The Territorial Dimension in United Kingdom Politics,* ed. P. Madgwick and R. Rose (London: Macmillan, 1982).

31. J.P. Nettl, "The State as a Conceptual Variable," *World Politics* 20 (1968): 559-81. See also K.H.F. Dyson, *The State Tradition in Western Europe* (Oxford: Martin Robertson, 1980).

32. Leslie Wolf-Phillips, *Constitutions of Modern States* (London: Pall Mall, 1968), p. 182.
33. S.E. Finer, *Five Constitutions: Contrasts and Comparisons* (Harmondsworth: Penguin, 1979), p. 34.
34. See, e.g., S.A. de Smith, *Constitutional and Administrative Law* (Harmondsworth: Penguin, 1971), chap. 30; and E.C.S. Wade and A.W. Bradley, *Constitutional Law* (8th ed.; London: Longman, 1970), chaps. 30-33.
35. Cf. The Royal Commission on the Constitution, *Report,* chaps. 31-32.
36. See the constitutional preambles as contained in Wolf-Phillips, *Constitutions of Modern States.*
37. A reader of this chapter in draft, W.R. McKay, pointed out that while there is one Crown in law, there are physically two sets of royal regalia. The Scottish crown is in Scotland—but it lacks the political symbolism, that, say, the crown of St. Stephen has had for Hungarians.
38. Nicholas Mansergh, *The Commonwealth Experience* (London: Weidenfeld and Nicolson, 1969), p. 29.
39. See Richard Rose and Dennis Kavanagh, "The Monarchy in Contemporary Political Culture," *Comparative Politics* 8, no. 4 (1976).
40. Wade and Bradley, *Constitutional Law,* p. 171.
41. Ivo D. Duchacek, *Power Maps* (Santa Barbara, Calif.: Clio Press, 1973), p. 96.
42. Quoted in Finer, *Five Constitutions,* p. 36.
43. James G. Kellas, *The Scottish Political System* (Cambridge: Cambridge University Press, 1973), p. 4.
44. Cf. Royal Commission on the Constitution, *Report,* pp. 161, 155; J.P. Mackintosh, *The Devolution of Power* (Harmondsworth: Penguin, 1968); A.H. Birch, *Political Integration and Disintegration in the British Isles* (London: Allen & Unwin, 1977), p. 156f; William H. Stewart, "The Function of Models and Metaphors in the Development of Federal Theory" (paper to the 1979 Meeting of the American Political Science Association, Washington, D.C.); and S. Rufus Davis, *The Federal Principle: A Journey through Time in Quest of Meaning* (Berkeley: University of California Press, 1978), p. 204.
45. Lord Cooper, in *MacCormick* v. *Lord Advocate* (1953 SC 396). More generally, see J.D.B. Mitchell, *Constitutional Law* (Edinburgh: W. Green, 1964). But compare R.S.V. Heuston, *Essays in Constitutional Law* (London: Stevens, 1961).
46. James W. Fesler, *Area and Administration* (Tuscaloosa: University of Alabama Press, 1949), p. 10.
47. See Richard Parry, *United Kingdom Public Employment* (Glasgow: University of Strathclyde Studies in Public Policy No. 62, 1980), table 1; and Jindrich Veverka, "The Growth of Government Expenditure in the United Kingdom Since 1790," *Scottish Journal of Political Economy* 10, no. 1 (1963): table 1.
48. Cf. J.G. Kellas, *The Scottish Political System* and George Pottinger, *The Secretaries of State for Scotland 1926-76* (Edinburgh: Scottish Academic

Press, 1979). William Ross, "Approaching the Archangelic?" in *The Scottish Government Yearbook 1978,* ed. H.M. Drucker and M.G. Clarke (Edinburgh: Paul Harris, 1978), pp. 1-20; Mary MacDonald and Adam Redpath, "The Scottish Office, 1954-79," in *The Scottish Government Yearbook 1980,* ed. H.M. Drucker and N.L. Drucker (1979), pp. 101-34; J.M. Ross, *The Secretary of State for Scotland and the Scottish Office* (Glasgow: University of Strathclyde Studies in Public Policy No. 87, 1981), and C. Hood, A. Dunsire and S. Thompson, "Comparing the Scottish Office with Whitehall," *British Journal of Political Science* 9, no. 3 (1979): 257-80.

49. Sir John Colville, *Footprints in Time* (London: Collins, 1978), p. 250.
50. R.H.S. Crossman, *The Crossman Diaries* (London: Magnum Books, 1979), p. 63. For a careful academic analysis of the confusion of motives, see Ian Thomas, *The Creation of the Welsh Office* (Glasgow: University of Strathclyde Studies in Public Policy No. 91, 1981).
51. See Royal Commission on the Constitution, *Minutes of Evidence,* vol. 1 (London: HMSO, 1970), pp. 10ff; and Denis Balsom and Martin Burch, *A Political and Electoral Handbook for Wales* (Farnborough, Hants: Gower, 1980), part 2.
52. See Buckland, *A Factory of Grievances;* Harry Calvert, *Constitutional Law in Northern Ireland* (London: Stevens, 1968), and R.J. Lawrence, *The Government of Northern Ireland: Public Finance and Public Services, 1921-1964* (Oxford: Clarendon Press, 1965).
53. Richard Rose, *Governing without Consensus: An Irish Perspective* (London: Faber & Faber, 1971), p. 301.
54. On these institutions, see Derek Birrell and Alan Murie, *Policy and Government in Northern Ireland* (Dublin: Gill & Macmillan, 1980). On the politics, see Richard Rose, *Northern Ireland: Time of Choice* (London: Macmillan, 1976).
55. See Rose, "Is the United Kingdom a State?"
56. Northern Ireland is a political exception, for the bulk of officials there belong to the Northern Ireland civil service, a creation of Stormont. But the officials most closely advising the Secretary of State on crucial political and security matters are normally part of London-based services.
57. L.J. Sharpe, "'Reforming' the Grass Roots: An Alternative Analysis," in *Policy and Politics,* ed. D. Butler and A.H. Halsey (London: Macmillan, 1978), p. 106.
58. Gallup Poll, *Political Index* (London: No. 249, 1981), p. 12.
59. Royal Commission on the Constitution, *Report,* pp. 332, 353, 333.

3. Integration by Party Competition

Party politics is about differences of opinion; the question is not whether the United Kingdom divides at a general election, but how it divides. If national cultural differences were dominant, parties would divide along lines of national identity and religion. Alternatively, insofar as functional economic differences are important, then parties should divide along class lines. Tensions between class and cultural loyalties are found in many European societies; class differences may become dominant only after political conflicts of national identity and religion are resolved.[1]

In a multinational state, class divisions can cause political integration. Working-class voters can support the same party whatever their nation, and middle-class voters support its opponents. Class differences can divide neighbours and nations while uniting members of the same class having different national identities.

Until the 1970s, class was taken for granted as the basis of political divisions in the United Kingdom. Northern Ireland was dismissed as an unnatural exception—notwithstanding the evidence (now conveniently overlooked) of the importance of religion in pre-1914 politics.[2] Well-publicized by-election and general election victories of Welsh and Scottish Nationalist candidates since 1966 and an upsurge of violence in Northern Ireland have made evident the potential for Nationalist politics to divide the United Kingdom. But, since 1921, Unionist and not Nationalist parties have consistently dominated all parts of the United Kingdom. Moreover, the 1979 general election saw Nationalists lose seats in both Scotland and Wales.

The purpose of this chapter is to consider whether and to what extent the competition for votes in the United Kingdom is more likely to lead to the maintenance *or* the disruption of the United Kingdom. The first section sets out the extent of the domination of functional parties. The second section examines how the nations of the United Kingdom have again and again voted for Union, and the third section considers how party competition contributes to the maintenance of the United Kingdom.

The Dominance of Functional Parties

Political parties can appeal to the electorate in very different ways. A functional appeal emphasizes that a party stands for the economic interests of particular groups in society: manual workers, the middle class, farmers, and so on. A religious appeal emphasizes that the party stands for Protestants, Catholics or freethinkers opposed to clerical influence in politics. A linguistic party can stand for the claim of people with a distinctive language to use that language in everyday public activities. A Nationalist party presses distinctive claims for a national community. Since each of these appeals is limited to a fraction of the electorate, there are also catchall parties that appeal to the whole electorate or to a coalition of interests without any common thread.[3]

In the United Kingdom, the Conservative and Labour parties between them usually alternate control of government, and they are functional parties. The Labour Party is most obviously so, because of its explicit adoption of Socialist rhetoric and its close institutional ties with trade unions. The Conservative Party presents a different image, that of a "national" party, that is, a catchall party that seeks votes from everyone. Normally Conservatives gain about half their votes from manual workers, and most leading politicians (Mrs. Thatcher being an exception) eschew rhetoric that would identify the party more or less exclusively with middle-class interests. The Conservatives win a disproportionate amount of their vote from the middle class and Labour from the working class. Both parties concentrate on the economy in electioneering.[4] The Liberals stand athwart the two parties of government, rejecting identification with a single class. But the Liberal Party has paid a high price because of the lack of an electoral base; for more than half a century it has been a failed catchall party. The Social Democratic Party founded in 1981 hopes to enlarge the vote for a "centre" or catchall party.

The Conservative, Labour and Liberal parties are only incidentally concerned with the issue of Union, that is, the maintenance of the United Kingdom, and questions of national identity tend to be ignored. (The Social Democratic Party has used the "small is beautiful" rhetoric of devolution, but it is no less Unionist than are Liberals committed to a federal United Kingdom.) Each of the parties takes for granted the identity of Britain. Equally important, the parties do not believe in making a particular issue about the claims or needs of the English nation, the largest partner in the Union. To give major importance to questions of national identity would distract attention from functional issues. Taking the United Kingdom for granted as a constant of the political system allows the parties to concentrate on issues that are their primary concern.

Because the Conservative, Labour, Liberal and Social Democratic parties are "unthinkingly" British, very little attention is given to the Constitution of the United Kingdom in normal political circumstances. The best-known British politician who today articulates views about the United Kingdom's national identity, Enoch Powell, is ignored when he does so by parliamentary colleagues. Powell is dismissed as obsessively unbalanced, and as trying to work his passage in Northern Ireland as a late arrival in the Ulster Unionist Party. This lack of attention makes it difficult to establish what a party thinks about the United Kingdom, beyond commitment to Union, because it is not clear whether parties think about it at all.[5]

Unthinking Unionism means that as and when party leaders speak about the maintenance of the United Kingdom, they may speak with more than one voice or may utter contradictions. The devolution debate revealed the readiness of politicians in all the major British parties to take and change positions quickly (cf. chapter 8). It also emphasized divisions within the Conservative and Labour parties, especially the latter, which had legislative responsibility as the government of the day. But the spasms of interest and boredom have never led to questioning commitment to the maintenance of Great Britain; only in Northern Ireland have parties qualified their commitment to maintain the United Kingdom.

The Conservative, Labour and Liberal parties can claim to be the three principal British parties because they are the only parties that have organized throughout Great Britain.[6] In organization, the Labour Party is the most centralist; its basic unit of organization is the constituency, and all constituencies are represented at the party's Annual Conference. The party's National Executive Committee (NEC) has members divided into five sections representing trade unions, constituencies, women, Socialist societies and Young Socialists. There are no representatives on the NEC of territorial divisions of Great Britain or of local government. The Labour Party's Scottish Council was formed in 1915 as a British region. In 1977 its status was enhanced in anticipation of devolution by the appointment of a political secretary in addition to a regional organizer. In Wales, the South and North West Federations of Labour parties were not amalgamated until 1947 as the Welsh Regional Council. The word *regional* was dropped in 1959. In Northern Ireland, Transport House sought to sustain a Northern Ireland Labour Party for years, but since 1974 it has been closer to the pro-Irish unity Social Democratic and Labour Party. Varying arrangements for the Scottish and Welsh regions of the British Labour Party do not detract from the party's centralist bias. There are disputes about where authority rests within the party, but all of the alternatives—Parliament, Annual Conference or the NEC—make no territorial distinction within Great Britain.[7]

Ironically, the Conservative Party officially styles itself the Conservative and Unionist Party, but it has never been a union covering all parts of the United Kingdom. The Conservative Party organization in Wales is the same as that of an English area, with an area council and, since 1972, an annual area conference. Conservative Central Office is the head office for the party in England and Wales. In Scotland, the party is organized separately. Its modern foundation dates from amalgamation in 1912 of Scottish Conservatives and the Liberal Unionist Association under the name of the Scottish Unionist Association. The word Conservative was only added to the title in 1965. A supplementary election manifesto has been issued since 1970. Since the rise of the Scottish Nationalists, Scottish Conservatives have increasingly become more integrated with the party in England and Wales. Since 1977, Scottish constituency associations have been entitled to send representatives to the autumn Conservative Party conference, along with English and Welsh constituencies. In Northern Ireland, the Conservatives have allowed Ulster Unionists to send representatives to the Annual Conference of the party of England and Wales, but this has rarely been done. At present, the Conservative Party is organized as a party of England and Wales, with increasing integration with its concurrent party institutions in Scotland, and disintegration vis-à-vis its longstanding alliance with Ulster Unionists.

The Liberal Party for decades has had difficulties in maintaining any organization in parts of England. Since 1935, the party has been led by an MP from Scotland or Wales (Sir Archibald Sinclair, Clement Davies, Jo Grimond and David Steel), except for the period from 1967 to 1976 when Jeremy Thorpe, MP for Devon North, was its leader. From 1945 until 1974, half or more of all Liberal MPs did not sit for English constituencies. The parliamentary leader of the Liberal Party has always seen himself as a British party leader — and one who must necessarily be particularly susceptible to all-Britain pressures. Organization in Northern Ireland has been minimal, although occasional Liberal standard-bearers have fought elections, albeit polling few votes. The Liberal revival since the early 1960s has been primarily an accession of relative strength in England. From 1964 to 1979 the Liberals on average have fought 76 percent of seats in England, 63 percent in Wales and 52 percent of Scottish constituencies.

At every Westminster election, wherever voters live in Great Britain, they have a choice between major British parties. An election is not primarily a choice between parties representing different nations; it is a choice between parties that represent different functional interests relevant throughout the United Kingdom. Notwithstanding minor organizational differences, Conservative, Labour and Liberal candidates fight as British candidates concerned with the direction of government at Westminster.

The major British parties are not the only parties that contest Westminster elections. F.W.S. Craig's chronicle of minor parties contesting seats at British general elections since 1885 identifies seventy-three such parties.[8] The minor party usually nominating the largest number of candidates is also a Unionist party, the Communist Party of Great Britain. As its name emphasizes, the Communist Party is as much a British party as the Conservative or Labour parties (and, like Labour, the Communists are also split by the national issue in Northern Ireland). Communist organization is biased toward Scotland and Wales. Since 1964, Communists have fought an average of 18 percent of constituencies in Scotland and in Wales, as against 5 percent of English constituencies. But the Communist Party of Great Britain emphasizes top-down direction.

The Nationalist parties that contest seats in Scotland, Wales and Northern Ireland are fundamentally different from the main British parties, as well as from evanescent or minor parties that occasionally introduce candidates at general elections. By definition, none contests or wishes to contest the majority of seats at stake at a Westminster general election. Thus, none of the Nationalist parties can ever win a majority of seats in the House of Commons. At most, Nationalist parties can be influential only temporarily, holding the balance of power at Westminster when support for the British parties is so divided that none wins an overall majority. However, the Nationalist parties differ from minor parties in that they *do* contest a majority or all the seats at stake in their own nation. Moreover, as Nationalist parties, they appeal for votes on cross-class rather than functional grounds. Both middle-class and working-class voters are asked to support the party of their nation, and Nationalist parties succeed in drawing support on a cross-class basis.[9]

Plaid Cymru (the party of Wales) is the oldest of the Nationalist parties. It was founded in 1925 to secure self-government for Wales and promote the culture, language and economic life of Wales. It first contested a parliamentary election in 1929, but did not nominate candidates for half the 36 seats in Wales until the 1959 general election. Since its leader, Gwynfor Evans, won a seat at the Carmarthen by-election in 1966, it has nominated a full slate of 36 candidates at each general election. In addition to seeking national independence, the party's emphasis on the language issue makes it distinctive from other Nationalist parties, as well as from the British parties. Plaid Cymru draws support on a cross-class basis; two-thirds of its vote comes from manual workers, who constitute about two-thirds the population of Wales. Its primary base of electoral support consists of Welsh-speakers; three-quarters of Plaid Cymru voters are Welsh-speakers. But since its vote is smaller, it also means that four-fifths of Welsh-speakers vote for British parties.[10]

The Scottish National Party was formed in 1928 as an amalgamation of Nationalist groups seeking self-government for Scotland. The party first contested general elections in 1929 and won its first by-election in April 1945. The

SNP did not begin contesting parliamentary elections seriously until after party reorganization in 1962. It won the Hamilton by-election in 1967, even though at the 1966 general election it had nominated candidates for less than one-third of Scottish seats. Since 1970 the SNP has nominated candidates for nearly every seat at a Westminster general election. The party emphasizes independence for Scotland above all other issues; it is not a cultural party in the way that Plaid Cymru is specially concerned with language and way of life. The SNP draws votes on a cross-class basis; nearly two-thirds of its supporters are manual workers. Its primary base of electoral support comes from those who identify themselves as Scottish, not British — but only one-fifth of voters who think of themselves as Scots vote for the SNP.[11]

In Northern Ireland, all the parties winning seats are distinctive to Northern Ireland and do not fight elections elsewhere in the United Kingdom or the Republic of Ireland. The principal parties of Protestants — the Ulster Unionists and Ian Paisley's Democratic Unionist Party — are, as their name implies, "loyalist" parties aggressively determined to maintain the Union of Great Britain and Northern Ireland. By contrast, the principal party of Catholics, the Social Democratic and Labour Party, is dedicated to the creation of a united Ireland. Since its foundation in 1970, the SDLP has inherited much of the support given to the old Irish Nationalist Party. The principal elections in the province are not Westminster but proportional representation ballots, thus encouraging a multiplicity of parties offering candidates in multimember constituencies.

Northern Ireland is the great exception to a pattern of functional party dominance elsewhere in the United Kingdom. In Ulster the principal parties are communal parties, that is, each party takes nearly all its support from a single community identified by religion and national identity. Among those voting for the SDLP, 99 percent are Catholics. Among supporters of the Official Unionists and the Democratic Unionist Party, 99 percent are Protestants. The parties are cross-class; each draws upwards of two-thirds of its support from manual workers. But the parties differ in the national identity of their supporters. Among SDLP supporters, 76 percent see themselves as Irish, compared to 5 percent of Unionists and 3 percent of Democratic Unionists. Loyalist voters normally see themselves as British.[12]

The dominance of functional parties in Great Britain reflects the conscious commitment to class politics of the chief parties contesting seats throughout Great Britain. But it is equally important to emphasize the weakness of Nationalist parties. Whereas such weakness in England may be explained by the absence of a Nationalist party, in Scotland and Wales such weakness is the more impressive because it is demonstrated by the failure of Nationalist parties to succeed in competition with functional parties.

The Nations Vote for Union—Again and Again

The 1970s saw an unusual number of electoral tests of popular support for the Union. In addition to the Westminster general elections of February and October 1974, when Nationalist parties made breakthroughs, there was a post-devolution election in May 1979. During the decade, referendums were held in Scotland, Wales and Northern Ireland about major changes in forms of governance. Only in England has there been no test of commitment to the United Kingdom, since English voters have not had the opportunity to vote for a party or referendum proposing home rule or independence for England.

In Scotland, Wales and Northern Ireland, the tests of the Union have been real tests because fundamentally conflicting alternatives have been placed before the electorate. Voters have been asked not only which functional party they prefer but also *whether* they prefer a Nationalist or a functional party, and *whether* they prefer the constitutional status quo or a major change. Repeated tests of electoral opinion in the four nations of the United Kingdom emphasize the scale of commitment to the maintenance of the United Kingdom (see table 3.1). The vote for British parties is complete in England, if only by default. What is more impressive is the extent to which support for British parties, as against Plaid Cymru, averaged 90 percent of the Welsh electorate. In Scotland, the vote for British parties averaged 80 percent, and volatile support for Scottish National Party candidates 20 percent. In Northern Ireland, the proportion of the electors voting for candidates allied to a British party dropped from 68 percent to virtually nil from 1970 to 1979. (It could equally be argued that English voters no longer support United Kingdom parties, since the Conservative and Labour parties have severed their links with parties in

TABLE 3.1. VOTE FOR BRITISH PARTIES BY NATION, 1970-79

	1970	February 1974	October 1974	1979	Average 4 elections	Change in % 1970-79
	(As % of total national vote)					
England	100	100	100	100	100	0
Wales	89	89	89	92	90	+3
Scotland	89	78	70	82	80	−7
Northern Ireland						
a. Parties linked with Britain	68	2	3	1	18	−67
b. All pro-Union	73	70	69	72	71	−1

SOURCE: Rose and McAllister, *United Kingdom Facts*, pp. 89-90.

NOTE: a. 1970: Ulster Unionists, Northern Ireland Labour; NI Liberal; February 1974, NI Labour; October 1974, Unionist Party of Northern Ireland (UPNI); 1979, UPNI.
b. Parties linked with Britain plus, in 1970, Protestant Unionists; February 1974, all Loyalists, Pro-Assembly Unionists and Alliance; October 1974 and 1979, all Loyalists, Alliance and NI Labour Party.

Ulster.) Very steady and high support for Union is nonetheless registered in Northern Ireland; an average of 71 percent votes for groups pledged to support Union. To suggest that Northern Ireland voters do not want to or should not remain in the United Kingdom because "only" 71 percent voted for parties of Union in 1979 implies a standard for minority veto that would justify allowing Scotland to secede if the Scottish National Party again reduced support for pro-Union parties to 70 percent of the Scottish electorate, as happened in October 1974.

Equally significant, the vote for British parties has remained high throughout a decade when Westminster gave maximum political attention to claims of Nationalist parties. In Wales, support for British parties rose from 89 to 92 percent from 1970 to 1979; Plaid Cymru has consistently been able to secure only one-tenth of the Welsh vote. In Scotland, the vote for the SNP has been much more volatile. The core of SNP support is larger than that of Plaid Cymru, but the core of support for British parties in Scotland is three to four times as great as that for the SNP. In Northern Ireland, support for pro-British parties has been extremely consistent, notwithstanding the political turbulence of the decade. None of the major parties contesting the 1979 Westminster election in Northern Ireland had fought under the same label in 1970. Notwithstanding this, the pro-British parties polled 72 percent in 1979, only 1 percent less than the pro-British vote cast in 1970.[13]

The consistency with which Scots, Welsh and Ulstermen vote for British parties does not mean that they vote in the same proportion for each of the British parties. Voters in Wales are disproportionately inclined to favour Labour; at every general election from 1945 until February 1974, Labour won more than half the Welsh vote. On average, Labour's vote in Wales has been 11 percent higher than its share of the total United Kingdom vote, a difference greater than can be accounted for by differences in class structure between Wales and the rest of Britain. In Northern Ireland, the Ulster Unionist's position as spokesman for the Protestant majority meant that it consistently secured a majority of the province's total vote. From 1945 through 1970, the vote for the Ulster Unionists was on average 18 percent higher than the Conservative share of the total United Kingdom vote, a difference that cannot be explained by class differences. In Scotland, neither the Conservative nor Labour party has consistently polled better than its United Kingdom average. From 1945 through 1955, the Conservatives were slightly above average; since 1959, the Conservatives have on average polled 7 percent less in Scotland than their United Kingdom share. In seven of the eleven general elections since 1945, Labour has polled above average in Scotland and in four, below average. Scotland does not have a hegemonic party in terms of popular votes; only once (in

1955) did one party (the Conservatives) win half the vote. In six of the last eleven elections, both the Conservative and Labour parties polled a larger share of the vote in England than in the United Kingdom as a whole.[14]

The logic of competition within a party system means that when one party gains or loses votes, this affects other parties in the system. In the 1970s the vote for both major British parties, the Conservatives and Labour, tended to decline. Furthermore, both parties also tended to lose support in the non-English parts of the United Kingdom. In consequence, both parties reacted (or, their critics would say, overreacted) by endorsing, or appearing to endorse, devolution (cf. chapter 8). In doing this, the parties thought they were showing sensitivity to majority opinion outside England. But this was a misreading of the situation in Scotland, Wales and Northern Ireland. Referendum and general election ballots reaffirmed the strength of Unionist opinion there.

In the abstract, a Nationalist party might be thought capable of winning nearly 100 percent of the vote within a non-English nation of the United Kingdom, since its rhetoric and programme assert a claim to represent the whole of a nation. But in practice, a Nationalist party is usually created in circumstances that link it with only one part of the nation it claims to represent. This gives it a core of support—but also limits the extent of its appeal.

In Wales the 1 March 1979 referendum on devolution produced a resounding vote for the status quo of Union. Only 20 percent of those voting favoured the 1978 Welsh Devolution Act. The rejection of the Act occurred notwithstanding support for devolution by most of the political parties active in Wales and the Welsh establishment, as well as by the Westminster House of Commons. Only Welsh Conservatives came out unambiguously against devolution. The reasons for rejection were multiple, including dissatisfaction with the earlier reform of local government in Wales, the unpopularity of the Labour Party at the time, and fears of a "slippery slope" course to independence or compulsory bilingualism.[15] The important point here is the size of the vote for the *Union as it is;* about nine-tenths of those normally voting for British parties opposed devolution. Support for devolution was slightly higher than support for the pro-independence party, Plaid Cymru. This is as it should be, given that Welsh devolution was perceived as a limited change in the government of the principality under the Crown.

The most important structural feature of electoral politics in Wales is that Plaid Cymru's support is concentrated among a minority of the electorate, Welsh-speakers. In 1979 Plaid Cymru campaigned for an independent Wales and downplayed its commitment to the Welsh language. But the electorate believed the party stood for the Welsh language as well as independence. This has put a ceiling on support, since census figures indicate that as of 1971 only

21 percent of the population spoke Welsh. While there are signs of goodwill for *voluntary* bilingualism in Wales, compulsory bilingualism (e.g., as a condition of holding a job in a public agency) would immediately disadvantage the four-fifths of the population that does not speak Welsh. Among its core group of supporters, that is, Welsh-speakers in Welsh-speaking areas of Wales, Plaid Cymru normally draws only one-fifth of the votes; it gains a smaller share of votes elsewhere. Concentrated strength can win parliamentary seats; in October 1974 Plaid Cymru won three seats and in 1979, two seats. But this also means the British parties took 34 of the 36 Welsh seats at the 1979 general election. As long as Plaid Cymru is associated with promoting the cause of Welsh-speakers, then the party faces a self-imposed ceiling of about one-fifth of the vote, for few voters who speak only English will support a party that promises to legislate a major language change to their disadvantage.

In Scotland, the 1 March 1979 devolution referendum divided the electorate almost evenly. Among those voting, 52 percent favoured the Devolution Act, and 48 percent opposed. But among those deemed eligible to vote, the standard set by Parliament, the largest single group, 36 percent, did not cast a vote; 33 percent voting for devolution and 31 percent against. The Act was repealed by Parliament; endorsement by 52 percent of voters on a 63 percent turnout was not deemed adequate positive support for devolution.[16]

Consistently since 1974, opinion polls have shown that there is no positive majority in Scotland about future institutions of governance (see table 3.2). This is made clear by examining replies to Opinion Research Centre sur-

TABLE 3.2. DIVISIONS OF SCOTTISH OPINION ABOUT FUTURE INSTITUTIONS OF GOVERNMENT

	April 1974	December 1975	October 1976	February 1977	April 1979	Average
	(% favouring each alternative)					
1. Keep the present system	21	14	23	32	35	25
2. Assembly made up of representatives of regional councils	19	14	8	13	8	12
3. Directly elected Assembly handling some matters and responsible to Westminster	24	19	20	16	13	18
4. Scottish Parliament handling most Scottish affairs, leaving Westminster dealing with defence, foreign affairs and international economic policy	16	28	27	20	28	24
5. Independence	17	21	18	14	12	16
6. Don't know	3	5	4	5	4	4

SOURCE: Opinion Research Centre polls for *The Scotsman* (Edinburgh), as reported in Rose and McAllister, *United Kingdom Facts*, pp. 116-17.

veys which ask Scots to state their preference among five constitutional alternatives. At no time has any of the five alternatives been endorsed by more than 35 percent of respondents. Equally noteworthy, each of the five alternatives uually receives the endorsement of more than 10 percent of Scots interviewed. The ambiguous referendum result thus accurately reflected the absence of a dominant majority view in Scotland.

The constitutional views of Scots can be grouped into three broad categories. The proportion against any elected assembly (categories 1 and 2 in table 3.2) was 40 percent of those surveyed in April 1974. After the devolution debate, the proportion five years later was virtually unchanged at 43 percent, the largest single group of Scots. There is also a substantial "middle" group that wants change, but change within the Union. This group (options 3 and 4) is divided about how much change is enough. A federal Scotland (option 4) is almost invariably more popular than a directly elected Assembly with powers along lines proposed by the 1978 Scotland Act. But debate in Parliament indicates that federalism is not a politically practical alternative. Independence is the preferred choice on average of one-sixth of Scots. Overall, an average of 37 percent want no real change, 18 percent want change on the scale of devolution, and 40 percent want more change than Parliament has been willing to offer, a federal Britain or independence.

Voting in Scotland was volatile in the 1970s, in keeping with the multiple divisions of opinion about devolution. Voters moved between the principal British parties and between British parties and the Scottish National Party. The SNP has the ability to draw some protest votes from persons who do not necessarily endorse independence, as well as having a core of support who favour independence. The range of support for the SNP is very much greater than for Plaid Cymru. If Scottish voters divided along functional lines, the SNP would get no votes, for it consciously straddles the class divide. If Scots voted strictly according to national identity, the SNP would gain the support of more than 50 percent of the Scottish electorate.[17] The potential support for the Scottish National Party is high because it is not identified with any internally divisive issue, such as language in Wales or religion in Northern Ireland. Insofar as it divides the Scottish electorate, it does so by being pro-independence, a cause of lost votes in 1979. It also fails to gain support from many who think of themselves as Scots because it is not seen as relevant to the principal axis of division of politics in Scotland, which remains functional.

Ironically, Northern Ireland is considered the most un-British part of the United Kingdom because the principal political division in the province is about whether it should remain British, that is, part of the United Kingdom. Protestants, constituting two-thirds of the population of Northern Ireland, have shown time and again the strength of their commitment to maintaining the Union; Unionist and Loyalist parties agree in commitment to the Union. In 1973 a referendum was held to test opinion about the constitutional future of Northern Ireland. The referendum result showed the strength of the Protestant commitment to the United Kingdom. The poll produced a 90 percent turnout of Protestants, and nearly 100 percent voted yes. The referendum also showed the opposition of the Catholic third of the population to the United Kingdom, for there was virtually a 100 percent Catholic boycott of the ballot (see table 3.3).

TABLE 3.3. THE CONSTITUTIONAL FUTURE OF NORTHERN IRELAND: 1973 REFERENDUM

	N	% electorate	% vote
Do you want Northern Ireland to remain part of the United Kingdom?	591,820	57.5	98.9
Do you want Northern Ireland to be joined with the Republic of Ireland outside the United Kingdom?	6,463	0.6	1.1
	598,283	58.1	100.0

SOURCE: Cmnd. 5875 (London: HMSO, 1973).

Northern Ireland is the great challenge to the United Kingdom because the organized majority in favour of Union is opposed by an equally persistent minority against the Union. For a century, Catholics have been voting for politicians seeking a fundamental change in the United Kingdom. Since the creation of Stormont in 1921, Catholics have usually voted for representatives committed to a united Ireland. Until 1965, the Nationalists at Stormont refused to take the title of a Loyal Opposition. The Social Democratic and Labour Party, founded in 1970, has differed only in working *by stages* toward a united Ireland. The goal of withdrawal from the United Kingdom remains unchanged. At Westminster elections from 1950 to 1955, the old-fashioned Nationalist and Sinn Fein candidates won an average of 26 percent of the vote; from 1974, a mixture of SDLP and Republican candidates has won an average of 28 percent of the vote. The SDLP did consistently win the majority of Catholic votes in the 1970s, but it is not the only party winning Catholic votes. In 1979, the SDLP vote was about three-fifths that of the Catholic community. The remainder was divided between more militant Republican and Nationalist candidates, plus a small portion for the bi-confessional Alliance Party. In two 1981 by-elections in Fermanagh and South Tyrone, the SDLP showed its deference to Irish unity by failing to put up a candidate against a Republican supporting an IRA hunger strike. The Catholic voters in the constituency elected Bobby Sands, an IRA hunger striker, and after his death, Owen Carron, his election agent.

Consistently public opinion surveys show that there is no consensus among a majority of Protestants and a majority of Catholics about the constitution and government of Northern Ireland. Because of the larger size of the Protestant community and the commitment to the United Kingdom among Protestants, support for the Union is clearly and consistently registered by two-thirds or more of the electorate in Northern Ireland.[18]

Overall, the four nations of the United Kingdom each show a consistent and strong support for Union. The level of Unionist voting differs from 100 percent in England to about 70 percent in Northern Ireland. The fact that some people vote for the breakup of the United Kingdom in Wales, Scotland and Northern Ireland is worth noting, but even more important is the fact that Nationalist voters are a minority. Moreover, in Wales and Northern Ireland the constellation of issues they stress is likely to condemn Nationalist parties to a continuing minority status within the nation they claim to represent. The Unionist parties divide the majority of the electorate along functional lines — but unite in maintaining support for Union.

Effects of Party Competition

Given the authority of the Crown in Parliament, any party seriously competing to win office must seek an absolute majority of seats in the House of Commons. This the Conservative and Labour parties consistently do, and the Liberals also contest seats throughout Britain in an effort to influence government. In the competition for a parliamentary majority, the nations are inevitably unequal, because of inequalities in population. England has 516 of the 635 seats, Scotland 71, Wales 36 and Northern Ireland 12, rising to 17 in the next general election. Notwithstanding the overrepresentation of Scotland and Wales in the ratio of seats to electors, the non-English nations of the United Kingdom together have only 19 percent of seats in Parliament.

In the competition for power at Westminster, the views of English voters will never be neglected, for English constituencies must provide the great bulk of seats that any party needs to win a parliamentary majority. This is not the consequence of a conscious English attempt to dominate non-English parts of the United Kingdom. It is a consequence of the democratization of the franchise. As long as the vote is based on the broad principle of equal representation, then with 83 percent of the registered electorate, voters in England should always elect the great majority of MPs. It is important to note that the single-member constituency system for electing MPs means that MPs are not elected to represent England. Instead, MPs represent a 1/516 part of England; they sit as MPs for English constituencies, not as English MPs.[19]

Election campaigning takes place under conditions of great uncertainty. The day an election campaign starts, no party can be confident about how many seats it is likely to win. The degree of uncertainty has widened with the loosening of standing party loyalties in the 1970s. The so-called marginal seats that parties most want to win are not in a fixed location, nor are they easily identified. The majority are in England—but so too is the majority of a party's hopeless seats. A party that campaigned only in England would have little chance of winning a majority of seats in the House of Commons. It would need to win 62 percent of English constituencies to do so. Only once since the war has a party won so many English seats, Labour in its landslide victory of 1945, when it also won a majority of seats in Scotland and Wales. In advance of the declaration of an election result, no party can be sure of how many seats it can win or where its chances are best to gain the seats necessary to give it a parliamentary majority.

The electoral strategy of the major parties is inclusive: Each campaigns on functional lines throughout Great Britain. This is deemed the most effective and economical way of securing a British-wide electoral swing in the party's favour. In an era of rapid and comprehensive communications through the mass media, parties cannot run separate campaigns in each nation, for what is said in one part of the United Kingdom is immediately repeated in other parts. The same broad issues and appeals move voters in a national swing—and the nation is Great Britain. The 1970s introduced complications in the movement of voters, for Nationalist parties challenged the major British parties to fight on a territorial front. But British parties can respond by stressing functional issues, arguing that the success of the economy throughout Britain provides the best answer to the particular problems of whatever constituency they are immediately addressing, whether it is in England, Scotland or Wales.

The consequence of parties campaigning on British-wide issues has been different in the four nations of the United Kingdom.[20] The Conservatives have tended to be more successful than Labour in England. In the eleven general elections since 1945, the Conservatives have eight times won a majority of English constituencies. The extent of the Conservative advantage in England has been growing since 1970. In elections from 1945 through 1966, the Conservatives averaged a lead of three over Labour in English constituencies. Since then, the Conservatives have averaged a lead of fifty-two over Labour in English seats, even though Labour has won two of the past four elections. Nonetheless, competition between the Conservative and Labour parties is consistently closest in England. On average, the Conservatives have won 51.5 percent of the seats in England in postwar general elections.[21]

In Northern Ireland, the Conservatives enjoyed an average advantage of ten seats through 1970, thanks to an alliance with Ulster Unionists. The Conservatives, like Labour, have won no seats in Northern Ireland since that time, because of the withdrawal of Ulster Unionists from alliance with the Conservative Party after the suspension of Stormont in 1972. The proposed increase in Northern Ireland representation to 17 seats in Parliament will make it a little bit harder for either the Conservative or the Labour parties to win an overall majority.

The Labour Party has consistently won an electoral advantage in Wales, which has returned a majority of Labour MPs at every general election since 1935. Previously, the Liberals were the dominant party; the Conservatives last won a majority of Welsh seats in 1859. The biggest advantage that Labour gained was in 1966, taking 32 of 36 Welsh seats; its smallest was in 1979, when Labour won 22 seats. The extent of Labour's advantage over the Conservatives has fluctuated in part according to the success of Liberal and Plaid Cymru candidates. In the period from 1945 to 1966, Labour had an average advantage of 22 seats over the Conservatives in Wales. Since 1970, its advantage has averaged 15 seats.

Party advantage in Scotland has shifted in more than one direction since 1945. The Conservatives have been the only party to win half the Scottish vote at a postwar general election, taking 50.1 percent of the vote in 1955. The Conservatives won as many or more seats than Labour at two of the first four postwar elections. In 1959, a secular swing to Labour commenced in Scotland, leading Labour to a maximum of 46 seats in 1966, a 26-seat advantage over the Conservatives. Since then, Labour's share of the vote has dropped significantly, but its share of Scottish parliamentary representation has remained high because the Scottish National Party has won a larger share of votes than seats. In 1979, Labour enjoyed a 44 to 22 advantage over the Conservatives in seats won in Scotland and a 41 to 31 percent advantage in votes.

Neither the Conservative nor Labour Party has gained a decisive advantage in the United Kingdom from the relative advantage that each party has in different nations. The two parties have divided eleven postwar elections almost evenly; Labour has won six contests and the Conservatives five. The Conservatives have usually won most seats in England, but have not been able to finish close enough to Labour in Scotland and Wales to translate this advantage into a consistent pattern of victories at Westminster. In the 1974-79 Parliament, Labour MPs argued that securing Labour majorities in Scotland and Wales against the Nationalist challenge was essential to maintaining a Labour government in Westminster, even though Labour had actually won more seats than the Conservatives in England at the October 1974 general election! Arguments about national advantage can easily be reversed. It is meaningless to talk about one party winning or losing control of Parliament because of an advantage in one of the four nations in the United Kingdom. The Westminster Parliament is truly a United Kingdom Parliament; an advantage won in one nation may be offset by losses elsewhere, or vice versa.

The dynamics of party competition set each of the major British parties a twofold task: to maintain or increase their advantage in areas of greatest strength, and to advance (or at least not lose further ground) where the party is historically weaker. The Conservative Party must not write off Scotland and Wales to Labour, otherwise it would start with a handicap of upwards of 100 seats in every election. Equally, the Labour Party cannot write off England to the Conservatives; to do that would be to concede an election to the Conservatives. Both major parties must fight general elections on a Britain-wide basis.

From a perspective that is both national and Unionist, the important question to ask is whether a nation is consistently excluded from a share in Westminster government. The answer is clear: No. In the period from 1945 to 1979, three of the four nations of the United Kingdom have usually voted for the governing party, most but not all the time, and occasionally have divided their representation equally between the two major parties (see table 3.4). England is most likely to vote for the winning party; the party in government has been in accord with a majority of its MPs for 78 percent of the time since 1945. Scotland has backed the winning party for 74 percent of the period and has backed a loser less than England. Wales and Northern Ireland have consistently backed one party. It is the swing of the pendulum on a United Kingdom-

TABLE 3.4. NATIONAL SUPPORT FOR THE GOVERNING PARTY, 1945-79

| | A majority of a nation's MPs support | | |
| | Government | Tie | Opposition |
	(% of months, July 1945-May 1979)		
England	78	4	18
Scotland	74	15	11
Wales	51	0	49
Northern Ireland	45	0	55

SOURCE: Calculated from F. W. S. Craig, *British Electoral Facts 1832-1980* (Chicester: Parliamentary Research Services, 1981).

NOTES: By-elections taken into account in calculating national majorities in the 406-month period.
     Northern Ireland Unionist and Loyalist MPs reckoned as in opposition to the government from the suspension of Stormont in March 1972.

wide basis that has determined whether Wales or Northern Ireland supports
the governing party of the United Kingdom.

Northern Ireland demonstrates how party competition can contribute to
integration or discord within the United Kingdom, depending upon circumstances. As long as the Ulster Unionists and British Conservatives were in alliance, then Northern Ireland could be considered like Wales, a one-party nation
within the United Kingdom party system. In reaction against the Conservative
advantage there, the British Labour Party encouraged the Northern Ireland
Labour Party to attempt to make the province a two-party system, albeit without success. Since the suspension of Stormont in 1972, Northern Ireland has
become a "pariah party system." None of the parties contesting seats in Great
Britain wishes to contest seats in Northern Ireland, nor do parties contesting
seats in Northern Ireland contest seats in Great Britain. In Northern Ireland
the dominant parties are for Union, but the Union to which they are loyal is
different from that which the parties in Great Britain support. In such circumstances, the Northern Ireland electorate cannot unconditionally support the
government of Great Britain—nor can the party in government at Westminster claim support in Northern Ireland.

The effects of party competition on Nationalists are just as important for
the maintenance of Union as the effects on major British parties. By definition,
a party that contests seats only in Scotland, Wales or Northern Ireland has no
chance of controlling government at Westminster. Nationalist parties are con-
demned to the status of minority parties in Parliament. But the Nationalist
parties do not fear perpetual frustration, for their object is to secede from
Westminster and establish their own Parliament as an independent nation.
The Scottish National Party campaigns to win a majority of seats in Scotland,
Plaid Cymru to win a majority of seats in Wales, and Irish unity candidates in
hope of eventually winning a majority of seats in Northern Ireland.

By the very fact of contesting elections, however, Nationalist parties give
tacit acceptance to the importance of the Westminster Parliament. To avoid
doing this, the Republican movement in Northern Ireland refuses to recognize
Westminster, not contesting elections or having its candidates abstain rather
than take a seat in the event of victory.[22] The IRA prefers the use of physical
force as a means of influence. *Cymdeithas yr Iaith Gymraeg*—the Welsh Language Society—carries out illegal and legal protests rather than fight elections.
In Scotland, Nationalists have in the past had recourse to petitions to Parliament as well as organized electoral competition.[23]

Nationalists decide to contest Westminster elections because of the importance of decisions taken there for all nations of the United Kingdom. This
includes decisions of immediate importance about levels of public expenditure

as well as exceptional measures of special national concern. For example, Irish unity MPs from Northern Ireland cannot ignore the presence of the British Army in Northern Ireland, Scottish Nationalists cannot ignore the impact upon North East Scotland of oil policies decided at Westminster, and Welsh-speakers are concerned with government decisions about language use on television.

In contesting elections, Nationalist parties seek to win a large number of votes, both for the sake of securing parliamentary representation and to validate their claim to be national spokesmen. But the SDLP and Plaid Cymru focus on minorities within their national electorates. For the SDLP to attempt to appeal to Unionists or for Plaid Cymru to appeal to Welsh voters who speak only English could dilute the party's principles to the point of self-destruction. In any event, it would be ineffective electorally. The Scottish National Party does not have this problem, but like its counterparts elsewhere in the United Kingdom, it too wins only a minority of the vote within its nation.

The activities of Nationalist parties in the non-English parts of the United Kingdom emphasize the strength of commitment to Union. *By fighting elections, Nationalists register the weakness of their support in their own nation.* Because of the disproportionately large size of England, no one would expect Nationalist parties to poll a large share of the vote throughout the United Kingdom. But Nationalist parties cannot reject the evidence of ballots within the nation they claim to speak for. The support for Nationalist parties varies from nation to nation within the United Kingdom. But the common factor is that within their own nations, Nationalist parties are *minority* parties. When the maintenance of the United Kingdom is in question, it is the Unionist parties that can fairly claim to speak for the great bulk of the electorate in each and all the nations of the United Kingdom.

NOTES

1. See, e.g., Richard Rose, "Comparability in Electoral Studies," in Rose, ed., *Electoral Behavior* (New York: Free Press, 1974), p. 17; and idem, *Governing Without Consensus* (London: Faber & Faber, 1971), chap. 14.
2. W.L. Miller and Gillian Raab, "The Religious Alignment at English Elections Between 1918 and 1970," *Political Studies* 25, no. 2 (1977): 227-51; and W.L. Miller, "The Religious Alignment in England at the General Elections of 1974," *Parliamentary Affairs* 30, no. 3 (1977): 258-68.
3. See Richard Rose and D.W. Urwin, "Social Cohesion, Political Parties and Strains in Regimes," *Comparative Political Studies* 2, no. 1 (1969): 7-67.
4. See Richard Rose, *Do Parties Make a Difference?* (London and Chatham, N.J.: Macmillan and Chatham House, 1980); and Richard Rose, *Class Does Not Equal Party: The Decline of a Model of British Voting* (Glasgow: University of Strathclyde Studies in Public Policy No. 74, 1980).

5. For attempts to deal with this issue, see Jim Bulpitt, "Conservatism, Unionism and the Problem of Territorial Management," and J. Barry Jones and
   Michael Keating, "The British Labour Party: Centralisation and Devolution," both in *The Territorial Dimension in United Kingdom Politics,* ed.
   Peter Madgwick and Richard Rose (London: Macmillan, 1982); and L.J.
   Sharpe, "The Labour Party and the Geography of Inequality: a Puzzle,"
   in *The Politics of the Labour Party,* ed. Dennis Kavanagh (London: Allen
   & Unwin, 1982).
6. For background on the territorial organization of parties and territorially
   organized parties, see Richard Rose and Ian McAllister, *United Kingdom
   Facts* (London: Macmillan, 1982), chap. 3. The Social Democratic Party
   also seeks to achieve this status by 1984.
7. For an introduction to the tangled skein of Northern Ireland politics and
   Labour parties in the plural, see E. Rumpf and A.C. Hepburn, *Nationalism and Socialism in Twentieth Century Ireland* (Liverpool: Liverpool
   University Press, 1977), pp. 195-208; and Rose and McAllister, *United
   Kingdom Facts,* pp. 75-85.
8. F.W.S. Craig, *Minor Parties at British Parliamentary Elections, 1885-
   1974* (London: Macmillan, 1975), pp. 115-27.
9. See Rose, *Class Does Not Equal Party,* table 24; and Ian McAllister, "United Kingdom Nationalist Parties: One Nationalism or Three?" in Madgwick and Rose, *The Territorial Dimension in United Kingdom Politics,*
   table 7.6.
10. Calculated from D. Balsom, P. Madgwick and Denis van Mechelen, "The
    Red and the Green: Patterns of Partisan Choice in Wales" (paper to the
    Annual Conference of the Political Studies Association, Hull, 1981), table
    19. On Plaid Cymru, see Alan Butt Philip, *The Welsh Question* (Cardiff:
    University of Wales Press, 1975); and Phillip M. Rawkins, *Minority Na-
    tionalism and the Advanced Industrial State: A Case Study of Contempo-
    rary Wales* (Toronto: University of Toronto Ph.D. thesis, 1975).
11. See McAllister, "United Kingdom Nationalist Parties," table 5; and, more
    generally, J.A. Brand, *The National Movement in Scotland* (London:
    Routledge & Kegan Paul, 1978); and William L. Miller, *The End of Brit-
    ish Politics? Scots and English Political Behaviour in the Seventies* (Ox-
    ford: Clarendon Press, 1981).
12. See E. Moxon-Browne, "Northern Ireland Attitude Survey," pp. 13-14.
    More generally, see Ian McAllister, *The Northern Ireland Social Demo-
    cratic and Labour Party* (London: Macmillan, 1977).
13. The electoral strength of the parties varies within nations at a given elec-
    tion. The coefficient of variability, calculated for each party's 1979 vote
    by region within England, Scotland and Wales, is, for the Conservatives
    0.11, 0.19 and 0.20 respectively; Labour 0.19, 0.43 and 0.27; the Liberals
    0.22, 0.98 and 0.42; the SNP 0.38; and Plaid Cymru 0.87. Calculations
    from data in Rose and McAllister, *United Kingdom Facts,* table 9.21.
14. See Rose and McAllister, *United Kingdom Facts,* p. 93; and W.L. Miller,
    "Variations in Electoral Behaviour in the United Kingdom," in Madg-
    wick and Rose, *The Territorial Dimension in United Kingdom Politics.*

15. See J. Barry Jones and R.A. Wilford, *The Welsh Veto: the Politics of the Devolution Campaign in Wales* (Glasgow: University of Strathclyde Studies in Public Policy No. 39, 1979).

16. For a criticism of the method used to derive the number of registered electors for purposes of calculating turnout, see Vernon Bogdanor, "The 40 Per Cent Rule," *Parliamentary Affairs* 33, no. 3 (1980): 249-63.

17. See McAllister, "United Kingdom Nationalist Parties," table 7.5.

18. See Rose and McAllister, *United Kingdom Facts,* p. 92; Moxon-Browne, "Northern Ireland Attitude Survey"; Richard Rose, Ian McAllister and Peter Mair, *Is There a Concurring Majority about Northern Ireland?* (Glasgow: University of Strathclyde Studies in Public Policy No. 22, 1978).

19. The same is also true of MPs from Scotland, Wales and Northern Ireland, but these MPs also have a greater "national" awareness. See *infra,* pp. 89ff.

20. Calculated from Rose and McAllister, *United Kingdom Facts,* chap. 4.

21. See R.M. Punnett, *The Inefficient Secret of British Politics* (Glasgow: University of Strathclyde Studies in Public Policy No. 94, 1981), table 10.

22. See Cornelius O'Leary, "The Wedgwood Benn Case and the Doctrine of Wilful Perversity," *Political Studies* 13 (1965): 65-78.

23. See McAllister, "Party Organization and Minority Nationalism."

4. The Institutions of the Mace

Conventionally, sovereignty represents the ultimate power of government. In international law, sovereignty—the unique and exclusive responsibility of a government within a defined territory—is important. This fact is accepted both by governors of the United Kingdom and by Nationalists seeking independence from Westminster. But within a country, identifying the locus of authority is easier said than done; the institutions that exercise the authority are multiple and diverse. In aggregate they may appear more like a maze, lacking any central point of reference, than like a pyramid of power with the supreme wielders of authority at the top.

In a political system that lacks both a sense of the state and a Constitution, the Mace is the appropriate symbol of political authority. The medieval origin of the Mace is a reminder of the long historical process that created the United Kingdom. In physical form, the mace is a five-foot-long silver gilt representation of prepotent power in days when kings and knights literally did meet in hand-to-hand combat. In the words of Ambrose Bierce, a mace is "a staff of office signifying authority. Its form, that of a heavy club, indicates its original purpose and use in dissuading from dissent."[1] As well as representing the harder face of power, the Mace symbolizes a gentler representative face, for only when the Mace is in position on the table of the House of Commons is it deemed to be in session. In the contemporary United Kingdom, authority can be exercised only with the consent of freely chosen popular representatives. Notwithstanding its traditional associations, the Mace today is a symbol of the power of representative government in the name of the Crown in Parliament.

The symbolic character of the Mace leaves open the identification of the hands or institutions that effectively wield the power of the Mace within the United Kingdom at a given time and place. At first glance, it might seem easy to find a single locus of authority. But government is, as Queen Victoria recognized, a plural noun. An infinity of institutions can be brought together under this heading. *Whitaker's Almanack* devotes 75 double-column pages to listing Government and Public Offices, starting with the Advisory Conciliation and Arbitration Service located near Whitehall and ending with the White Fish Authority in Edinburgh. The great bulk of its next hundred pages also refer to public institutions, for example, the Royal Commissions, courts, the armed forces, local government, the universities, and the Church of England. Paging through this catalogue of Government and Public Offices is like exploring a seemingly endless maze.[2]

In the midst of a maze of institutions, each sufficiently distinct to merit attention on its own — Whitehall ministries, nationalized industries, local government, and the health service — the presence or absence of an integrating force is easily overlooked. The Mace is important because it sets limits to the actions of each of these institutions, and its authority can resolve differences between them. In a system such as the United States, there is no single authoritative institution to resolve conflicts between different institutions of government; they are meant to regulate one another by a system of checks and balances. In the United Kingdom, the Mace represents a force strong enough to give direction to disparate institutions.[3]

The Cabinet wields the authority of the Mace today. Government at Westminster — that is, the House of Commons meeting at the old Palace of Westminster and government ministries in Whitehall — draws together parties, MPs and Cabinet ministers at the head of particular departments. To describe these groups separately is to ignore the importance of the links between them. Parties choose MPs, and Cabinet ministers are drawn from the ranks of leading MPs in the majority party in Parliament. There is a multiplicity of sources of authority, but even more important, there is a collective institution to integrate them.

Since this book must inevitably emphasize territorial divisions of United Kingdom government, it is of first importance to consider explicitly how disparate territorial institutions are united under the Crown in Parliament. The first section of this chapter considers Parliament's role in sustaining the cross-national integration of the United Kingdom, notwithstanding the fact that each MP represents a different territorial constituency. The second section analyses the Cabinet's role as the *de facto* custodian of the *de jure* authority of the Mace.

The Parliament of a Union

By definition, the United Kingdom consists of all the territories electing representatives to Parliament, no more and no less. MPs do not represent other levels of government as do members of the United States or Australian Senate or the German second chamber, the *Bundesrat*. The House of Commons is an institution of the Union, bringing together elected representatives from all parts of the United Kingdom for the purpose of collective governance.

By seeking election to the House of Commons, Scottish, Welsh and Northern Ireland politicians, whatever their party or political outlook, pay practical tribute to the unique importance of Westminster. This is as true of Nationalist candidates rejecting its authority as it is true of the great majority of MPs upholding its authority. Every Member of Parliament is elected in the name of a particular geographical constituency, but the constituency is not conceived as a community. Instead, it is defined by the abstract criterion of numbers; it is meant to be a unit of a given number of electors. The great bulk of parliamentary constituencies are not natural communities, that is, geographical areas with which people readily identify; a constituency is much larger than a neighbourhood within a city or a village or a suburban town. Frequent redistribution of parliamentary constituencies further reduces a sense of identification, altering constituency boundaries and names.[4] Constituencies are far smaller than a nation. An MP from Scotland or Wales or Northern Ireland does not represent a nation but a constituency that is 1/12, 1/36 or 1/71 of a nation.

Party competition emphasizes functional or class loyalties, not geographical loyalties. More than 95 percent of all MPs (and until the breakaway of Ulster Unionists from the Conservatives in 1972, more than 99 percent) are elected as representatives of British parties divided by functional interests. As representatives of the Conservative, Labour or Liberal parties, MPs see themselves and are seen as concerned with economic issues relevant everywhere in the United Kingdom. The principles and interests an MP represents are not those of a territorial constituency; rather, they are broad concerns that unite people in all parts of the United Kingdom. For example, constituency activist pressures upon Labour MPs after the 1979 election have *not* been an expression of territorial sentiment but of British-wide differences between left and right within the Labour Party. Similarly, divisions within the Conservative Party reflect "wet" and "monetarist" economic views, not territorial differences between English and non-English MPs or suburban and rural MPs.

The great bulk of MPs do not have a personal connection with the constituency they represent prior to selection as a parliamentary candidate. Among candidates in winnable constituencies, less than one-quarter can claim a direct personal connection when nominated.[5] The parliamentary system of representation is, in Sharpe's words, "a carpetbaggers' paradise."[6] The rule is, in the words of lobby correspondent James Margach: "Start at the centre and work outwards."[7] A young person who gains recognition as a promising politician in circles around Westminster and at party conferences seeks nomination in a safe constituency in any direction from London.

The majority of MPs have no prior local government experience before election to Parliament. Among Conservatives, 74 percent of MPs are without local government experience; and among Labour MPs, 55 percent. Nor is local government experience necessarily evidence of constituency involvement. For example, whereas 30 percent of a sample of Conservative MPs have had local government experience, only 7 percent had local government experience related to their constituency. Among Labour MPs, 41 percent have had local government experience, but only 26 percent with a local authority in their constituency.[8] The local councillor who becomes an MP for the area is not only atypical of councillors but also of MPs—and is almost invariably an unimportant backbench MP.

MPs who become leading Cabinet ministers are least likely to build a career from constituency grass roots. Of the 17 Prime Ministers since Balfour entered office in 1902, 12 made their way in the House of Commons as carpetbaggers, representing an average of 2.3 constituencies in their career. Sir Winston Churchill held the record, in the course of a long career representing five different constituencies from Dundee to suburban London. Ramsay MacDonald sat for four constituencies scattered across England, Scotland and Wales. Cabinet ministers are also less likely to have local government experience than their backbench colleagues. In the February 1974 Labour Cabinet, only 4 of 21 Labour ministers had been councillors; and in the 1979 Conservative Cabinet, only 4 of 22. In this century, only two major politicians, Neville Chamberlain and Herbert Morrison, launched a Westminster career after becoming important figures in local government.

Once elected to the House of Commons, MPs find that the business of the House emphasizes functional concerns. Debates usually concentrate attention upon such problems as the economy, foreign affairs, employment, education, housing, social services, trade and industry. The fourteen Select Committees established after the 1979 general election similarly concentrate attention on functional areas of policy as well as providing forums about Scotland and Wales. If an MP wishes to be listened to by colleagues from other parts of the United Kingdom, then he must speak in terms relevant to their interests, that is, in terms that cut across constituency boundaries. To talk only about Scotland or Wales or Northern Ireland is to risk losing the ear of the 90 to 98 percent of MPs who do not represent that nation. To speak of unemployment or inflation is to address a concern that is common to all constituencies.

MPs speak out about matters that concern their constituency or constituents, but they normally do so in functional terms. Only one-tenth of Scottish and Welsh MPs see voicing "pork barrel" demands for constituency benefits as important.[9] Unusually among British MPs, they can articulate economic problems in terms of a national territorial interest, that is, as the problems of Scotland or Wales, rather than as the problem of an ill-defined English region or a very narrowly defined constituency.[10] However, only by linking Scottish or Welsh concerns to functional issues, such as industrial change or unemployment, can MPs hope to interest most of their colleagues.

MPs usually spend more time dealing with the problems of individual constituents than those of their constituency as a whole. MPs are subject to a stream of requests for assistance with problems of housing, pensions, interpretations of government regulations and so forth. If anything, MPs from Scotland, Wales and Northern Ireland are more likely to be subject to such requests. While responding to constituent requests may help in insulating an individual MP to some extent against nationwide electoral swings, it also diminishes the MP's attention to larger issues. This is particularly the case for Scottish, Welsh and Northern Ireland MPs, for nearly all of their questions about the problems of individual constituents are likely to be handled by a single territorial ministry rather than a variety of functional ministries.[11]

An MP is interested in being reelected by his constituency; a virtual precondition of reelection is that the MP continues to be a candidate of a British-wide party.[12] Hence, any actions taken on behalf of a constituency in the House of Commons must be within the bounds of party policy or toleration. An MP cannot expect to vote a constituency rather than a party line, except upon rare occasions when such a deviation will not affect the political outcome or where there are peculiar local concerns (e.g., redrawing constituency or local government boundaries).[13] A good constituency MP is an MP who cultivates publicity and friendly relations in the constituency and is known to be helpful in response to personal requests. It is not a person who votes a local as against a party line.[14]

Any MP who entered Parliament in the mistaken belief that his role was to represent a constituency or nation immediately learns from the whips that he was elected to represent a party. Party discipline cuts across territorial boundaries, uniting MPs from all parts of Britain into voting blocs. MPs are expected to look to party whips for instructions about voting and not to their constituency. MPs cannot act like congressmen seeking benefits for their constituency, for they have no vote to trade for favours in Parliament. While the nominal subject of parliamentary divisions varies, the lens of Parliament continuously focuses attention upon one question of unique importance to all MPs: Which party is to be the government of the United Kingdom? For an MP to vote on constituency rather than party lines would court rejection by the party and subsequent electoral defeat in the constituency, whereas an American congressman doing this would expect to guarantee his reelection.[15]

The authority of government is greatly strengthened by having a single party controlling a majority of the House of Commons. With the single party in charge of both the Commons and the Cabinet, the initiative of one set of leaders can produce both executive action and endorsement by the majority of elected representatives. In the absence of a parliamentary majority in the hands of a single party, government must proceed by negotiation between partners to coalition. The effects of this were spectacularly demonstrated when Irish Nationalists held the balance of power in pre-1914 Parliaments. The absence of a parliamentary majority for the 1974-79 Parliament was exceptional. The formation of the Social Democratic Party in 1981 and its alliance with the Liberals is a reminder that a party holding the balance of power can be functional rather than Nationalist. Should the SDP and Liberals achieve their hopes for a breakthrough, then the potential for influence by Nationalist and Ulster MPs would be swamped by the much greater weight of a British-wide "third" party.

Given exposure to discipline in Westminster along party and functional lines, MPs from Scotland, Wales and Northern Ireland could react in either of two ways. On the one hand, the experience could promote a sense of alienation, insofar as they believe their primary political concerns are problems distinctive to their nation. Alternatively, Scots, Welsh and Northern Ireland MPs elected to Westminster could thereby become fully integrated in United Kingdom political divisions.

In fact, Scottish and Welsh MPs are *more* likely than their English colleagues to participate in Westminster, as measured by voting in divisions. This generalization holds true for all three British parties, Conservative, Labour and Liberal (see table 4.1). Among Conservatives, Welsh MPs are most likely to vote in divisions, with Scots second. Among Labour MPs, Scots are most likely to vote in divisions, with English MPs second. Among Liberals, Welsh MPs are most likely to vote in divisions. There is no persisting tendency for one nation's MPs to participate more than the other; party is the greater influence. In the 1977-78 session, English MPs were less likely to vote than Scots or Welsh because the latter included a greater share of Labour supporters of the governing party. In the 1979-80 session, English MPs were more likely to vote because a disproportionate number of English MPs were supporters of the Conservative government.

Nationalists elected to Westminster face two dilemmas. The first is *whether* to participate in Parliament at all. To participate actively at Westminster is to make independence appear less important than integration in a British political system. Yet the alternative—to abstain from Westminster—makes an individual MP appear of no significance and loses Nationalists the opportunity to press their cause, even if it is upon a government not to their liking. When the Nationalists held the balance of power with the Liberals in the 1977-78 ses-

TABLE 4.1. PARTICIPATION OF MPs IN DIVISIONS BY PARTY AND NATION

Labour Government session 1977-78

	England	Scotland	Wales	N. Ireland
	(average MP's participation as % of 324 divisions)			
Conservatives	54	54	66	n.a.
Labour	64	69	62	n.a.
Liberals	62	62	64	40 (Unionist and Loyalist)
Nationalists	n.a.	56	64	11 (Ir. Unity)
All Parties	59%	62%	63%	35%

Conservative Government session 1979-80

	England	Scotland	Wales	N. Ireland
	(average MP's participation as % of 500 divisions)			
Conservatives	64	66	72	n.a.
Labour	53	53	49	n.a.
Liberals	56	44	61	25 (Unionist and Loyalist)
Nationalists	n.a.	41	37	12 (Ir. Unity)
All parties	59%	55%	55%	23%

SOURCE: Compiled from *The Political Companion*, no. 28 (1978): 131-56; nos. 30/31 (1981): 96-121.

sion, the Scottish and Welsh Nationalists were readier to participate in divisions than the chief Opposition bloc, Conservative MPs representing English constituencies (see table 4.1). In the 1979-80 Parliament, when Nationalists had no hope of influencing a Conservative government with a clear majority, Nationalist MPs were less likely to vote than the chief Opposition, Labour. Lesser attention to Parliament also reflected party pressures on Nationalist MPs to spend more time in their national bailiwicks than in the Imperial Parliament.

A second dilemma facing Nationalists is *how* to vote. To vote with the government of the day is to endorse British authority. To vote against it is to condemn the party to being permanently on the losing side. To abstain is to be irrelevant. Like Liberals who face the same dilemma, Nationalist MPs react by sometimes voting with the government and sometimes against it, sometimes voting with other third-force parties or by themselves, and sometimes abstaining and sometimes splitting. The specific action taken depends upon the parliamentary situation and the issue at hand. For example, during the devolution debate the Nationalists were prepared to support a minority Labour government in 1977-79, but voted for its downfall when it became clear that the Labour government would not implement the Devolution Acts in the light of the March 1979 referendum results.[16]

The exceptional position of Northern Ireland representation in the House of Commons is made evident by the tendency of Ulster MPs to stay away from

Parliament. This cannot be ascribed to their membership of a minority party, for Northern Ireland MPs participate far less than Liberals, Scottish Nationalists or Welsh Nationalists. Nor can it be explained simply as a function of distance, for air travel time to Westminster from Belfast is less than the train journey from some less accessible English or Scottish constituencies. In the 1977-78 session of Parliament, pro-British Ulster Unionists and Loyalists participated in only 40 percent of divisions. In the 1979-80 Parliament, when none of the minor parties could influence a majority government, participation in divisions dropped far more on the Northern Ireland side than elsewhere. Ulster Unionists and Loyalists participated on average in 25 percent of divisions, and pro-Irish unity MPs in 12 percent. Both Unionists and Irish unity representatives differ from each other as well as from British MPs. At one extreme, Frank Maguire, Irish unity MP for Fermanagh and South Tyrone, appeared to vote only 13 times in 1977-78 and 18 times in 1979-80. On the other side, the Unionists, led by James Molyneaux and Enoch Powell, are pro-integrationist, and some vote as much as the average British MP. But Ian Paisley's Democratic Unionist Party group does not; in 1977-78 Paisley himself voted only 76 times; and in 1979-80, the three DUP MPs voted in only 11 percent of divisions, less than the two pro-Irish unity MPs.

To participate in Parliament is the right of every MP; to participate in government is the privilege of approximately one-third of MPs. Yet the opportunity of becoming a minister is of great importance. Together, ministers and would-be ministers dominate the ethos of Parliament, an ethos that jealously defends the authority of the Mace. MPs who aspire to ministerial position must show that they understand and respect the preeminent claims of the Mace.

In pursuit of ministerial ambitions, Scottish and Welsh MPs start with one distinctive advantage: Positions in the Cabinet are reserved for territorial Secretaries of State for Scotland and Wales, and junior ministerial posts too. Thanks to reserved seats in territorial ministries, Scottish and Welsh MPs tend to be overrepresented in the ranks of ministers. Whereas 31 percent of all MPs in the period from 1945 to 1974 had held an appointed office,[17] 36 percent of Scottish MPs and 43 percent of Welsh MPs have held office in the period. Northern Ireland MPs, by contrast, are pariahs: Only 1 of 57 has held a ministerial appointment, notwithstanding the identification of Ulster Unionists with Conservatives until 1972.

Ministerial posts given Scottish and Welsh MPs do not appear confined to "ghetto" posts of Secretary of State for Scotland and Wales. Of 15 Scottish MPs who have been Cabinet ministers since 1945, 7 were in Cabinet in functional ministries and 12 had held non-Scottish Office posts, even if junior. Of the 12 Welsh MPs who have been Cabinet ministers, 8 were in Cabinet without a territorial brief,and only 1 had never held a brief outside the Welsh Office. Leaders of the Northern Ireland Office have a difficult task, but it is a task that has been deemed to require a relatively senior politician; of the first six incumbents, all were able to hold other senior posts as well. Of the nine post-1945 Prime Ministers, one sat for a Scottish constituency (Sir Alec Douglas-Home), and another for a Welsh constituency (James Callaghan). Given the small proportion of MPs from Scotland or Wales and the limited ration of Cabinet posts, especially senior posts, the record of Scottish and Welsh MPs can be said to be about average.

The fact that Scottish and Welsh MPs of all parties participate fully in Parliament emphasizes the extent of their integration in the institutions of the Crown in Parliament. In no sense can they claim to dominate Parliament, given their relative fewness of numbers among 635 seats. The opposite is the case: Participation in Parliament makes Scots, Welsh and Ulster politicians into British politicians.[18]

The Cabinet as the Custodian of the Mace

The Cabinet expresses both diversity and unity in government.[19] Individually, Cabinet ministers represent specific functional or territorial departments. Ministers are divided by their departmental differences and individual ambitions. The Cabinet joins and reconciles these differences. The Cabinet is pre-eminently a political institution; it embodies in practice the unity of authority symbolized by the Mace. The doctrine of collective Cabinet responsibility requires individual ministers to accept publicly whatever policy is adopted. In the everyday business of government a Cabinet decision can be treated as the final word, for all ministers and ministries are committed to accept it. Moreover, endorsement by Parliament is reasonably sure because a Cabinet also contains the leaders of the dominant party in Parliament. Although ministers individually speak with many voices and tongues, collectively Cabinet can speak with only one voice at one time. The Mace is mute; the Cabinet is its voice.

The Cabinet can restore differences that arise between the territorial and functional institutions into which government is divided. Without an institution with the authority of Cabinet, conflicts would be endless, for departmental interests inevitably conflict. The job of Cabinet is to be the supreme arbiter of these differences. As in any court, the participation of disputants signifies their readiness to accept the authority of the arbiter. This is specially important in territorial politics. Policies of the Scottish, Welsh and Northern Ireland

Offices must be endorsed by the Cabinet collectively; they are not decisions taken by territorial ministers solely on national grounds. Territorial ministers have limited policy discretion; they can act only within limits acceptable to the Cabinet.

Acting as the executive committee of the party dominant in Parliament, the Cabinet positively authorizes and negatively limits the freedom of action of individual ministers. Because each minister must act in the name of the government as a whole, any matter likely to cause serious political controversy is normally discussed in Cabinet or in a Cabinet committee. A Cabinet minister is not free, as may be the case in Washington, to take what initiatives he wishes, subject only to constraints imposed by pressure groups or legislators. Functional ministers must bring major policies forward for discussion and endorsement by a Cabinet where territorial ministers sit. Territorial ministers must secure Cabinet endorsement for their measures too.

While all ministers are equal, some are more equal than others. By most measures of political standing, territorial ministers are not in the front rank of Cabinet. The front-ranking ministers are those responsible for the central concerns of government, the Chancellor of the Exchequer, the Foreign Secretary, the Minister of Defence, the Home Secretary, and the managers of the government's business, the Leader of the House of Commons and the Chief Whip. Such individuals see the Prime Minister most often, and discuss government business of broadest importance. Depending upon personalities and the temporary salience of issues, a few other ministers may also be of special significance in Cabinet. For example, the Northern Ireland Secretary, William Whitelaw, was a major figure after Stormont was suspended in 1972, but subsequent to the establishment of "temporary" direct rule, the post has declined in significance.

One crude indicator of the status of Cabinet ministers is their precedence in the list of ministers announced at the opening of each Parliament. The first name on the list is always the Prime Minister, and the second can claim to be deputy Prime Minister. The Secretaries of State for Scotland, Wales and Northern Ireland almost always appear in the bottom half of this list. On average, the Secretary of State for Scotland has ranked 11 out of 20 since 1945; the Welsh Secretary, 15 out of 22; and the Northern Ireland Secretary, 17 out of 22.[20]

Mechanisms for exercising the authority of Cabinet are multiple. Party loyalty is fundamental for the existence of the Cabinet as an effective decision-making body. A minister who speaks for a view unpopular in the majority party will have an uphill task carrying colleagues with him. In particular, territorial ministers cannot espouse policies likely to be unpopular in England, for the majority of Labour or Conservative MPs inevitably represent English constituencies. Indifference is a frequent response to proposals by territorial ministers to adapt to national circumstances programmes within their responsibility. As long as territorial ministers keep their proposals within the limits of tolerated indifference, then Cabinet endorsement can be gained more or less on the nod for limited initiatives.

If legislation is wanted, territorial ministers must look to Cabinet for sanction for any measures that they might wish to take that involve exceptions to standing policies or simply statutory variations in concurrent policies. If the requests of territorial ministers are accepted, then a request must be made to the future legislation committee of Cabinet for a share of the limited ration of parliamentary time available for enacting legislation. Even though procedural means can be invoked to reduce the time that the whole House of Commons spends considering legislation dealing with smaller nations of the United Kingdom, parliamentary time is normally in short supply and territorial legislation limited (see table 6.1).

When money is required, spending ministers — and territorial ministers are preeminently this — must again look to Cabinet for annual money grants needed to sustain continuing programmes. Treasury approval must also be sought for new programmes making claims on public money. The Treasury sets aggregate spending limits for ministers in the light of an annual public expenditure review which reflects Treasury policy for the management of the United Kingdom economy as a whole. In addition, territorial ministers are also constrained, insofar as their claims for money are comparable with equivalent functional ministries responsible for England. From a territorial minister's view, the amount of increase for a given concurrent programme in England, with an appropriate adjustment for population differences, constitutes a minimum demand. But anything more becomes conspicuous; the floor can also become a ceiling. When a large block grant is received, a territorial minister has more scope to move money between programmes because he will be responsible for a greater variety of functions than any one functional ministry.[21] But with a given block grant total, increasing expenditure priorities on one programme, such as housing, necessarily means less money for other functional policies, such as education or transport.

The growth of government has affected the conduct of Cabinet business, particularly the responsibilities of the Scottish, Welsh and Northern Ireland Offices. Most ministers individually bear a relatively small portion of the burden of increased responsibility, since their functions are limited to a small portion of governmental activity (e.g., health, education or housing). By contrast, territorial ministers have had a disproportionately large expansion of their responsibilities, for the Scottish, Welsh, and Northern Ireland Offices cover policies equivalent to half a dozen or more Whitehall departments. Because their responsibilities are concurrent with many ministries making policies in England, a territorial minister's work is disproportionately widespread.

In response to an increase in problems requiring collective discussion, much government business is now discussed in Cabinet committees. Even before the Second World War, there were about two hundred Cabinet committee meetings a year on home affairs, and more on defence and Imperial affairs.[22] At any given time, there are likely to be two dozen or more Cabinet committees and subcommittees discussing matters sufficiently broad and significant to merit the collective attention of a number of ministers. Many issues are settled in Cabinet committees, being reported to but not discussed at Cabinet. A minister whose views have been rejected in committee will find it difficult to secure the reversal of a committee discussion by a full Cabinet. Even more important, a minister who is not a member of a Cabinet committee will find it difficult to reverse or to influence significantly recommendations reported from a committee to a full Cabinet, as long as committee members are prepared to defend the bargain arrived at there.[23] Cabinet committees are formally divided into two types: standing committees dealing with continuing major concerns of the government, such as the economy; and ad hoc committees dealing with problems of temporary importance, such as devolution. Because the names of committees often change with the Prime Minister and the workings of committees are shrouded by the mystique of the Official Secrets Act, Cabinet committees cannot be analyzed from their records. But ample is known from memoirs and occasional writings to establish points important here.

The most important Cabinet committees are those least likely to have the Scottish, Welsh or Northern Ireland Secretaries as members. These are committees dealing with matters of persisting major concern to the government — the management of the economy, defence and foreign affairs and government business in Parliament. The committees are important because they are chaired by the Prime Minister or other leading ministers; they deal with matters of pervasive impact upon the government of the day, and have a major substantive impact too. Territorial ministers are likely to be on a social affairs committee because of their social policy responsibilities.

Territorial ministers can expect to be on a host of standing and ad hoc Cabinet committees dealing with industrial policy, given the importance of industrial policy and nationalized industries within their territory. Moreover, they can expect to be on any committee dealing with agriculture and fishing, given its relative importance within their territory. A Scottish Secretary can also claim, ex officio, a seat on any committee dealing with energy and oil.

The Northern Ireland Secretary, when issues are "hot" in the province, will find a special ad hoc Cabinet committee concerned with his territory. But significantly, the Northern Ireland Secretary will not chair the committee; this responsibility will be vested in a higher-ranking minister, such as the Home Secretary or even the Prime Minister. Equally, there are many Cabinet committees that territorial ministers do not (or do not want to) sit on, though their decisions may have some consequences for their department. There are limits to the time that a minister can spend each week attending Cabinet committee meetings.

The majority of Cabinet ministers see themselves as responsible for functional policies, not as promoters of territorial interests. Their territorial responsibilities—whether for the United Kingdom, Great Britain, England and Wales, England or some combination of these—are only incidental. Moreover, politics within Scotland and Wales is usually about functional issues: health, education, employment, the cost of living, and so on. Territorial ministers want to claim the full benefits of United Kingdom policies. In doing this, they must also accept the standards laid down by Westminster; they cannot claim benefits without also incurring obligations.

An issue that reaches a Cabinet committee is likely to involve both functional and territorial questions. If administration of a policy is in the hands of different ministers in different nations of the United Kingdom, as is the case in most major welfare state programmes, territorial as well as functional ministers will be members of the committee. But the presence of two types of questions and ministers does not mean that both are equally important. The first question is: What action can and should the Cabinet endorse in the face of a specific functional problem? If an action is worth taking, then it will be presumed to be worth taking throughout the United Kingdom. If it is not, then it should not be adopted in any part. For example, if the school-leaving age should be raised a year, then it is assumed it should be raised in all parts of the United Kingdom. The territorial extent of a given measure is usually a secondary question. Deliberations normally start from the assumption that any policy should apply to the whole of the United Kingdom, but the administration may be divided between functional and territorial ministries.

Within Cabinet, the initiative on a given issue normally rests with the functional ministry primarily concerned with a policy. For policies uniform throughout the United Kingdom, this is easily identified: the Treasury, the Foreign Office or Defence. For other policies the "lead" department, to adopt a useful Washington term, is normally the department responsible for a function in England because of the relative weight of its claims upon resources and its administrative expertise, reinforced by the weight of English representation in the majority party in Parliament. It would be unusual for a Scottish or Welsh Secretary of State to chair a Cabinet committee or subcommittee instead of a functional minister responsible for England or England and Wales or Great Britain.

Organizations tend to define policy goals. Just as a Secretary of State for Scotland thinks of Scotland, so a Secretary of State for Education will think first about education. The lead minister on a given issue will promote it in functional terms. This means that, first, it will be viewed without reference to territory. For example, the desirability of raising the school-leaving age or providing more nursery education will be considered in terms of general principles and not in terms of Scottish, Welsh or English children. Insofar as general principles are not explicitly contradicted by national conditions in the United Kingdom (e.g., different national religious settlements in education), then territorial ministries will follow the lead department. For example, Rate Support Grant settlements have tended to make similar assumptions about what is the "adequate" provision of services by local government in different parts of the United Kingdom. At one time, the Rate Support Grant memorandum from Whitehall to Welsh local authorities was literally identical in wording with that sent to English local authorities.[24]

The pre-eminence of a lead department, in terms of manpower and money, is reinforced by the likelihood that its head will be a politician of greater weight than territorial ministers for Scotland, Wales and Northern Ireland and will be served by a department with greater functional expertise. For example, when the Chancellor, the Secretary of State for Industry and territorial ministers gather, the first two will invariably be more influential politicians. This is equally likely to be the case in welfare fields, if only because the functional minister, say, for Education, will know education policy far better than the multifunctional territorial minister, who will be working to a brief provided by a junior minister in day-to-day charge of education in a multifunctional department.

The pressure on different ministries to keep in step is strongly reinforced by the predisposition of civil servants at policy-making level to maintain harmony. Civil servants wish to avoid awkward questions being raised about putative reasons for national differences in a Cabinet policy. Minimizing differences that do not have already accepted precedents can be considered good per se. Civil servants are also strategically placed to promote harmony, for they meet in committees that shadow Cabinet committees. They meet to go over the ground for discussion between departments, to agree on statements of facts and settle some outstanding difficulties and refer what they deem major issues for collective ministerial consideration.

The officials representing the territorial ministries speak on behalf of different departments, but they belong to a single civil service. They are recruited and promoted on a United Kingdom-wide basis and their first loyalty is to the Crown, rather than to a single department or nation within the Union. There is no separate Scottish or Welsh civil service, nor was one authorized by the 1978 Devolution Acts. Senior civil servants, whatever their departments, are expected to be loyal to the collective Mace. Moreover, it is in their immediate self-interest to be so. Promotion may well involve transfer between departments and is authorized centrally by Whitehall. Insofar as the experience of civil servants differs, then the functional element can be more important than the territorial. A senior Scottish Office civil servant comments:

> An experienced civil servant transferred from, say, the Department of the Environment to the Scottish Education Department would acclimatise more quickly than if he were transferred to the Ministry of Defence or the Department of Industry. In the first case, he would be dealing as before with social policies operating through the agency of local government and having the general public as their clientele. In the second, he would be dealing with economic or strategic issues in a highly scientific and technological context. . . . On many points there are greater differences between Departments *within* the Scottish Office than there are between these Departments and some Whitehall Departments.[25]

Within an interplay of conflicting interests, territorial ministers usually have two concerns. The first is a substantive concern with the level and form of policies. Territorial ministers normally start from the assumption that "more" means "better" when government is providing welfare state or economic benefits. Hence territorial ministers, whatever their party, develop a repertoire of arguments about why their part of the United Kingdom deserves more of the benefits (or less of the costs) of a given policy, invoking insofar as possible putative special needs of their territory. Arguing for differences in the form of policy is ambiguous. To vary a functional policy among nations of the United Kingdom can leave a territorial Secretary of State open to awkward questions: Why can't our nation be treated just like other parts of the United Kingdom? This complaint is particularly pointed when it comes from integrationist Unionists in Northern Ireland, who believe in reducing rather than enhancing Ulster's differences from Great Britain.

There are strong limits upon varying substantive expenditure. Most benefits provided from the Treasury to the nations of the United Kingdom are a by-product of functional decisions taken on policy priorities and assessments of needs (see table 5.4). Benefits are allocated to nations because they are part of a Union. A politician may allow the belief to spread in Scotland, Wales or Northern Ireland that he is personally responsible for producing the whole of his department's expenditure, but this is "imaginary patronage."[26] In fact, a territorial minister could hardly stop the flow of government money to Scotland, Wales or Northern Ireland. On *a priori* terms, it might be expected that territorial ministers would pursue "pork-barrel" politics, that is, promote measures that are seen as benefits for a given territory (e.g., the location of a government office or building a bridge). For a territorial minister to canvass for pork-barrel benefits for one nation is likely to be self-defeating, for he can quickly mobilize the nonbeneficiaries, a majority of the Cabinet ministers, against a proposal.[27] To promote pork-barrel benefits for the whole of the United Kingdom is possible, for example, an extensive road-building programme. But it is also very expensive, and would require a major Cabinet decision about resources.

The limits for varying the formal content of a policy are also great. The high degree of socioeconomic homogeneity among the nations of the United Kingdom reinforces the presumption of common functional policies, just as the existence of cultural differences permits exceptions where cultural concerns are at issue. The basic concept is that no variation should be allowed that would cause strong objections by any Cabinet minister. This is, first, a guarantee against territorial ministers being discriminated against by their Cabinet colleagues. They can always claim parity of treatment. Second, it limits variations from the functional standard accepted by other ministries. Other ministers cannot be expected to be happy about giving visibly abnormal benefits to one part of the United Kingdom.

The second concern of territorial ministers is administrative: Who will carry out a measure? Whereas the case for exceptional treatment in substantive policy is difficult to make in a Cabinet, the case for the administrative division of responsibilities is easily and often pressed. The very existence of territorial ministries is a presumption of their competence. If territorial ministries never have functions taken from them (and this seems to be the rule), then change must be in only one direction: upwards. Since a big addition to St. Andrews House or the Welsh Office is only a small diminution in a functional ministry (and sometimes, a welcome relief), such claims can often be successful. As long as major lines of policy are collectively agreed in a Cabinet committee and reinforced by legislation, Treasury monitoring and implementation by a unified civil service, it is easy for a functional ministry to accept territorially distinctive administration in the smaller nations of the United Kingdom.

The administration of industrial development policy illustrates the resulting administrative maze, involving both territorial and functional institutions.[28]

There are territorial institutions such as the Scottish Development Agency, the Northern Ireland Development Agency and a Welsh Office Industrial Department. Each territorial ministry gives a high priority to its responsibility for promoting industrial development within its boundaries, but major decisions affecting industrial development are usually made with a functional ministry as the lead ministry. The Treasury is the lead ministry for policies affecting economic conditions. It also determines tax policies relevant to investment and allocates the funds that territorial agencies use to encourage regional development. The Department of Industry is important inasmuch as it is concerned, along with the Department of Energy, with major nationalized industries whose employment and investment policies are particularly important in Scotland and Wales. The Department of Industry is also responsible for industrial assistance programmes on an all-Britain basis, or concurrently with territorial ministries. The Department of Industry negotiates policies with the Treasury. It is concerned with maintaining a reasonable consistency in actions taken by the Scottish Economic Planning Department, the Welsh Office Industry Department and its own English regional offices. When the particular responsibilities of territorial ministries are compared with those of functional ministries, the dominant role of the latter in making industrial policy is clear.

The more important the issue, the narrower the tolerance for territorial variations in policy. For example, when the 1964-70 Labour government sought to promote an end to selective secondary education, it did so for Welsh and Scottish education, as well as English — and in the 1974-79 Parliament it sought to extend this policy to Northern Ireland, though it had won no votes there. Equally, when the 1970-74 Conservative government sought to make major changes in council house rents, it did so by enacting measures affecting Scotland and Wales as well as England, even though Conservative MPs were a minority in these two nations. When a functional ministry with Great Britain or United Kingdom responsibilities disagrees with a territorial minister (say, the Department of Energy and the Scottish Office, or the Treasury and territorial ministers), the functional ministry will be more likely to carry the Cabinet. The scope for policy differentiation by territorial ministries is thus aptly summarized by a retired Scottish Office official: *"The Scottish administration is distinguished from its English equivalent more by how it does things than by what it does."*[29]

The collective character of Cabinet government confers significant benefits as well as constraints upon territorial ministries. The less their political status, the more they are enhanced by being elevated to the Cabinet, even if in a "second eleven" post. If the Welsh Office did no more than take low-status regional offices from a variety of functional departments and bring them together with a common territorial concern, this itself is a substantial change because it creates a Welsh seat on many Cabinet committees. Growth in administrative responsibilities can be significant in implementing and maintaining policies with a minimum of friction, especially when other institutional differences between nations of the United Kingdom are involved. Having administrative responsibility within a common policy framework can become an important (and realizable) alternative to promoting substantive variations in policy. The obligation imposed on a territorial minister is not unique to him. In the words of the first Permanent Under Secretary of the Welsh Office:

> The position of the Welsh Office and the position of the Secretary of State is almost exactly the same as the position of any other department or any other minister. We have a constitutional situation in which government operates collectively. Therefore, on any big issue ministers sitting together in the Cabinet may decide to overrule a departmental minister and insist on a particular policy.[30]

Usually, a territorial minister does not find his views overruled by Cabinet because they are not discussed at Cabinet. Within Cabinet committees, it is his political task to identify the extent to which his ministry will benefit from combining with functional ministers to press for a substantive programme common for the whole of the United Kingdom, albeit differently administered. It is also his task to judge to what extent and under what circumstances variations in policy can be secured. To ask for nothing is to be little more than a passive figurehead.

In every political sense, *the territorial ministries are much more part of Whitehall than they are part of Scotland, Wales or Northern Ireland.* This starts with their direction by a minister vested by the authority of the Westminster Parliament, and it extends through most departmental operating procedures. Geographical distance is not important politically. St. Andrews House, Edinburgh, although 400 miles from Trafalgar Square, is more immediately subject to Westminster's authority than is the Greater London Council, an assembly of locally elected politicians meeting at the other end of Westminster Bridge from Whitehall. A Prime Minister can dismiss a recalcitrant Scottish Secretary, but cannot dismiss an elected local government leader.

The names of ministries can be misleading. It is tempting but wrong to think that a ministry with a territorial name must pursue a distinctive national policy. For example, it is a misperception to see the Scottish Education Department as primarily and autonomously concerned with distinctive policies for education in Scotland. It is first of all concerned with *education,* and with problems of education that are common throughout the United Kingdom and beyond. The existence of differences from the Department of Education and Science, say, on secondary-school-leaving examinations and state sponsorship of separate schools for Catholic and non-Catholic pupils should not detract from even greater similarities, starting with a common commitment to promoting reading, writing and knowledge of arithmetic. Nor would Scots welcome a statement from a Secretary of State for Scotland that, say, the minimum school-leaving age in Scotland was to be reduced by a year from that in England in order to finance more spending on housing in Scotland. The Scottish Office is supposed to provide policies at "British" standards.

There is government aplenty in Scotland, Wales and Northern Ireland, but there is no such thing as a Scottish government, a Welsh government or a Northern Ireland government today. Decisions about what policies apply to which particular parts of the United Kingdom are the prerogative of those who hold the power of the Mace. The same is true about decisions concerning which institutions will administer the policies thus endorsed. Policies in the United Kingdom are usually formulated by a particular functional minister and approved by territorial ministers with concurrent responsibilities. But both types of ministers gain authority for their actions only insofar as they are the actions of Her Majesty's Government as endorsed by the Crown in Parliament.

NOTES

1. Ambrose Bierce, *The Enlarged Devil's Dictionary* (Harmondsworth: Penguin, 1971), p. 216.
2. See *Whitaker's Almanack 1979* (London: J. Whitaker & Sons, 1978). More generally on the boundary lines of government, see B. Guy Peters and Martin Heisler, *Government: What Is Growing and How Do We Know?* (Glasgow: University of Strathclyde Studies in Public Policy No. 89, 1981).
3. See Richard Rose, "Government against Sub-governments," in Rose and E. Suleiman, eds., *Presidents and Prime Ministers* (Washington, D.C.: American Enterprise Institute, 1980), pp. 284-347.
4. Richard Rose, *The Problem of Party Government* (London: Macmillan, 1974), pp. 148ff.
5. Michael Rush, *The Selection of Parliamentary Candidates* (London: Nelson, 1969), pp. 74, 181, 288.
6. L.J. Sharpe, "The Labour Party and the Geography of Inequality," in *The Politics of the Labour Party,* ed. Dennis Kavanagh.
7. James Margach, *The Anatomy of Power* (London: W.H. Allen, 1979), chap. 4.
8. Colin Mellors, *The British MP* (Farnborough: Saxon House, 1978), pp. 90-98.

9. William Mishler and Anthony Mughan, "Representing the Celtic Fringe: Devolution and Legislative Behavior in Scotland and Wales," *Legislative Studies Quarterly* 3, no. 3 (1978): 389.

10. See John F. McDonald, *The Lack of Political Identity in English Regions* (Glasgow: University of Strathclyde Studies in Public Policy No. 34, 1979).

11. See Michael Keating, *A Test of Political Integration: The Scottish Members of Parliament* (Glasgow: University of Strathclyde Studies in Public Policy No. 6, 1977); and David Judge and D.A. Finlayson, "The Scottish Members of Parliament: the Problem of Devolution," *Parliamentary Affairs* 28, no. 3 (1975): 278-92.

12. Note that an MP leaving one party is more likely to join another rather than fight for reelection as an independent. The introduction of proportional representation by single transferable vote would weaken the link between MP and party and strengthen it between MP and constituents. But the introduction of proportional representation by party list system would do just the opposite.

13. Note the absence of territorial concerns in the great majority of divisions chronicled in Philip Norton, *Dissension in the House of Commons, 1945-74* (London: Macmillan, 1975).

14. See Bruce E. Cain, John A. Ferejohn and Morris P. Fiorina, "The House Is Not a Home: MPs and Their Constituencies," *Legislative Studies Quarterly* 4 (1979): 501-24.

15. Cf. R. Douglas Arnold, *Congress and the Bureaucracy* (New Haven: Yale University Press, 1979).

16. For detailed breakdowns, see "How SNP MPs Voted," *Scots Independent,* September 1978; and "How SNP MPs Voted," ibid., May 1979.

17. Figures on ministerial participation calculated from David Butler and Anne Sloman, *British Political Facts 1900-1979* (5th ed.; London: Macmillan, 1980). Britain-wide figures reported by Michael Rush, "The Members of Parliament," in *The House of Commons in the Twentieth Century,* ed. S.A. Walkland (Oxford: Clarendon Press, 1979), p. 92.

18. The opposite is not normally true. Membership in Parliament does not give English MPs any particular understanding of the territorial dimension in United Kingdom government. Perforce, ministers at the Northern Ireland Office must learn quickly about the tangled affairs of the province, but such a "crash" course is in no sense equivalent to the lengthy indoctrination into Westminster received by the average Scottish, Welsh or Northern Ireland MP.

19. For the development of the interpretation presented here, see Richard Rose, "British Government: The Job at the Top," in Rose and Suleiman, *Presidents and Prime Ministers,* esp. pp. 22-43.

20. Since the respective offices have been in existence for different periods of time, the average size of Cabinet fluctuates slightly. On the significance of precedence, see Harold Wilson, *The Governance of Britain* (London: Sphere Books, 1977), pp. 37, 64.

21. Cf. David Heald, "The Scottish Rate Support Grant: How Different from the English and Welsh?" *Public Administration* 58 (Spring 1980): 25-46.

22. S.S. Wilson, *The Cabinet Office to 1945* (London: HMSO, 1975), p. 12.

23. Cf. Wilson, *The Governance of Britain*, pp. 83ff; J.P. Mackintosh, *The British Cabinet* (2nd ed.; London: Methuen, 1968), p. 518; and Patrick Gordon Walker, *The Cabinet* (London: Jonathan Cape, 1970), esp. pp. 176-77.

24. Cf. *The Rate Support Grant Order 1977* (London: H.C. 57, 1977) and *1978* (H.C. 63, 1978) for England and Wales; and for Scotland, *The Rate Support Grant (Scotland) Order 1977* (H.C. 91, 1977) and *1978* (H.C. 40, 1978).

25. J. M. Ross, *The Secretary of State for Scotland and the Scottish Office* (Glasgow: University of Strathclyde Studies in Public Policy No. 87, 1981).

26. Paul Martin Sacks, *The Donegal Mafia* (New Haven: Yale University Press, 1976), p. 7.

27. Roy Gregory, "Executive Power and Constituency Representation in United Kingdom Politics," *Political Studies* 28, no. 1 (1980): 83.

28. See Brian W. Hogwood, "The Regional Dimension of Industrial Policy," in Madgwick and Rose, *The Territorial Dimension in United Kingdom Politics;* and Hogwood, *In Search of Accountability: the Territorial Dimension of Industrial Policy* (Glasgow: University of Strathclyde Studies in Public Policy No. 82, 1981).

29. Ross, *The Secretary of State for Scotland and the Scottish Office*, p. 18; italics in the original.

30. Sir Goronwy Daniel, in Royal Commission on the Constitution, *Minutes of Evidence* 1 (1970): 11.

5. Organizing for Public Policy

Government must be judged by what it does as well as by what it is. Conventionally, writings about the Crown in Parliament concentrate on the institutions of government, as if what government did was irrelevant to the authority of the Mace. Such an approach was understandable in Victorian times, when government did little. But it is not tenable today, for the great changes in government in the past half century have been less about what government is than what it does. Organizing the routine delivery of established welfare state policies is now the main day-to-day activity of government.

The Crown is a unitary concept, but policies exist in the plural. The Victorians were correct to regard government as a plural noun, for it is a multiplicity of organizations. The legal formula *La Reyne le veult* (the Queen wishes it) has endorsed far more policies than any one institution, let alone a single minister, could effectively deliver. The growth of the contemporary mixed-economy welfare state has involved the differentiation of organizations to deliver specific programmes that embody the intentions of policy makers.[1]

Government is a complex of programmes; organizations are but the means to the end of delivering programmes. The goods and services that government provides are heterogeneous in the extreme, ranging from military defence and steel to infants schools and "meals on wheels" for the elderly. In a country of 56 million people, the delivery of these policies is a formidable organizational task. It is also important, for public policies have a substantial impact on nearly every family everywhere in the United Kingdom.

Every government must be organized in both functional and territorial terms. Each institution of government is responsible for specific functional programmes authorized by Acts of Parliament and for a delimited territory, whether it be a local government area or the whole of the United Kingdom. In an ideal-type unitary government, responsibility for public policies would be divided functionally, and each organization, whatever its function — defence, industry, health or education — would have a uniform territorial scope. In a federal system, the principal division of responsibilities is by territory; each partner in the federal compact has specific (and sometimes overlapping) programme responsibilities. Although the Crown is unitary, the government of the United Kingdom is not organized strictly along unitary lines. As the Royal

Commission on the Constitution concluded, there is no ready answer to questions about the allocation of programme responsibilities along functional and territorial lines.[2]

The functional differentiation of the institutions of the Crown has occurred gradually across two centuries. The direction of change has been clear: the creation of a wide variety of organizations to carry out the increasing tasks of government and increasingly complex relations between these organizations. Today, the typical Whitehall ministry is not so much concerned with a single function of government as it is with coordinating activities of the many different units into which each ministry is subdivided. For example, the Home Office is divided into units concerned with fire, police, prisons, broadcasting and immigration. In addition, every ministry has some functional divisions for tasks common to all bureaucratic organizations, such as personnel management and finance.

Every functional organization also has a territorially delimited scope. There is a United Kingdom government, but most ministries are not United Kingdom ministries, that is, they do not deal with the whole of the United Kingdom. This status is normally reserved for those few ministries—the Foreign Office, Defence, and the Treasury—concerned principally with the defining activities of a sovereign government. The great majority of ministries have programmes limited territorially to one part of the United Kingdom. This is most obviously the case with the Scottish, Welsh and Northern Ireland Offices and their jurisdictions limit the territorial scope of ministries denominated in functional terms for England, England and Wales or Great Britain.

Territorial ministries are not functionless nor are functional ministries without territorial responsibilities. Each territorial ministry is internally organized into functional departments. The Scottish Office has five separately denominated departments—Agriculture, Development, Economic Planning, Education and Home and Health—and a central service unit. The Welsh Office comprises eight functional groups—Agriculture, Economic Planning, Land Use Planning, Industry, Transport, Education, Health and Social Work and Local Government. The Northern Ireland Office is organized into six functional departments—Agriculture, Commerce, Education, Environment, Health and Social Services, and Manpower, staffed by the Northern Ireland Civil Service—and a central unit, primarily Whitehall-staffed and serving the Secretary of State.

In local government, while the basic principle of organization is territorial, the actual work is organized functionally. At the boundaries of a local government area, a sign will define its limit; but within a local government building, signs emphasize functional divisions into such departments as education, housing, roads and transport, public health and social work. While each local government employee delivers programmes within a limited territory, many local government employees are hired as functional specialists, as teachers, policemen, social workers, and so forth. The links within each profession are strong and cut across local government boundaries, being sustained by professional associations and trade unions. Vertical links with sponsoring ministries are also strong, for example, between teachers and the education departments of central government. Such is the functional fragmentation that the reorganization of local government sought to promote "corporate management," that is, bringing the heads of different functional departments together to look at local government in terms of its collective impact upon an area.

Territory and function are complementary rather than conflicting attributes of government organizations. Every institution of the Crown has territorial and functional limits to its jurisdiction. Collectively, government can be conceived as a matrix of functional-cum-territorial and territorial-cum-functional organizations, depending upon which is the primary and which is the secondary principle of organization. Every Whitehall ministry is accustomed to having its functional competence limited by the functional competence of other ministries (e.g., Employment, not Education, is the ministry responsible for youth employment services). Equally, nearly every ministry is likely to find its territorial competence limited too (e.g., the Scottish, Welsh and Northern Ireland Offices are principally responsible for education in the non-English parts of the United Kingdom).

The purpose of this chapter is to examine systematically the nature of functional and organizational divisons of the Crown. This not only involves defining the functional characteristics that differentiate organizations but also assessing their relative importance by weighting them in terms of their command of public money and public employment. Attention is given first to differentiating policies according to their territorial scope. Second, organizations are examined in terms of the territorial scope of their functional responsibilities.

Differentiating Policies by Territory

Given the complexity of government, the question arises: What is the territorial scope of public policies in the United Kingdom today? Are programmes delivered on a United Kingdom basis by each organization of the Crown or is responsibility for a given programme normally confined to an institution concerned with only one nation of the United Kingdom? Just as we would not expect two government agencies, one delivering health care and another delivering nuclear weapons, to be organized in the same way, so we should not be surprised to find differences in the territorial scope of organizations delivering different programmes.

In functional and territorial terms, the institutions of the Crown can be divided into three groups. The first consists of organizations with United Kingdom-wide responsibilities: These are responsible for *uniform* policies, that is, measures that are the same in law and in the same organizational hands in all parts of the United Kingdom. Foreign policy and defence are examples of uniform policies. If two or more institutions are responsible for the same policy in different parts of the United Kingdom, whether under a single or parallel Acts of Parliament, this is a *concurrent* policy, for it is concurrently administered by different institutions. Education is a good example of a concurrent policy; division of responsibility for the service is shared among four Whitehall ministries, one functional (The Department of Education and Science) and three territorial (the Scottish, Welsh and Northern Ireland Offices). This is not meant to involve fundamental differences in education policy in different nations of the United Kingdom. *Exceptional* policies are measures that apply in only one nation of the United Kingdom, for example, the promotion of the Welsh language or security legislation for Northern Ireland.

1. *Uniform policies.* Major defining activities of government — representing a country abroad, defending its territory militarily, and maintaining the supply of money — can only be taken on a uniform basis.[3] Other countries expect the Crown to speak with a single voice about foreign policy, to have a single military force, and to have a single currency; responsibility cannot be divided among a functional ministry, the Foreign Office, and three territorial ministries, as can responsibility for education and housing, which are not collective public goods. The voice of the Crown abroad is kept clear by vesting responsibilities in a single organization speaking for the United Kingdom as a whole. The Foreign and Commonwealth Office, the Ministry of Defence and Her Majesty's Treasury each speak for the United Kingdom as a whole about their functional concerns. Even such a seemingly minor matter as the desire of the Scottish Development Agency to have its own overseas office to attract investment to Scotland causes Whitehall to oppose this in the name of a single uniform voice for the Crown abroad.

International relations is unique in the imperative pressures it creates for a uniform policy in international affairs; the whole of the United Kingdom is implicated by what happens to the country's military security, and by what happens to the currency or whether or not it is in the European Community. In the 1975 Referendum on the European Community, the proportion voting yes varied from 69 percent in England to 52 percent in Northern Ireland, but there must be a single United Kingdom policy about membership in the European Community, whether or not it is equally popular in all its parts.

A distinctive territorial feature of uniform policies is that government attention is directed *outside* the United Kingdom. This is most obviously the case in the Foreign and Commonwealth Office, which maintains representatives in more than one hundred different countries around the world. At any given time, it may have more staff working outside the United Kingdom than within it. The Ministry of Defence is also outward-looking. It has armed forces stationed from Germany to Hong Kong, and military attachés at many embassies abroad. In economic affairs some policies that concern the Treasury require a single collective decision (e.g., monetary policy), but many decisions about the economy do not in principle require a uniform policy. For example, there is no logical or political necessity for taxes to have the very high degree of uniformity that exists throughout the United Kingdom. It would have been possible for a devolved Scottish or Welsh Assembly to have taxation powers notwithstanding that shibboleth "the political and economic unity of the United Kingdom." It is the political power of the Treasury that creates pressures for uniformity.

2. *Concurrent policies.* These are here defined as programmes with the same function throughout the United Kingdom but delivered by different institutions in different parts. Concurrent policies are meant to run in harmony because they are adopted and administered under the authority of the Mace. Even if Cabinet and Parliament authorize differences, these may be regarded as minor adjustments justified by national circumstances but not detracting from its principal functional aims.

Concurrent policies depart from uniformity because they are delivered by different organizations in different parts of the United Kingdom. The practical importance of this to the recipient of a given policy may be limited, but there is always likely to be some variation, whether random or intentional, when administration is placed in different hands. The extent will depend upon the significance of administrative discretion for a given policy. For example, there is more discretion in administering land-use planning than in enforcing a statutory age for school attendance. Ministers in the Scottish, Welsh and Northern Ireland Offices believe that administrative discretion is worth having, even if limited to administrative responsibility for common ends endorsed by Parliament. Territorial pressure groups in Scotland, Wales and Northern Ireland also like concurrent policies because this improves their access to officials actually responsible for delivering policies affecting them.

Most policies of government in the United Kingdom are concurrent rather than uniform. Concurrent policies involving territorial ministries include nearly the whole of social policy (education, health, social security and housing), most policies concerned with housing, roads, transport, the environment and many industrial policies as well (see table 5.2). Since the local government system of each nation in the United Kingdom is under a different minister and is different in form, this means that any public policy delivered by local government in the United Kingdom is normally concurrent rather than uniform.

The reasons are multiple for vesting responsibility for the same policy objective in different administrative hands. In the case of Northern Ireland, a half century of separate Stormont responsibility for legislation embracing, *mutatis mutandis,* nearly all the programmes of the contemporary welfare state, creates a presumption that any new Westminster policy affecting an existing Northern Ireland programme will be assigned to the Northern Ireland Office, thus making it concurrent. The troubles of the province are an additional reason for Whitehall to insulate Northern Ireland affairs. Scotland may require so many minor amendments in a bill drafted in terms of institutions in England and Wales that separate legislation is preferable, a prima facie case for concurrent administration. The Welsh Office has added to the significance of concurrent jurisdictions by a conscious policy of "bureaucratic empire building," seeking to acquire responsibility in Wales for as broad a range of policy functions as the Scottish Office had gained. It advanced this goal on administrative grounds, not because it wished to vary substantially the objectives of such programmes. Particular local responsibilities that loom large in the eyes of the Welsh Office or Scottish Office may not loom large in the ministry responsible for England. Looking after a programme in England can be challenge enough, without worrying about what needs to be done in Auchtermuchty or Llanberis.

Concurrent policies are meant to be harmonious, that is, consistent with each other except for administrative differentiation. Authorization by a single Parliament is one guarantee that any differences of means will not raise politically unacceptable doubts about the pursuit of differing ends. Once a line of policy has been agreed, it is by implication the "best" or "British" way of doing things. For a territorial minister to act out of harmony with policies endorsed by the Mace would mean departing from a collective decision of the Cabinet and risking attack in Parliament and repudiation by the Cabinet. To do so would also invite challenge from the Treasury, insofar as departures involve significant costs. Administrative differentiation does not necessarily mean variation in the substance of a policy.

Political expectations and demands reinforce the presumption that concurrent policies will not differ in substance. Just as workers in Scotland, Wales or Northern Ireland do not want different wages if this means lower wages, so citizens do not want different provisions of public policy if this means less benefits, but only if it means more. Nationalist parties tacitly accept this claim. Usually they do not argue that major policies will be substantially different given independence, but rather that established benefits will continue or increase with independence.

3. *Exceptional policies.* These are adopted and administered for one nation of the United Kingdom without involving concurrent action elsewhere. Exceptional policies usually derive from distinctive historical or cultural circumstances of a nation. Government policy about religion provides a classic example, for there are four different policies for the four nations. In England, an Episcopal church is established, and in Scotland a Presbyterian church. There is no established church in Wales, and in Northern Ireland there is explicit legislation against religious discrimination.

Northern Ireland is the most obvious example of exceptional circumstances allowing exceptional policies, because of exceptional security problems. This has been the case from the days of rule from Dublin Castle. From 1921 to 1972 Stormont used separate legislative powers for two kinds of exceptional policies. First, it did not pass "modernizing" or "permissive" legislation in tandem with Westminster, for example, about abortion, divorce or the legalization of homosexuality. Second, it enacted measures with no counterpart in Great Britain, for example, such public order legislation as the Illegal Flags and Emblems Act, 1954, making the flying of the Irish tricolour in certain circumstances an offence. The Special Powers Act, used as the basis of internment in 1971, was exceptional but not un-British, having been based on previous Westminster legislation.[4] After 1945, Stormont did enact welfare state legislation more or less in line with legislation at Westminster; exceptions were made, but these were not of financial consequence.[5] Since suspension in 1972, Northern Ireland has been the subject of exceptional Acts approved at Westminster affecting the powers of security forces, such as the Northern Ireland (Emergency Provisions) Act and the Prevention of Terrorism Act, which allows the Home Secretary, if he deems it desirable, to prevent Northern Ireland residents from entering "mainland" Britain.

In Wales, language provides the chief ground for exceptional policies. The justification was greatest in the nineteenth century when the majority of Welsh were Welsh-speaking but exceptional policies were few. Today, the fact that Welsh is very much a minority language within the principality limits the scope for pursuing exceptional policies. Westminster has no wish to expand measures that would offend the majority. Nor is there a tradition of separate legislation for Wales, making it easier to cross the line between con-current and exceptional policies. Measures taken to promote the language tend to make additional provision for Welsh-speakers, with a minimum of compulsory involvement of the non-Welsh-speaking majority. For example, Welsh-medium television programmes need not be watched by those who do not speak Welsh. Compulsory bilingual policies necessarily affecting Anglo-phones as well as bilingual Welsh-speakers are very few.[6]

In Scotland, cultural distinctiveness is not as marked as in Wales or Northern Ireland, even though the existence of a separate Scottish legal system and a well-entrenched Scottish Office provides an institutional basis for excep-tional policies. The statute books record a substantial quantity of separate Scottish legislation, but for every Act that Parliament passes dealing only with Scotland, it passes nearly eight Acts incorporating programmes for Scotland within legislation applicable throughout Great Britain or the whole of the United Kingdom (see table 6.1). Completely exceptional policies or legislation[7] are likely to deal with matters of limited significance within Scotland—for ex-ample, the Sale of Venison (Scotland) Act, 1968, or the Crofting Reform (Scot-land) Act, 1976, both principally affecting parts of the Highlands. In matters that Westminster deems important—for example, the 1965 Labour govern-ment measure to integrate secondary school pupils without regard to academ-ic ability—no exceptions are allowed. On matters that Westminster today re-gards as unimportant—for example, the statutorily based segregation of Scot-tish pupils into Catholic and non-Catholic schools—Westminster tolerates an exception. Typically, differences are matters of degree. For example, Parlia-ment sanctions the sale of alcohol in both England and Scotland, but it lays down slightly different conditions for its sale in each nation.

Distinguishing between policies is important, but it is equally important to understand the relative importance in government of uniform, concurrent and exceptional policies. A rough indication of significance can be gained by tabulating the number of public employees and the amount of public expendi-ture devoted to each type of policy in the United Kingdom today. The theory of the unitary state implies that uniform policies should claim the bulk of mon-ey and personnel. Insofar as national differences result in policy differences, then exceptional policies should be important.

In fact, the major policies of the Crown today are concurrent policies (see table 5.1). This is true whether the measure used to rank policies is public ex-penditure (83 percent concurrent) or public employment (88 percent).[8] The growth of government in the twentieth-century United Kingdom has empha-sized welfare state programmes. Almost invariably there are concurrent poli-cies delivered to citizens wherever they live in the United Kingdom by a variety

TABLE 5.1. THE DISTRIBUTION OF PUBLIC EXPENDITURE AND PUBLIC EMPLOYMENT
BY TYPES OF TERRITORIAL POLICY

	Public Expenditure		Public Employment	
	£ (bn)	%	N (000)	%
Uniform[a]	13	16.7	900	11.4
Concurrent[b]	65	83.2	6,900	87.4
Exceptional[c]	0.1	0.1	100	1.3
	£78.1 bn		7,900	

SOURCES: Calculated from *The Government's Expenditure Plans 1980-81 to 1983-84* (London:
HMSO, Cmnd. 8175, 1981), table 1.1 and passim; *Supply Estimates 1979-80* (London:
HMSO HC 266, 1979); and updating to 1979 figures in Richard Parry, *United Kingdom
Public Employment* (Glasgow: University of Strathclyde Studies in Public Policy No. 62,
1980).

a. Includes Defence, Foreign and Commonwealth Office, Trade and Energy, Treasury and Inland Revenue, other miscellaneous public services.
b. Includes social security (£19.7 bn), separately administered for Great Britain and for Northern Ireland.
c. Includes miscellaneous expenditures arising out of the Northern Ireland emergency, aid to
Welsh language and Scottish aid to crofters.

of territorial and functionally denominated ministries, local authorities,
health services and nationalized industries. Uniform policies necessary to the
maintenance of government — for example, defence, foreign affairs and the
collection of taxes — are substantial in absolute terms, accounting for £13 billion and nearly 1 million public employees. But they are secondary relative to
concurrent welfare programmes. Exceptional policies appear small for two
reasons. The first is the limited amount of money and personnel devoted to exceptional policies within Northern Ireland, Wales or Scotland. The second is
the absence of exceptional policies for England, which, because of its population, claims most of the resources of the Crown. The result is Union but not
uniformity; public policies are authorized by a unitary Mace, but organizationally they are separate.

Differentiating Organizations by Territory

What is the territorial scope of functional institutions? Four different functional institutions produce and deliver the goods and services that collectively constitute the public policies of the Crown. Two are familiar and headed by elected politicians: Cabinet ministries and local government. Two are equally
familiar but different in direction: public corporations, of which nationalized
industries are the best-known examples, and the national health services.

Territorially, institutions of government can be divided into those responsible for policies on a United Kingdom-wide basis and those with a less

than United Kingdom scope. When organizations have their territorial competence circumscribed, this can be done in any of three ways: (1) Powers may be limited to one of the four nations of the United Kingdom (e.g., the position of the Scottish Office and, for the most part, the Department of the Environment); (2) powers can be confined to one part of one nation (e.g., the Highlands and Island Development Board in Scotland and every local government body from the Greater London Council to the Shetland Island Council); or (3) powers can cover more than one nation but less than the whole of the United Kingdom (e.g., the Home Office is responsible for police and prisons in England and Wales, and the Department of Transport is responsible for railways and ports in the three nations of Great Britain).

The logic of a unitary political system implies that Cabinet ministries (collectively known as Whitehall) would be differentiated by function, yet each would uniformly carry out its policies on a United Kingdom-wide basis. But the territorial organization of the Crown is historical, not logical. Whitehall ministries differ in the kinds of policies for which they are responsible, some concentrating on collective policies that must be uniform (e.g., the Foreign Office) and others on the delivery of particular services to individuals and families (e.g., Health and Social Security), which tend to be concurrent.

A complication is that most Whitehall ministries are *internally heterogeneous;* for some functions they operate on a Great Britain or United Kingdom-wide basis, and for others, only in England or England and Wales. For example, the Department of Education and Science is principally concerned with primary, secondary and further education in England, but it is also responsible for universities throughout Great Britain and for research councils throughout the United Kingdom. Given heterogeneity within ministries, it is necessary to disaggregate Whitehall departments into their principal parts, each responsible for discrete policies and programmes, in order to determine their territorial scope.

The systematic analysis of major policy responsibilities *within Whitehall ministries* (see table 5.2) reveals how few ministries are exclusively concerned with the United Kingdom as a whole: four of the eighteen functional ministries in Cabinet, the Foreign Office, the Treasury, Defence and the Civil Service Department. Equally, it shows that only one ministry is territorially mixed, operating some policies nationally, some binationally for England and Wales, some for the three nations of Great Britain and some for the whole of the United Kingdom. It is particularly noteworthy that heterogeneity is part of the organic structure of Great Britain. Northern Ireland adds to but is not the cause of the typical Whitehall department having a territorially heterogeneous range of programmes.

TABLE 5.2. THE TERRITORIAL JURISDICTION OF WHITEHALL DEPARTMENTS

Department	Programme Responsibilities		
	United Kingdom	Great Britain	National or Binational (E, W, S, NI, E & W)
Agriculture	EEC policy Food standards Price support	Animal health	Research (E & W) Fisheries (E) Forestry (E) Advisory services (E) Administering price supports (E)
Civil Service	All functions	—	—
Defence	All functions	—	—
Education & Science	Research councils	Universities	Primary and secondary (E) Arts (E)
Employment	—	Industrial relations Health & safety	Manpower services (E)
Energy	Oil Atomic energy	Gas Coal	Electricity (E & W)
Environment	Property services	—	Housing (E) Planning (E) Local government (E)
Foreign & Commonwealth	All functions	—	—
Health & Social Security	—	Social security	Health (E) Personal social services (E)
Home Office	Citizenship Immigration Broadcasting	—	Police, Fire (E & W) Prisons (E & W) Crime (E & W)
Industry	Post Office	Regional aid Nationalized industries	Selective financial assistance (E)
Law Officers & Lord Chancellor	—	—	Court administration (E, W & NI)
Northern Ireland Office	—	—	(See table 5.3)
Scottish Office	—	—	(See table 5.3)
Trade	Trade policy Shipping Civil aviation	Companies Consumer protection	Tourism (E)
Transport	International vehicle licensing	Railways Ports	Roads (E) Bus transport (E)
Treasury	All functions	—	—
Wales	—	—	(see table 5.3)

SOURCE: Compiled from *Civil Service Yearbook 1980* (London: HMSO, 1980).

NOTE: *E* = England only scope; *E & W* = England and Wales; *W* = Wales; *S* = Scotland; *NI* = Northern Ireland.

Territorial ministries are multidepartmental ministries because they have functional responsibilities far greater than the typical Whitehall department (see table 5.3). Within the territorial ministries, the term *department* refers to its functional divisions; the Office itself is a conglomerate holding company. The Northern Ireland Office has functional responsibilities for concurrent policies carried out by thirteen different ministries concerned with "mainland" Great Britain. Because of the prior existence of Stormont, the Northern Ireland Office even has its own Northern Ireland Civil Service and a Ministry of Finance with some functions equivalent to the Treasury. The Scottish Office has responsibilities that parallel functions of eleven different Whitehall ministries. The Welsh Office has responsibilities that parallel eight Whitehall departments.

TABLE 5.3. THE FUNCTIONAL JURISDICTION OF TERRITORIAL DEPARTMENTS

Functional Departments (England)	Territorial ministry has some functional jurisdiction		
	Scotland	Wales	Northern Ireland
Agriculture	Yes	Yes	Yes
Civil Service	No	No	Yes
Defence	No	No	No
Education & Science	Yes	Yes	Yes
Employment	Yes	Yes	Yes
Energy	Yes	No	Yes
Environment	Yes	Yes	Yes
Foreign & Commonwealth	No	No	No
Health & Social Security	Yes	Yes	Yes
Home Office	Yes	No	Yes
Industry	Yes	Yes	Yes
Law Officers	Yes[a]	No	Yes
Trade	Yes	Yes	Yes
Transport	Yes	Yes	Yes
Treasury	No	No	Yes
TOTALS	11	8	13

SOURCE: As in table 5.2

a. The Lord Advocate's Department is separate from the Scottish Office, but it is very much a territorial department with functional jurisdiction.

The authority of the Mace is unitary, but the institutions of the Mace are divided territorially as well as functionally. While any given programme in any part of the United Kingdom can be identified as the responsibility of one particular ministry, it is not normal for a ministry to be responsible for a programme throughout the United Kingdom. Altogether, the eighteen ministries of Whitehall fall into nine different territorial categories. At one extreme are four United Kingdom-wide ministries responsible for uniform functions. At the other extreme are three territorial ministries, each concerned with a variety of functions for a single nation. The majority of ministries are territorially heterogeneous. One ministry, Agriculture, operates with its territorial scope defined four different ways; some programmes concern the United Kingdom as a whole, others Great Britain, a third group England and Wales, and a fourth group only England. Four ministries have three different sets of territorial boundaries: Education, Industry, Trade, and Transport. Each has some responsibilities for England, some for Great Britain and some for the whole of the United Kingdom. Energy has a slight variant with programmes for England and Wales, Great Britain and the United Kingdom. Two departments, Employment and Health and Social Security, each divide their major functions into two categories—programmes in England only and programmes for Great Britain. The Home Office is principally a ministry for England and Wales, but it also has some United Kingdom responsibilities. Environment too has United Kingdom-wide responsibilities as well as a principal concern with local government in England. The Lord Chancellor's Department and the Attorney General and Solicitor General are concerned with England and Wales and also with Northern Ireland; Scotland has a separate Lord Advocate's Department. Given the preeminence of mixed ministries, at the centre of the government of the United Kingdom, there are few departments actually organized to act on a United Kingdom-wide basis. But there are also few organized on an exclusively national basis.

A rough indication of the relative importance of departments with different types of territorial responsibility can be gained by examining the distribution of public expenditure and civil service employment.[9] Ministries concerned uniformly with the whole of the United Kingdom account for about one-sixth of the total public spending; their share of civil service employment is about one-twelfth. The territorial ministries collectively account for about one-tenth of public expenditure and 2 percent of total civil service employment. Ministries with mixed territorial responsibilities claim nearly three-quarters of total public expenditure and an even larger share of civil service manpower. In sum, the custodians of the Mace collectively cover the whole of the territory of the Crown, but individually their territorial responsibilities are both limited and mixed.

When attention is turned to other institutions of the government of the Crown, territory heterogeneity remains the dominant characteristic. *Public corporations* are functional organizations providing basic services such as energy, transport and communications. While the function of a particular public corporation is usually easy to identify, there is no general principle determining what "nation" a nationalized industry covers. The only generalization is negative: There is no uniformity.

Most public corporations are intended to be functional rather than territorial agencies. They are organized to carry out particular economic activities. Energy, Industry, Trade and Transport are the sponsoring ministries for most public corporations, reinforcing their functional emphasis. But it would be wrong to suggest that nationalized industries are without any incidental, even if unintended, territorial impact. This is most evident in the effect on public employment of such industries as coal, steel and shipbuilding (see pages 139ff). It is also explicitly evident in the territorial concerns of such public corporations as the Scottish Development Agency, the Welsh Development Agency and the Northern Ireland Development Agency.

The majority of nationalized industries and other public corporations are neither national nor are they United Kingdom-wide. Of their 2 million employees, 48 percent work for the nation of Great Britain (e.g., British Rail, British Steel, and the National Coal Board).[10] Public corporation employees serving the whole of the United Kingdom (25 percent of the total) do so under a variety of territorial labels or none (e.g., the British Broadcasting Corporation, the Bank of England, and the General Post Office). Another 17 percent of public employees work for agencies that are confined to a single nation, principally England or "England and Wales." Eight percent work for public corporations that are less than national in scope, principally passenger transport executives and New Town development corporations.[11]

The National Health Service (NHS) is in a class by itself, both in the scale of its claims on government resources and in its organizational form. The NHS is intended to provide health and hospital care for people throughout the United Kingdom. Although cultural or historical differences would not be thought to create "English" appendicitis, "Welsh" measles or "Scottish" heart attacks, responsibility for health care is divided into four national services: the Department of Health and Social Security, the Scottish Office, the Welsh Office and the Northern Ireland Office.

While health service programmes differ little in form from nation to nation within the United Kingdom, there are organizational boundaries within national boundaries. Given the large scale of the hospital service (which accounts for three-quarters of health service expenditure), each ministry decentralizes responsibilities for administration. The principle of ministerial supervision but not administration is analogous to local government. However, the medical profession successfully avoided coming under local government when the health service was established. Effective power in delivering health services is carried down to the level of the hospital and the general practitioner's surgery. Because of the claims of the health service on the public purse (9 percent of public expenditure) and on public employment (16 percent of total public employment) the organization of health is specially important as an example of concurrent policy.

By definition, each local government is confined to a small portion of territory of the United Kingdom, but collectively the whole of the United Kingdom is covered by local government institutions. Given a common need for local government throughout the United Kingdom, it would appear logical to have a uniform system of local government. But this is not the case. The structure of local government is determined by history. Local government has evolved from different origins in England and Wales, Scotland, and Northern Ireland. The result is that United Kingdom local government consists of four national systems of local government, and there are four Whitehall departments—Environment, Northern Ireland, Scotland and Wales—each responsible for one nation.

Local government varies both between nations and within nations. No two nations of the United Kingdom have the same system of local government. Ironically, the simplest system is found in Northern Ireland, where local government is least significant. The whole of Northern Ireland is divided into 26 districts, each with its own exclusive territory, but none with any significance. Some significant programmes, such as education, are vested in area boards and others retained by institutions appointed by the Northern Ireland Office. Wales also has a relatively simple local government system. The whole of Wales is treated uniformly, being divided into 2 tiers of local authorities, 8 counties and 37 districts; the boundaries of several districts are contained within a single county. In Scotland, there are three different sets of local government units. The bulk of the Scottish population is divided into regions, which are subdivided into districts. The principal programmes are assigned to the regional councils. There are three island councils, with specially defined powers, and also "peripheral rural districts" which lack the planning powers of districts. Altogether, Scotland has 65 units of local government. In England, there are three principal forms of local governments, each embracing a substantial portion of the population: nonmetropolitan (or shire) counties, with district councils as their lower tier; metropolitan counties (large urban conurbations), with lower-tier metropolitan districts councils; and the Greater London area, with distinctive provisions for inner and outer London boroughs, for the City of London and for education. In total, there are a dozen different types of local government within the United Kingdom, each with its own distinctive set of policy functions.[12]

The organization of local government in the United Kingdom is as complex as that of Cabinet ministries, and similarly lacking in uniformity and logic. The initial differences are national. Within each nation, different types of local government units are found, depending upon the nation *and* the area within the nation. A person moving from England to Scotland, Wales or Northern Ireland would expect to receive approximately the same locally provided programmes—but would do so from different organizations. A person moving within England would also find significant differences in the local government organization of services, if moving between a major conurbation, London or the shires—but would also expect to find much the same provision of services.

When the complex of institutions of government is viewed together, territorially limited organizations clearly dominate. Local government, the health services, public corporations and ministries with functions limited to a single nation together account for 64 percent of total public employment and 48 percent of total public expenditure (see table 5.4). With the evolution of the contemporary welfare state these are the institutions responsible for the biggest public programmes. Ministries and public corporations operating throughout Great Britain have substantial expenditure because pensions are paid in this way, but they are low in employees because they provide relatively few services besides cash transfers. United Kingdom-wide organizations of the Crown rank lowest in the amount of money they spend, and are relatively low in their share of public employment. The most important public employer in the United Kingdom is the most decentralized: local government.

TABLE 5.4. THE ALLOCATION OF PUBLIC EMPLOYMENT AND EXPENDITURE BY TERRITORY

Scope of Organization	Public Employment		Public Expenditure	
	N (ooo)	%	£bn	%
1. United Kingdom-wide	1,510	19	12.5	16
2. Great Britain	1,365	17	27.7	36
3. National				
a. Ministries, public corporations and health service	1,925	25	15.8	20
b. Local government units within nations	3,070	39	21.8	28
	7,870	100	£77.8	100

(National categories a and b bracketed: Public Employment 64%; Public Expenditure 48%)

SOURCE: Calculated by updating to 1979 Richard Parry, *United Kingdom Public Employment;* and for 1979-80, from *The Government's Expenditure Plans 1981-82 to 1983-84* (Cmnd. 8175).

NOTES: 1. United Kingdom-wide includes uniform policies and services of Whitehall departments and public corporations.
2. Great Britain: Principally social security, some public corporations and Department of Industry.
3. National categories include, in addition to territorial units for Scotland, Wales and Northern Ireland, the national health services, some public corporations and functional ministries confined principally to England.

When government is examined in terms of what it is, its complexity is often obscured by the opaque simplicity of constitutional language. As a Central Policy Review Staff survey of relations between central and local government notes,"For most practical purposes, the concept of central government is an abstraction which conceals reality."[13] The Crown is unitary, but the authority of the Crown in Parliament is exercised by a multiplicity of organizations, some based in Whitehall, others in town halls, public corporations and the health services. The number of distinct organizations tabulated is a matter of choice. A Whitehall ministry such as the Home Office or the Scottish Office can be viewed as a single unit or as a holding company for many units. Local government in England can be counted as one system with many subsystems or as 411 separate units. The number can be further increased by subdividing each local government functionally according to its responsibilities for education, social services, housing, and so forth.

When government is examined in terms of what it does, the significance of the territorial dimension is equally clear. Even though in theory every public policy in the United Kingdom could be provided by regional branches of functionally organized ministries, in practice this is not done. Parliament normally endorses programmes that are meant to provide much the same benefits in all parts of the United Kingdom, but provides them through territorially distinct institutions. Local authorities are more likely than Whitehall ministries to be the immediate provider of major public services. The separate health services of the four nations of the United Kingdom employ more people than the whole of the United Kingdom civil service. Within Whitehall, there are territorial as well as functional ministries. Even though Scotland, Wales and Northern Ireland account for only one-sixth of the population of the United Kingdom, they more than double its organizational complexity. The United Kingdom is a collection of territorial puzzles. Moreover, the puzzles interlock, for any institution with a distinctive jurisdiction in one territory necessarily subtracts from the territorial jurisdiction of another.

NOTES

1. The term *policy* is used here to refer to the intentions and broad purposes of a set of programmes that are specific activities authorized by particular Acts of Parliament. Thus, housing *policy* consists of a number of separate housing *programmes*. See Richard Rose, *Disaggregating Government* (Glasgow: University of Strathclyde Studies in Public Policy No. 86, 1981), pp. 11-13.
2. Royal Commission on the Constitution, *Report,* p. 214.
3. See Richard Rose, "On the Priorities of Government," *European Journal of Political Research* 4, no. 3 (1976): 250.

4. See Harry Calvert, *Constitutional Law in Northern Ireland* (London: Stevens, 1968), p. 201.
5. Cf. R.J. Lawrence, *The Government of Northern Ireland* (Oxford: Clarendon Press, 1965); and Derek Birrell and Alan Murie, *Policy and Government in Northern Ireland* (Dublin: Gill & Macmillan, 1980), pp. 141, 220ff, 269ff.
6. Cf. Phillip Rawkins, *Implementation of Language Policy in the Schools of Wales* (Glasgow: University of Strathclyde Studies in Public Policy No. 40, 1979).
7. For a complete list of separate Scottish, Welsh and Northern Ireland legislation, see Richard Rose and Ian McAllister, *United Kingdom Facts* (London: Macmillan, 1981), pp. 61-65.
8. While the measures used in table 5.1 can be only rough guides, the conclusion in unambiguous. Even if social security expenditure, separately administered in Northern Ireland and Great Britain, were reclassified as uniform on the grounds that it was "virtually" identical, 55 percent of policies by expenditure would still be concurrent policies, as well as five-sixths of public employment.
9. The figures calculated from sources listed in table 5.1 can be only approximate guidelines, bearing in mind that mixed ministries include territorial responsibilities and that the civil service is only a fraction of total public employment.
10. Calculated from 1979 update of data in Richard Parry, *United Kingdom Public Employment* (Glasgow: University of Strathclyde Studies in Public Policy No. 62, 1980).
11. Calculations of public expenditure for public corporations are not useful indicators of scale, for many corporations are trading bodies that generate most of their revenue from sales, whereas a few, such as the BBC, do not.
12. See Edward C. Page, *Comparing Local Expenditure: Lessons from a Multi-National State* (Glasgow: University of Strathclyde Studies in Public Policy No. 60, 1980).
13. Central Policy Review Staff, *Relations between Central Government and Local Authorities* (London: HMSO, 1977), p. 21.

6. Distributing the Resources of Public Policy

A famous definition describes politics as being about "who gets what when and how."[1] The resources that government can distribute are multiple: laws, money and the services of public employees.[2] The responsibility for distributing resources is readily identified: It rests with Her Majesty's Government. Laws are the most centralized of government's resources: Only Parliament can enact laws. Revenue raising is also unusually centralized: The Treasury is directly responsible for raising 89 percent of all United Kingdom tax revenue. Only in public employment is there decentralization: The proportion of civil servants directly responsible to Whitehall departments is relatively small.[3]

To define politics in terms of conflicts about the allocation of resources prompts the question: By what criteria, territorial and functional, are resources allocated? As chapter 5 has shown, both territorial and functional influences are important in the organization of government. How does this complex structure affect the territorial distribution of the resources of government? Do people who live in different nations of the United Kingdom receive more or less than their proportionate share of resources because of the nation in which they live?

The distribution of government's resources is normally viewed functionally. British political parties speak of distributing benefits to different classes or income groups; they differ about how relatively equal or unequal the distribution between classes should be. This presupposes that it is easy to identify the individuals and families who are the recipients of programme benefits. In fact, 55 percent of public expenditure, including spending on defence, police and fire, aids to industry and trade and interest on the public debt cannot be attributed to individuals or families. Public policies that have identifiable beneficiaries, such as health, social security and education, are important, but claim less than half of money allocated by government.[4]

In federal systems of government, territory is often the initial basis for allocating resources. Each of the lower-tier partners in a federal system will have lawmaking and revenue-raising powers and a substantial number of employees. Central government may also allocate a portion of its resources to the states, provinces, or Länder of the federal system, which in turn allocate these resources to local government and directly to citizens. In the United States, even the scale of such important welfare state benefits as unemployment pay is left to the states to determine. In the United Kingdom, politicians normally expect Westminster to set and finance more or less common standards of benefits throughout the United Kingdom. But this still allows some scope for territorial differentiation of policies, for example, in a decision about priorities in investment in the steel industry, where specific decisions must be made about giving money to particular places.

The potential for varying the distribution of public resources by territory depends upon the type of policy. By definition, uniform policies must be applied the same in all parts of the United Kingdom, and exceptional policies imply resources being allocated differently between the parts. Concurrent policies imply the possibility for territorial variation in the provision of money and public services, above and beyond the division of administrative responsibilities. The question is: How much is the distribution of resources among the four nations of the United Kingdom affected by the policies and institutions of the Crown in Parliament?

Because there is no agreed standard for distributing resources, the first section of this chapter reviews different and sometimes contradictory criteria for distributing public policies. Subsequent sections review the territorial distribution of laws, public expenditure and public employees in order to test to what extent, if any, the different nations of the United Kingdom benefit differently in the sharing out of the major resources of government.

How Should Resources Be Distributed?

The question: How are the resources of public policy distributed? cannot be separated from the question: How should these resources be distributed? This is most obvious in disputes about whether government should provide the goods and services of a modern welfare state. The work of government today is less concerned with ideological theories about whether government should intervene in the marketplace than with how it should determine the nonmarket allocation of resources.[5] There is no agreement among social scientists or politicians about what are or ought to be the best criteria.

The simplest territorial criterion—allocation according to nation—is rarely used within the United Kingdom because of the gross disparity of population between nations. England is more than eight times the size of Scotland, and Scotland is more than three times the size of Northern Ireland and almost twice the size of Wales. Resources allocated on the basis of "one per nation" are atypical and approximate; for example, the Copyright Act requires that a publisher provide at least one copy of every book published in the United Kingdom for libraries in each of four nations — England has three copyright libraries, as against one each for Scotland, Wales and Ireland.[6] Similarly, the British Broadcasting Corporation has what it calls "national regional" councils and members for Scotland, Wales and Northern Ireland — but it has no English national member, and its English regional headquarters in Birmingham is not on a par with non-English nations. The closest example of the "one per nation" formula is found in sports; each of the four nations of the United Kingdom fields one football team to compete internationally. But in rugby this pattern is broken, for one of the four national rugby teams represents pre-1921 Ireland.

A fiscal exchange model of policy suggests that people should get what they pay for, that is, that government should allocate money to the parts of the United Kingdom in proportion to the tax revenue derived from each part.[7] In this model, government would do what was to be done collectively, but it would leave unaltered the distribution of resources among the nations of the United Kingdom. There are considerable problems, however, in attributing revenue accurately by territory, as was shown by attempts to calculate the basis for national taxation post-devolution.[8] The profits of corporations can be earned in one part of the United Kingdom but declared by headquarters elsewhere. Individuals making large income tax payments may have more than one address, and their tax address may differ from the address at which they usually consume public services. Moreover, taxes such as value-added tax (VAT) involve a multiplicity of stages of payments and rebates. The principles of fiscal exchange can also be challenged as inegalitarian, because returning benefits in proportion to taxes paid means "to him that hath shall be given."

Distributing benefits according to population is appropriate to the constitution of the United Kingdom as a unitary state. Population is readily measured; the population of Scotland and Wales has been remarkably stable as a proportion of the United Kingdom for more than a century, and the population of Northern Ireland has been relatively constant. But the composition of each nation's population is not identical; for example, because of emigration, Northern Ireland has a disproportionate amount of young and elderly people. It is therefore argued that resources should be distributed proportionate to a "standardized" population, allowing for such factors as differences in age structure, which particularly affect spending on education and the health services.

An alternative approach is that people should get what they need. Distribution according to need starts from the assumption that people and places have different needs; therefore, to treat everyone the same is wrong. For example, the musically gifted need one kind of education, the deaf another, and the ordinary youth yet a third. The needs of a prosperous London suburb will differ from a Welsh hill farming district or a Fife mining village. A town with lots of slums may be low in the rate revenue but need much revenue from rates on property to improve housing. With some major concerns, such as unemployment, regions can be ranked from the neediest to the least needy area of the United Kingdom. Other differences do not imply inequalities; they may concern incommensurables that cannot easily be ranked as better or worse, like the contrast between urban and rural living. The assessment of tolerable degrees of differences in the allocation of policy resources to meet social needs is a political, not a technical, question.

The conventional way to evaluate how government distributes resources is to measure public policy inputs, that is, the amount of money and personnel devoted to a given policy. But inputs cannot be translated directly into outputs of benefits. Higher inputs of resources can be demanded for areas of high need to achieve the same outcomes as in areas of less need. For example, to secure the same proportion of adequate housing in all parts of the United Kingdom, more resources must be directed to clearing slums in areas with a disproportionate number. With some public policies, it is not so easy to see how to alter resource inputs in order to secure the same outputs. For example, links between health service spending and health are not so automatic that more money spent means more good health, as distinct from more treatment for ill health. Nor can differential costs be ignored. To reduce unemployment in Northern Ireland to the level of the best region in England may be technically possible, but it could involve so great a cost to the Treasury that other desirable programmes would have to be sacrificed.

Criteria for distributing the benefits of public policy imply two very different political judgments about the scope for central authority. Decentralizing or devolving decision making implies an acceptance of differences in public policy and living conditions between parts of the United Kingdom justified by history, by geography, as a consequence of market forces or on all these grounds. From such a perspective, the role of government is to ensure minimum standards but not equal standards in the provision of public policies. For example, more money could be spent to remove slum housing in areas where it is greatest, and more could be done to combat unemployment in areas where it is greatest, without expecting complete equalization. Such an approach would promote a degree of "levelling up," by raising the standards of less fortunate areas and groups. But it accepts a continuing degree of difference or inequality; the choice of the label depends upon the observer.

By contrast, the doctrine of territorial equality, or "territorial justice" as it is sometimes called,[9] assumes that central government should distribute resources to all parts of the United Kingdom in order to remove differences or inequalities arising from history, geography or market forces. Just as Socialists declare they favour redistributing wealth and income between classes, so too a case can be made for redistributing the benefits of public policies in favour of less-well-off parts of the United Kingdom. For example, government can direct to regions of high unemployment industries that would not locate there on normal market criteria, and it can provide economic and social infrastructure to make depressed areas economically attractive, in an effort to raise living standards there. In economic boom times, the fiscal dividend of growth makes it possible to reduce differences by spending more on less-well-off areas. In times of fiscal stress, this is not easily done. When money is tight, the doctrine of territorial equality prescribes that levelling should continue, if necessary by reducing standards in better-off regions while raising those in below-average regions.

Judgments about how resources should be distributed territorially rest upon political values — and thus generate value conflicts.[10] Not only do value differences underlie criteria described above, there are also conflicts between values articulated at different times and places by the same politicians or parties. To favour local autonomy and equality of policy outcomes is inconsistent. Insofar as central governments must reallocate resources to redress imbalances, this inevitably reduces local autonomy. To favour arithmetic equality in distributing resources may be consistent with local autonomy but is inconsistent with equality of policy outcomes, given differences in needs between areas in the United Kingdom. Nor is government itself consistent. Education and health services are virtually free in all parts of the United Kingdom, although it will cost more to provide such services in remote parts of the Scottish Highlands than in the South East of England. But nationalized transportation is not free; charges are related to distance, thus making transport costs vary greatly from one end of Britain to the other.

Entitlements by Law

Laws are a unique resource of government, and the unitary status of the United Kingdom is most clearly affirmed in Parliament's status as the sole lawmaking body in the United Kingdom.[11] Unlike public expenditure, which is reviewed and reauthorized every year, laws remain on the statute books indefinitely; they are monuments to the persisting influence of past as well as present governments. The cumulative total of legislation now in effect in the United Kingdom is very great. Moreover, the amount of legislation has grown greatly since the end of the Second World War. Two-thirds of all Acts of Parliament now in effect and more than four-fifths of all Statutory Instruments have been enacted since 1945.

The great bulk of legislation today confers benefits rather than enforces obligations. The law is less concerned with criminal actions or the procedural rights of individuals than it is with providing benefits. The Acts of Parliament of greatest importance in everyday life are those that entitle people to receive such benefits of the welfare state as education, health care, pensions, housing subsidies and industrial grants for businesses. People in all parts of the United Kingdom share a uniform expectation of receiving the benefits of welfare state legislation. This political expectation of uniform benefits reinforces constitutional doctrines of unitary authority.

Because the great bulk of legislation confers benefits, it is also noncontroversial. The government usually does not bring forward a bill until after it has been carefully discussed with affected interest groups in all parts of the United Kingdom. Notwithstanding the adversary system of parliamentary debate, more than three-quarters of government bills are not opposed on principle in second reading debates in the Commons. Moreover, very few Acts of Parliament are repealed when government changes from Conservative to Labour hands, or vice versa. The measures of successive governments are incorporated in a "moving consensus."[12]

Whilst the theory of Parliament emphasizes the unitary nature of authority, the procedures of Parliament provide scope for territorial exceptionalism. This most obviously has been the case in Northern Ireland; for half a century the existence of Stormont meant that Westminster was debarred from legislating on any policy transferred to Stormont. It could act only by suspending the Constitution as a whole. Since suspension in 1972, the great bulk of Northern Ireland legislation affecting matters previously in the hands of the Northern Ireland Parliament is promulgated by Westminster as Orders in Council, published in draft form to allow public consultation and debate in the Northern Ireland Committee before becoming binding.

The existence of a distinctive legal system in Scotland has accustomed Westminster to devise distinctive legislative procedures for Scottish bills. A limited number of Scottish bills are taken on the floor of the House of Commons when controversial, for example, the Devolution bill. Most Scottish legislation is debated in principle in the Scottish Grand Committee, which can sit in Edinburgh as well as London, and the committee stage of Scottish bills is taken by Scottish Standing Committees. In these committees, Scottish MPs are numerically preponderant. There is no distinctive legislative procedure for

Wales, and it is rarely the subject of exceptional legislation. A Welsh Grand Committee exists as a standing committee of the House of Commons to debate matters exclusive to Wales, but it meets rarely and normally discusses but does not vote on legislation. Select committees established in the 1979 Parliament for Scottish Affairs and Welsh Affairs make enquiries and attract publicity for their reports, but they are not legislative committees.

A review of the territorial extent of Acts of Parliament in the 1970s emphasizes the lack of uniformity in legislation (see table 6.1). Of the 607 Acts of Parliament enacted from 1970 to 1979, 49 percent were uniformly applicable throughout the United Kingdom, and 22 percent uniform throughout the whole of Great Britain. The remaining 29 percent of legislation was confined to one of four nations—Scotland, Northern Ireland, Wales or a nation *(sic)* still significant for legislative purposes, England and Wales. The proportion of acts of limited territorial scope was virtually the same under the 1970-74 Conservative government and the 1974-79 Labour government. In all, 71 percent of legislation was British, and was thus the responsibility of functional ministries. Functional rather than territorial considerations are the primary concern of most legislation.[13]

Scotland requires a small but steady flow of distinctive legislation because it has a separate legal system and because the organization of government in some ways differs, for example, in the assignment of functions between the

TABLE 6.1. THE TERRITORIAL EXTENT OF ACTS OF PARLIAMENT, 1970-79

	1970-74		1974-79		Total	
	N	%	N	%	N	%
United Kingdom[a]	131	52	164	46	295	49
Great Britain[b]	56	22	79	22	135	22
Limited national application	N	%	N	%	N	%
1. England & Wales[c]	33	13	54	15	87	14
2. Scotland	19	8	37	10	56	9
3. Northern Ireland[d]	12	5	18	5	30	5
4. Wales	1	—	3	1	4	0.5
	65	26	112	31	177	29

SOURCES: Compiled by Richard Parry from *Public General Statutes* (London: HMSO, annual volumes).

NOTES: *a.* Includes 8 Acts which contain parallel provisions for Great Britain and for Northern Ireland, and 4 doing so for England and Wales,Scotland and for Northern Ireland.
b. Includes 13 Acts which contain distinctive provisions for England and Wales and for Scotland, and 2 doing similarly for England, Wales and Scotland.
c. Includes 2 Acts applicable to England and Wales and to Northern Ireland.
d. Excluding Acts of the Stormont Parliament suspended in 1972 and subsequent Orders in Council. Note that in the last full session of Westminster prior to suspension, no Acts exclusive to Northern Ireland were adopted.

two tiers of local government. In consequence, half a dozen or so Acts of Parliament are adopted each year that refer only to Scotland. The scope of most Scottish bills is narrow, often concerning technicalities of Scots law or arising from the existence of concurrent institutions for functional policies. Even more important, Scottish legislation is normally not controversial. Of the 56 Scottish bills introduced by the government from 1970 to 1979, only 8 were voted against at second reading by the opposition. Scottish legislation thus reflects an even higher degree of consensus than average in Westminster, notwithstanding the political controversies arising from devolution.

Northern Ireland has been subject to very different legislative procedures before and after the suspension of Stormont. An analysis of Stormont legislation by Ulster officials for the 1965-69 period concluded that 40 percent of all Stormont Acts were "legislation peculiar to Northern Ireland," 19 percent were "parity legislation" matching Westminster Acts, and an additional 41 percent of Acts fell in an intermediate category or were strictly technical.[14] This classification must be interpreted with care, however, for measures classified as "peculiar to Northern Ireland" included such matters as the Museum Amendment Act (NI), 1965, or the Poultry Improvement Act (NI), 1968. These are not matters that make an Englishman regard Northern Ireland as "peculiar." Stormont officials appear to have classified any measure not specifically drafted to follow a Westminster Act as "peculiar." In fact, only a handful of Stormont measures can be classified as directly derived from the "peculiar" public order problems of the province, for example, the Londonderry Corporation Act (NI), 1970, which followed the suspension of elected local government there after civil rights demonstrations.[15]

Westminster's assumption of legislative authority for Northern Ireland in 1972 provides a test of the extent to which Northern Ireland requires legislation different from that of the remainder of the United Kingdom. The test is particularly suitable, since Westminster has had three main choices for enacting measures: an Act applying to the whole of the United Kingdom including Northern Ireland, an Act applying only to Northern Ireland, or an Order in Council subject to affirmative or negative resolution in Parliament and registered as part of Northern Ireland Statutes. In fact, the great bulk of legislation enacted for Northern Ireland has been uniform rather than exceptional legislation, notwithstanding the exceptional circumstances in the province and the conscious desire of the government to maintain the distinction between Westminster and Stormont legislation. Of 327 Acts enacted by Westminster from 1970 to 1979 and applicable to Northern Ireland, 91 percent have been United Kingdom legislation, as against 9 percent exceptional measures pertaining only to Northern Ireland. When Orders in Council are taken into consideration, the pattern is altered, for there have also been 170 Orders in Council from 1972 through the 1978-79 session of Parliament, as well as 26 Acts of Parliament specially for the province. Of all laws made binding in Northern Ireland since suspension of Stormont in 1972, 62 percent have been uniform United Kingdom legislation, and 38 percent have involved distinctive Northern Ireland Orders in Council or Acts of Parliament, such as exceptional security measures suspending trial by jury, which Westminster has not applied elsewhere in the United Kingdom.

Wales has no administrative justification for separate legislation and has had four centuries of automatically being subject to legislation also applying in England. In the period reviewed here, only four measures were uniquely applicable to Wales—the Welsh National Opera Company Act, the Welsh Development Agency Act, the Development of Rural Wales Act and the 1978 Devolution Act. The creation of a Welsh Office permits the discussion of Welsh concerns prior to the presentation of legislation to Parliament by a functional minister. In drafting functional legislation, the Welsh Office is asked to respond to a lead from a functional ministry. Statutes primarily concerned with England, Great Britain or the United Kingdom as a whole may occasionally include provision for varying their application in the principality, in line with proposals made by the Welsh Office and approved by the functional ministry and Cabinet.

Diversity in legislation illustrates the mazelike properties of the Crown in Parliament. Every Act of Parliament reviewed here requires separate examination to determine its territorial scope. There is no *a priori* way to determine territorial extent, but historically a pattern emerges. The scope of legislation emphasizes the unitary nature of the Mace. Of the 607 Acts of Parliament reviewed, 86 percent applied to Wales, 85 percent to England and 81 percent to Scotland. A majority of Westminster's Acts (54 percent) were also applicable to Northern Ireland. The overall pattern is thus uniform legislation for the government of Great Britain. The limited and usually uncontroversial variations embodied in concurrent legislation do not derogate from the authority of the Mace but simply show Westminster's flexibility—as long as this does not create conflicts of principle about functional policies.

Public Expenditure: Adjusting for Need and Political Muscle

In the mixed-economy welfare state, the distribution of money is inevitably important politically. Government policies greatly affect how the national product is allocated, for about 40 percent of the national product is collected in taxes. Government not only assumes responsibility for economic well-being in the aggregate but also for national levels of unemployment and differences in growth rates between nations within the United Kingdom. Both economic growth and recession are territorially ambiguous: Change may increase or decrease differences between parts of the United Kingdom.

The nations of the United Kingdom differ in the production of national income. Consistently, England ranks first, Scotland second, Wales third and Northern Ireland fourth (see table 6.2). But differences among nations are limited, and are declining through time. In 1966 the gross domestic product per head in England was 14 percent above Scotland; in 1979, the difference was 5 percent. Wales, too, has had its gross domestic product rise by two points toward the United Kingdom average. Northern Ireland, substantially less well off than any other part of the United Kingdom, has seen its national product increase both relatively and absolutely from 1966 to 1979, although it still remains 22 percent below the United Kingdom average.

Examining regional figures for gross domestic product shows that the chief economic differences within the United Kingdom are not national, but between the South East of England and the rest of the United Kingdom. The 21 percent distance between the South West, the least-well-off English region, and the South East, is about the same as that between Northern Ireland and the United Kingdom average. The South East generates 14 percent more income than the second most productive region of England. Scotland is ahead of six English regions in its per capita product. Of course, if income could be disaggregated by region within Scotland, this would show big variations too. Distributing public moneys according to the national product could concen-

TABLE 6.2. THE TERRITORIAL DISTRIBUTION OF GROSS DOMESTIC PRODUCT PER CAPITA

Nation/Region	1966	1971	1979	Change
	(UK = 100)			
South East England	114	114	113	− 1
England	103	102	102	− 1
East Midlands	92	96	99	+ 7
Scotland	89	93	97	+ 8
West Midlands	108	103	96	− 12
North West	98	96	96	− 2
Yorkshire & Humberside	96	93	95	− 1
East Anglia	96	95	94	− 2
North of England	88	87	93	+ 5
South West England	87	94	92	+ 5
Wales	86	88	88	+ 2
Northern Ireland	63	75	78	+ 15

SOURCES: *Abstract of Regional Statistics 1974* (London: HMSO), table 77; *Regional Trends 1981* (London: HMSO), table 15.1. The old regional boundaries for England are used for 1966 figures and for some regions in 1971.

trate on public spending in the South East of England, or in compensation raise the level of public expenditure in less well off regions.

Nations that produce more wealth should be expected to contribute more revenue to the Chancellor of the Exchequer, and this is in fact the case. Whilst Inland Revenue procedures prevent the exact attribution of taxes to the four nations of the United Kingdom, the Treasury has sufficient confidence in the bulk of data to publish estimates of tax revenue by nation. In the 1973-74 financial year, for every £100 per head raised in England, £88 was raised in Scotland and £88 in Wales. In the 1976-77 financial year, for every £100 raised in England, £90 was raised in Scotland, £84 in Wales and £73 in Northern Ireland. National differences in taxes broadly follow differences in national income. There are similar differences in tax revenues contributed by English regions to the Exchequer.[16] Insofar as taxes are regarded as a cost rather than a benefit of government, then Scotland, Wales and Northern Ireland do well; each contributes less than its share of the national product.

A revenue-based or fiscal-exchange approach to United Kingdom public expenditure would prescribe that England, and particularly the South East of England, should receive a disproportionate share of public expenditure, as the areas contributing a disproportionately large amount of taxes. But the benefits of public expenditure are distributed very differently from the burdens of taxation. The three non-English nations of the United Kingdom consistently receive a much larger share of public expenditure than their proportion of the population and their contribution to taxation. On Treasury calculations, in Northern Ireland the percentage share was 44 percent more than the United Kingdom norm in 1979, 19 percent more in Scotland and 12 percent more in Wales (see table 6.3). The differences are persisting, but there has been no consistent tendency for national spending patterns to grow. Spending increased by 17 percent per capita in Northern Ireland from 1972 to 1979, and 2 percent in Wales, and fell by 8 percent in Scotland. There are also great differences be-

TABLE 6.3. THE DISTRIBUTION OF TERRITORIALLY IDENTIFIED PUBLIC EXPENDITURE BY NATION

	1972/73	1976/77	1979/80	Change
	(UK per capita = 100)			
Northern Ireland	127	141	144	+ 17
Scotland	127	120	119	− 8
Wales	110	111	112	+ 2
England	96	96	96	0

SOURCES: 1972, 1976: *Social Trends*, no. 9 (London: HMSO, 1979), table 7.16; 1979: *Regional Trends 1981*, table 15.11. Territorially identified expenditure excludes debt interest spending on defence and overseas programmes; it thus includes about 75 percent of total public expenditure.

tween English regions, albeit less than in the United Kingdom as a whole. Short found a difference of 24 percent in regionally relevant public expenditure between the below-average East Midlands and the above-average North of England.[17]

Disparities in population among the four nations of the United Kingdom convert large percentage differences into relatively small cash differences. In per capita terms, spending in Wales was £176 more per head than in England; in Scotland, £265 more per head; and in Northern Ireland, £550 more per head.[18] But because England is so much larger in population than any other part of the United Kingdom, 79.5 percent of territorially identifiable public expenditure is spent there, compared to 11 percent in Scotland, 5.5 percent in Wales and 4 percent in Northern Ireland. Given that higher spending is concentrated upon the smaller nations of the United Kingdom, the total "cost" to the average Englishman of being part of the United Kingdom (i.e., receiving less in territorially identifiable benefits than the United Kingdom average) was £58 in 1980. By the same logic, a resident of London or the South East might reckon that remaining part of England is an unwarranted expense. For example, if the South East withdrew from England and became part of France, it would lose the burden of subsidizing the North of England and could also claim the benefits of being in France, with its higher average income!

A needs-based approach to public expenditure provides a very different interpretation of territorial differences in public expenditure. Such a philosophy starts from the assumption that different needs justify different levels of expenditure. In the words of a Treasury review:

> It is a long-established principle that all areas of the United Kingdom are entitled to broadly the same level of public services, and that the expenditure on them should be allocated according to their relative needs.[19]

This means that parts of the United Kingdom with an above-average proportion of children should have more money to spend on education; areas with more unemployed, more spent on unemployment benefit; and areas with an accumulation of housing problems, more spent on housing. It is particularly important to emphasize that the needs approach starts from what a Secretary of State for Scotland has called "British functional programmes."[20] Instead of thinking in terms of spending in Scotland, Wales or Northern Ireland, the first question is: How much should be spent on a given public policy? A particular functional programme total is authorized by Cabinet as part of a series of decisions about priorities between functional programmes and macro-economic priorities. These decisions imply marginal changes in the total to be spent in each nation of the United Kingdom.

The prospect of devolution, which would have required the Treasury to set public expenditure totals for the Scottish and Welsh assemblies, led the Treasury to produce a quantitative measure of how much each nation of the United Kingdom actually needed, in view of its specific characteristics of population, housing, geography, and so on. The analysis covered health and social services, education, housing and other environmental services, roads and transport, and law and order, all programmes normally under the direction of relevant territorial ministries. It excluded pensions and unemployment benefits, major programmes that territorial differences do not affect because there is a single standard benefit paid for the whole of the United Kingdom. The estimate of the "need" for a given amount of public expenditure was calculated by means that the Treasury describes as "a long way from wholly definitive" because there are "few explicit standards" for measuring needs for services. It has published its calculations as "the best that could be devised with the time and information available."[21] Treasury calculations for 1976-77 concluded that when per capita spending in England stood at 100, greater needs meant that public spending for the programmes analyzed ought to be 9 percent greater in Wales, 16 percent greater in Scotland and 31 percent greater in Northern Ireland.[22]

The actual amount of territorial public expenditure reflects political "muscle" as well as Treasury estimates of need. In the polite words of the 1975 Devolution White Paper, "No neat formula could be devised to produce fair shares for Scotland (and for England, Wales or Northern Ireland) in varying circumstances from year to year. The task involves judgments of great complexity and political sensitivity."[23] To put it in extreme terms, the less the objective evidence of special need, the greater the importance of political muscle for extracting from the Cabinet increased territorial spending. For example, the substantial increase in public expenditure in Northern Ireland from the mid-1960s to the mid-1970s did not reflect an increase in objective need, for Northern Ireland has always had relatively greater social needs than other parts of the United Kingdom. Instead, it reflected a greater political sensitivity in London to problems of the province, causing public spending in Northern Ireland to "catch up" to levels in other parts of the United Kingdom and then to pull ahead.[24] Equally important, a politically weak Secretary of State might cause his territorial ministry to receive less than its needs would justify because of a lack of political muscle in the fight for slices of the Treasury cake.

When the joint effects of both need and political muscle are taken into account, four very different patterns can be found (see table 6.4). First, England sets the minimum standard, since provision for functional ministries concerned with England provides a basis for arguing relatively greater need else-

TABLE 6.4. TERRITORIAL PUBLIC EXPENDITURE,
ADJUSTED FOR NEED AND POLITICAL MUSCLE

	English Norm	Needs Allowance	Political Muscle Allowance	Total per Capita
Northern Ireland	100	+31	+5	136
Scotland	100	+16	+7	123
Wales	100	+9	−8	101

SOURCE: Derived from *Treasury Needs Assessment Study*, pp. 5, 25; figures for 1976-77.

where.[25] Northern Ireland receives more money primarily because of its much greater assessed needs, not so much because of political muscle. For every £100 spent per person in England, an additional £31 is spent in Ulster to meet its estimated needs; the extra £5 spent for political muscle accounts for only one-seventh of its additional expenditure.[26] In Scotland, too, needs justify more additional spending than does political muscle. For every £100 spent per person in England, an additional £16 is spent in Scotland in recognition of its estimated needs, and another £7 as a tribute to political muscle. By contrast, Wales does badly because of a historic lack of political muscle. For every £100 spent per person in England, a total of £109 ought to be spent in Wales to meet its estimated needs; in fact, only £101 is spent. The creation of the Welsh Office was intended to give Wales political muscle by giving it a voice in Cabinet, but this has yet to eradicate a historic tendency to treat Wales like England for expenditure purposes, even though its estimated need for public expenditure is greater.

The distribution of public expenditure in the United Kingdom today is primarily determined by population. The evidence in table 6.4 shows that in Wales the per capita norm, determined by spending in England, accounts for 99 percent of identifiable public expenditure. Distinctive needs add 1 percent more — though they could add 9 percent, but for the defective political muscle of Welsh politicians. In Scotland, allocation according to population accounts for 81 percent of total expenditure, needs allowance for an additional 13 percent, and political muscle for 6 percent. In Northern Ireland, per capita expenditure is high, the needs allowance accounting for 23 percent of the budget, and per capita population for 74 percent. Political muscle (in part used in fighting that pushes up disproportionately the cost of law and order) accounts at most for 4 percent of total expenditure.

The paradox of territorially identified public expenditure is that it is *not* territorially determined: it is first and foremost functionally determined.[27] Spending on exceptional programmes affecting only one nation in the United Kingdom (e.g., bilingual education in Wales) has very little impact on total national or United Kingdom expenditure. The most important single influence upon how much money is spent on a programme in Scotland, Wales or Northern Ireland is the decision about how much is to be spent on the function in the first place. The decision that Cabinet sanctions is taken at the instigation of the functional spending minister in bargains with the Chancellor of the Exchequer. Territorial ministers may influence the bargain marginally. Territorial differences in spending priorities can be maintained where historic differences exist (e.g., housing in Scotland), but the scope for altering territorial spending priorities today is very limited, even though block grant allocations to territorial ministers make them appear possible. A Secretary of State may have the nominal power to decide to spend more than the functional norm on one policy—but this can be done only by spending less on another.

Territorial variations in public spending reflect historic differences; today they are at the *margin* of spending levels determined for the United Kingdom as a whole. A territorial minister cannot claim to "win" the money spent on housing or education in Scotland or Wales or Northern Ireland. Most of that money is provided as of right for functional services throughout the United Kingdom. The fact that spending under the jurisdiction of the territorial minister is normally above the United Kingdom mean is not to his particular political credit. Distinctive territorial needs provide the chief justification for spending advantages. Ironically, if Treasury calculations are correct, then the political muscle of a territorial minister is more important where it is weak, namely, in the Welsh Office. Notwithstanding this, public policies in Wales are funded to the same level as England, a by-product of policies being funded primarily on a functional United Kingdom standard.

Public Employment: Providing Goods and Services United Kingdom-Wide

Public employment is both a means to an end and a benefit in itself. Government employs teachers, nurses or civil engineers in order to achieve policy objectives; the jobs created are a means to the end of providing education, health or roads. But from the point of view of the employee, the job may be an end in itself, both in terms of professional satisfaction and as a source of livelihood. In an era of economic prosperity, job creation may be considered an incidental by-product of particular public policies. But in a time of economic recession, like the early 1980s, public employment can be an end in itself, particularly in areas of the United Kingdom where unemployment is relatively high and private sector jobs relatively hard to obtain.[28] This is particularly so if the job is better paid or more secure than alternative employment.

One criterion for the distribution of public employment is that it should be proportionate to population. This assumes that public employees primarily provide such welfare services as health and education directly to individuals; therefore, their numbers in a given place should be determined by its population. Alternatively, it could be hypothesized that public employment is distributed unevenly between the parts of the United Kingdom. A theory of overcentralization predicts that public employment should be greatest in England, and *a fortiori* in the South East of England, because it has the capital; government is assumed to have a disproportionate number of employees in the capital. Another explanation for concentration is that government is the primary generator of economic growth; the relatively greater prosperity of the South East of England would therefore reflect a high level of government employment. A contrary theory predicts that public employment will be above average in areas distant from London, expecially Northern Ireland, Scotland and Wales. This assumes that government has a responsibility to act as an employer where the regional economy is relatively weak and the need for jobs is greatest. It becomes disproportionately important by taking over declining industries and in default of a normal level of private-sector employment.

Given the scale of public employment in the United Kingdom today, each of these theories could be partially true. Public employment related to the welfare services could be spread throughout the United Kingdom more or less in proportion to population. Employment related to nationalized industries could be concentrated in a few areas, and employment associated with the administration of government disproportionately found in the South East of England. The fact that each of these explanations can be partially true does not make them equally important. For example, there are far more public employees delivering welfare services than there are administrative civil servants delivering advice to Cabinet ministers.

Public employment in the United Kingdom provides work for more than three in ten (31.4 percent) in the labour force. Local government is the largest single employer; the nationalized industries are second in size; the national health service, third. The principal central government employers, the civil service and the armed forces are least in size. The distribution of public employment varies substantially from nation to nation within the United Kingdom (see table 6.5). It is highest in Northern Ireland (40.5 percent of the labour force), one-quarter above the United Kingdom average; Wales (38.0 percent) is one-fifth above average, and Scotland (34.3 percent) a tenth above average. Public employment is below average in England.

Treating England as a single unit masks important regional variations within it, for the all-England figure is an average of figures for regions as dif-

TABLE 6.5. THE NATIONAL DISTRIBUTION OF PUBLIC EMPLOYMENT IN THE UNITED KINGDOM

	Public Employees (N)	Public Employees as % Nation's Labour Force	Index of Public Employment (UK = 100)
Northern Ireland	233,000	40.5	128
Wales	420,000	38.0	121
Scotland	765,000	34.3	109
England	6,294,000	30.0	97
UNITED KINGDOM	7,817,000a	31.4	100

SOURCE: Richard Parry, *The Territorial Dimension in United Kingdom Public Employment* (Glasgow: University of Strathclyde Studies in Public Policy No. 65, 1980), table 1, data for 1977. The labour force figures are for employed persons only.

a. Including 105,000 civil servants and members of the armed forces resident abroad and not attributed to any part of the United Kingdom.

ferent as the South East of England, with London its chief city, and the industrial North, bordering on Scotland and similar to Central Scotland in industrial structure. Subdividing public employment by region within England shows that differences in public employment among English regions are greater than differences between the four nations of the United Kingdom (see table 6.6). The difference in employment between England and Northern Ireland is 31 percent, but it is 41 percent between the North of England (122 percent of average) and the industrial West Midlands (81 percent of average). The extreme variations among regions reflect a variety of influences. Both the North of England and the West Midlands are industrial regions, but in the North of England a disproportionate number of industries are nationalized, whereas West Midlands engineering is primarily in the private sector. East Anglia ranks low because its labour force is disproportionately agricultural and few of its industries have been of the kinds subject to nationalization. Northern Ireland ranks high, even though it is disproportionately agricultural, because of the weakness of private sector employment. Notwithstanding the presence of the headquarters of nearly all major government agencies, the South East of England ranks eighth out of eleven areas in its share of public employment.

To explain the territorial distribution of public employment it is first necessary to account for the substantial proportion of public employees in each nation and region of the United Kingdom. We need to know why nearly one in four persons in the West Midlands and three in ten in England are in the public sector, as well as why two in five workers in Northern Ireland are publicly employed. Differences between nations and regions are differences of degree, not kind.

The most important single determinant of the number of public employees in a region is the population, because the programmes requiring the most

TABLE 6.6. THE REGIONAL DISTRIBUTION OF PUBLIC EMPLOYMENT IN THE UNITED KINGDOM

	Public Employees (000)	Public Employees as % Regional Labour Force	Index of Public Employment (UK = 100)
Northern Ireland	211	37.1	134
Wales	397	35.9	131
North of England	446	33.5	122
Scotland	664	29.8	108
Yorkshire and Humberside	617	28.9	105
South West	504	28.8	105
East Midlands	461	28.3	103
South East	2,095	26.3	96
North West	724	25.4	92
East Anglia	177	23.2	84
West Midlands	522	22.2	81
UNITED KINGDOM	6,818[a]	27.5[a]	100

SOURCE: Parry, *The Territorial Dimension,* table 3, data for 1976-78.

  a. There are slight discrepancies with United Kingdom totals given in table 6.5 because not all categories of public employment can readily be attributed to English regions and, for the sake of comparability, their counterparts were also removed from Scotland, Wales and Northern Ireland. The principal excluded categories are public transport and subsidiaries of the National Enterprise Board, exclusions constituting 13 percent of public employees.

workers tend to distribute their services according to population. This is true of the biggest employment category—local government—and specifically of education, the single biggest local government service. It is also true of the national health service. Local government and the health service together account for more than half of all public employment.

As long as Westminster lays down that education, health care, police and other local government services should be provided to all residents of the United Kingdom, then it follows that the numbers employed to provide the services should be roughly proportional to population demand. Of course, the proportions are not identical in every region. Education services vary according to regional characteristics; the South East of England is overprovided for by comparison with the United Kingdom average. There are also variations in health care, arising from very considerable regional differences existing prior to the creation of the national health service. But there remain variations around the theme of assured welfare and community services for all citizens in all parts of the United Kingdom. Coefficients of variation are low for the regional distribution of local government employment (0.08); for education (0.06) and for the health services (0.11).[29]

Nationalized industries tend to reinforce the distribution of public employment according to population, for three-fifths of such employment is in public utilities providing services to individuals and households, for example, electricity, the post office and the railways. The largest, the post office, accounts for more than one-quarter of nationalized industry employment attributable by region. In each of these public utilities, the bulk of the labour force must be close to the people who consume the services.

The importance in the United Kingdom of nationalized industries such as coal, steel, shipbuilding and aerospace is the major factor skewing the territorial distribution of public employment. Each of these particular nationalized industries is "lumpy," that is, production must be relatively concentrated. Geology dictates that miners can be employed only where there is coal in the ground, and geography dictates that ships be built on tidal water. The investment requirements of the steel and aerospace industries compel concentration of production in a limited number of very large factories, and access to raw materials and markets further differentiates regional locations. Labour governments have taken the lead in promoting nationalization and public assistance to industry, but Conservatives too have sustained loss-making nationalized industries. In the Labour Party, nationalization was initially seen as a means to modernization. Labour even called for the removal of inefficient factories, implying that jobs might be lost rather than created.[30] In the 1970s and '80s, nationalization can be undertaken for a different motive, as a means of maintaining employment and production in firms and industries that have become commercially unviable.

Among lumpy nationalized industries, the North of England has more than three times its proportionate United Kingdom share of employment, because it is a centre of coal mining, steel production and shipbuilding; it also lacks the private-sector engineering found in the West Midlands. Wales also has three times the United Kingdom average, because of the great concentration of steel mills and mining there; and the East Midlands and Yorkshire and Humberside have more than double the United Kingdom average of lumpy nationalized industries. At the other extreme, the South East of England has less than one-fifth of its proportionate share of these industries; and rural East Anglia, one-sixteenth. The coefficient of variation is thus extremely high, 0.84.[31]

The distinctive characteristics of lumpy nationalized industries account for a substantial portion of variation in public employment. If Wales had only the average share of employment in these industries, its total share of public employment would be 30.6 percent, slightly below the United Kingdom average. If the Northern region of England had an average share of lumpy industries, then 27.5 percent of its labour force would be in the public sector, the average for United Kingdom regions (cf. table 6.6). However, lumpy nationalized industries can only have major impact on regions with a relatively small proportion of the population, such as the North of England and Wales, for these industries account for only 9 percent of regionally attributable public employment.

Contrary to what might be expected, being the headquarters of government does not give the South East of England a great direct employment advantage. The civil service accounts for less than one-tenth of total public employment, and only 29 percent of these jobs (that is, 2.8 percent of total public employment) are of a headquarters type. Of headquarters jobs in the civil service, 101,000 are in the South East of England, but this is only 1.2 percent of the total labour force in the South East.[32] The great bulk (71 percent) of these "central" government jobs are United Kingdom-wide, that is, in every locality of any size. The distribution of civil service office staff around Great Britain shows a low coefficient of variation, 0.15, virtually the same as that for major welfare services.

Defence is the principal source of public employment concentrated in the South of England. Proximity to historic continental enemies caused a concentration of naval forces along the English Channel, and also RAF bases. The army requires rural areas for training bases, and the South of England, because of the absence of a concentration of urban, industrial areas, offers these. Excluding Northern Ireland, where special circumstances prevail, the two regions of Great Britain with above-average defence forces are the South West (index number 198) and East Anglia (146); whereas in the industrial North West and North, the armed forces are virtually absent (index number 5).[33] The interregional differences in the armed forces (0.82 coefficient of variation) are as great as in lumpy nationalized industries, but the numbers are today much smaller, 336,000 in the armed forces as against 633,000 in lumpy nationalized industries.

In the past three decades, there has almost certainly been a trend toward fewer differences in public employment between the parts of the United Kingdom. This is because the greatest growth in public employment has occurred (up 1,900,000) in those welfare state services such as health, education and social services in which public employment is most closely distributed in accordance with population. Employment has declined most in such territorially skewed fields as defence (down 624,000) and in lumpy production industries such as coal mining and steel (down 547,000).[34]

Public employment is not the only boost that government gives to regional employment. It also provides substantial sums for trade, industry, energy, employment, agriculture and fishing. Collectively, these policies account for about 6 percent of total public expenditure, but of this less than 1 percent is regional policy (e.g., development grants). The bulk of territorially identified government subsidy for economic activity goes to England — 64 percent of all subsidies for trade, industry, energy and employment, and 58 percent of all subsidies for agriculture, fisheries and forestry. But this also means that a disproportionate amount of spending goes to the other nations of the United Kingdom.[35] Most of this above-average economic assistance can be explained in functional terms. A disproportionate amount of agricultural and fisheries aid ought to go where agriculture and fishing is most important and of economic aid to areas of greatest need, in both cases the non-English nations of the United Kingdom.

The territorial dimension in public employment is limited, and a by-product of its primary purpose. The chief explanation for the pattern of public employment is functional: public officials are employed to provide services to individual families and communities. This is most obviously true of the local government and health services, but it is no less true of employees in public utilities. Two-thirds of central government civil servants must also provide services on a United Kingdom-wide basis. The exceptions to this — lumpy nationalized industries and defence forces — may also be explained in functional terms. Coal miners must dig coal where coal is to be found, and the defence forces must mass where attacks from the enemy are expected. The evidence clearly rejects the hypothesis that public-sector employment tends to reinforce centralization around London. It also rejects the hypothesis that public-sector employment tends to be associated with economic growth: it is below average in the most prosperous areas (cf. tables 6.2 and 6.6). In effect, public employment tends to compensate for lower levels of private-sector employment.

Overall, the distribution of resources by government throughout the United Kingdom is consistent with two principles. The first is the economic and social premise that the allocation of public policies should be in accord with functional imperatives. Since the great bulk of public money and employment is allocated to goods and services where demand tends to be determined by population, then the resources of public policy should be allocated in proportion to the distribution of population. Second, the political principle of territorial justice postulates that all persons within the United Kingdom, regardless of residence, should have the same chance of enjoying such benefits of public policy as education and health care. This principle sees the role of central government in compensating for the uneven distribution of some resources by countervailing policies. For example, the Rate Support Grant distributed to local authorities is intended to give an above-average grant to those local governments that have below-average rateable values. The distribution of funds for functional programmes in Scotland, Wales and Northern Ireland also

makes allowance for estimated higher levels of needs in major welfare programmes. Whereas the functional principle tends to reinforce existing differences between areas, the principle of territorial justice is redistributive, calling
for positive Whitehall action to equalize public policies in relation to population needs.

Both these principles depend upon the authority of the Mace. Functional
priorities recognize differences between policies, but not between territories
within the United Kingdom. All are expected to share in the consequences of
Acts of Parliament. Territorial justice is even more dependent upon the Mace
for the authority to redistribute resources. Standards of public policy for the
whole of the United Kingdom are set at Westminster, establishing what each
subject of the Crown can expect. An assessment of differential need is made
centrally, comparing different parts of the United Kingdom to each other, and
revenues collected from different parts of the United Kingdom according to
the ability to pay are then meant to be redistributed in accord with needs.

NOTES

1. Harold Lasswell, *Politics: Who Gets What, When, How* (New York:
   McGraw-Hill, 1936).
2. To analyse how these resources are then combined by government into
   programme outputs, which in turn can be evaluated for the benefits conferred upon recipients, is desirable—but the subject of another book. For
   a framework doing this, see Richard Rose, "What If Anything Is Wrong
   with Big Government?" *Journal of Public Policy* 1, no. 1 (1981): 7ff.
3. See Richard Rose, *Changes in Public Employment: A Multi-Dimensional
   Comparative Analysis* (Glasgow: University of Strathclyde Studies in
   Public Policy No. 61, 1980), table 6.
4. See *Economic Trends*, no. 327 (January 1981): 121.
5. See Richard Rose, *Do Parties Make a Difference?* (London and Chatham,
   N.J.: Macmillan and Chatham House, 1980).
6. Trinity College, Dublin, because copyright law dates from the pre-1921
   United Kingdom of Great Britain and Ireland.
7. See, e.g., James Buchanan, "Public Finance and Public Choice," *National
   Tax Journal* 28 (December 1975): 383-94; and "Taxation Is Fiscal Exchange," *Journal of Public Economics* 6 (July/August 1976): 17-29.
8. Cf. David Heald, *Financing Devolution within the United Kingdom* (Can-
   berra: Centre for Research on Federal Financial Relations, Research
   Monograph No. 32, 1980).
9. See Bleddyn Davies, *Social Needs and Resources in Local Services* (London: Michael Joseph, 1968).
10. See David Heald, *Territorial Equity and Public Finances: Concepts and
    Confusion* (Glasgow: University of Strathclyde Studies in Public Policy
    No. 75, 1980).

11. On laws as a resource of public policy, see Richard Rose, *Politics in England: An Interpretation for the 1980s* (3rd ed.; London: Faber & Faber, 1980), pp. 312ff.

12. Rose, *Do Parties Make a Difference?* p. 80.

13. If the 14 percent of England and Wales Acts, principally the concern of the Home Office and Department of Environment, are counted as functional bills, the total of legislation without any territorial dimension is 85 percent.

14. Royal Commission on the Constitution, *Minutes of Evidence* (1970), 3:176-85.

15. Cf. Richard Rose and Ian McAllister, *United Kingdom Facts* (London: Macmillan, 1982), pp. 64-65; and Derek Birrell and Alan Murie, *Policy and Government in Northern Ireland* (Dublin: Gill & Macmillan, 1980), pp. 280ff.

16. For English regional figures, see David N. King, *Financial and Economic Aspects of Regionalism and Separatism* (London: HMSO, Commission on the Constitution, Research Paper No. 10, 1973), p. 38. United Kingdom figures calculated from Heald, *Financing Devolution within the United Kingdom.*

17. John Short, in *English Regions,* ed. Brian Hogwood and M. Keating (London: Oxford University Press, 1982), tables 3 and 6. Short also found that this 1974-78 average figure showed a slight narrowing of the gap between English regions from the 1968-73 average, when it stood at 26 percent. For an important discussion of the problems of comparison of local government expenditure *within and between* nations, see Edward Page, *Comparing Local Expenditure: Lessons from a Multi-National State* (Glasgow: University of Strathclyde Studies in Public Policy, No. 60, 1980).

18. Calculated from *Regional Trends 1981,* table 15.10.

19. Treasury, *Needs Assessment Study—Report* (London: H.M. Treasury, 1979), p. 4.

20. George Younger, in House of Commons Committee on Scottish Affairs, Minutes of Evidence, *Scottish Aspects of the 1980-84 Public Expenditure White Paper* (London: HMSO, 1980), p. 56.

21. *Needs Assessment Study,* p. 1. For a critique, see David Heald, "Scotland's Public Expenditure 'Needs,'" in *The Scottish Government Yearbook 1981,* ed. H.M. and N.L. Drucker (Edinburgh: Paul Harris, 1980), pp. 60-84.

22. Treasury, *Needs Assessment Study,* p. 28.

23. Cmnd. 6348, p. 21. See also Younger, House of Commons Committee on Scottish Affairs, p. 60.

24. J.V. Simpson, "The Finances of the Public Sector in Northern Ireland, 1968-1978," *Journal of the Statistical and Social Enquiry Society of Ireland 1980-81* (forthcoming).

25. See Younger, House of Commons Committee on Scottish Affairs, pp. 54ff.

26. The semiofficial Northern Ireland Economic Council nonetheless argues that this extra expenditure is still "totally inadequate . . . to help over-

come our severe economic difficulties and allow the Province to catch up with social and economic conditions in Great Britain." See its *Public Expenditure Comparisons between Northern Ireland and Great Britain* (Belfast: Parliament Buildings, No. 18, 1981), pp. 15-16. Cf. Simpson, "The Finances of the Public Sector," which emphasizes the amount of "catching up" involved in the rapid rise of public spending in Northern Ireland in the 1970s.

27. Significantly, American studies, where political and territorial patronage might be expected to be higher than in the United Kingdom, have also found that functional criteria have dominated. See, e.g., Kenneth R. Mladenka, "The Urban Bureaucracy and the Chicago Political Machine," *American Political Science Review* 74, no. 4 (1980): 991-1006; and R. Douglas Arnold, *Congress and the Bureaucracy.* Cf. a tough-minded analysis of Ireland by Paul Sacks, *The Donegal Mafia* (New Haven: Yale University Press, 1976).

28. There is in fact a positive correlation of 0.74 between unemployment and public employment in United Kingdom regions; public employment is thus proportionately larger — and therefore disproportionately more important — where jobs are hardest to find.

29. See Richard Parry, *The Territorial Dimension in United Kingdom Public Employment* (Glasgow: University of Strathclyde Studies in Public Policy No. 65, 1980), tables 5, 6, and 8.

30. See F.W.S. Craig, *British General Election Manifestos, 1900-1974* (London: Macmillan, 1975), p. 127.

31. See Parry, *Territorial Dimension in United Kingdom Public Employment,* table 9.

32. Calculated from *Civil Service Statistics 1977,* table H.

33. Parry, *Territorial Dimension in United Kingdom Public Employment,* table 12.

34. See Rose, *Changes in Public Employment,* appendix table 2C.

35. Calculated from 1978-79 data reported in House of Commons, *Debates,* vol. 974, col. 517-20; *Written Answers* (26 November 1979).

7. The Mace and the Maze

Unity in theory is often complemented by diversity in practice. A politician expecting to wield the authority of the Mace to resolve a problem can be shocked to find the Mace less powerful than expected, as in many unsuccessful Treasury attempts to limit spending by non-Whitehall agencies. Alternatively, a politician who relies upon a maze of institutions to dilute the effect of a decision of the Crown in Parliament may feel the unqualified force of the Mace.

Constitutionally, the Mace symbolizes the unity of authority within the body politic. But it is such a high-order abstraction that it obscures the day-to-day workings of government in the United Kingdom.[1] The body politic is not a single body in which the head directs all other members of a mystical and singular body. The organizations of government are connected with one another, both constitutionally and operationally, but without a single head, as the metaphor implies. To observe government in action is to see a complex of organizations delivering a wide variety of public policies throughout the United Kingdom. When both territory and functions of government are combined, the absence of clear straight lines of responsibility resembles a maze, rather than the "straight line" hierarchical authority symbolized by the Mace.

The models of the Mace and the maze each start from the assumption that many organizations are involved in the provision of public policies. The differences between the two models can be made clear by considering the different answers that each implies to four basic questions about relationships between organizations.

1. *How many organizations does government consist of?* The Mace depicts government as a single authoritative structure; the unity of the Crown implies a single integrated set of institutions. By contrast, the maze assumes that the country has a plurality of governments; local government institutions are seen as *apart from* rather than a part of central government; so too are nationalized industries and other public corporations.

2. *What is the formal status of governmental organizations?* The Mace views particular institutions (e.g., local government or nationalized industries) as dependent agents of the Mace. When government is viewed as a maze,

each institution is considered autonomous with a will and freedom to act independent of nominally superior bodies.

3. *What is the relationship between organizations?* The Mace defines government in hierarchical terms. Given a hierarchy of authority, subordinate institutions are supervised and directed by superior institutions. By contrast, in a maze no institution can command all others; relations between organizations are resolved by political bargaining.

4. *How is power distributed?* The unity of authority under the Mace assumes an inequality of power; the custodians of the Mace have overriding authority. By contrast, the maze implies that power is fairly equally dispersed between organizations, inasmuch as cooperation of each is required by others, and each can use its specific resources when bargaining on its own behalf.

In the idealized world of pure central authority, rationally and perfectly administered, government by the Mace would involve a single integrated organization, with operating agencies subordinate agents of central authority. By contrast, government in the maze would involve a multiplicity of organizations, each with its own autonomy, making policies by bargaining among equals, as in the idealized world of the marketplace. In fact, no model of government exactly fits the imperfect world of politics. In criticism of the model of pure hierarchy, Hood describes government as "multi-organizational suboptimization."[2] Equally, government is not a free market of organizations. Even relatively democratic systems have inequalities between organizations, just as inequalities exist in real-world marketplaces. This is especially true in the United Kingdom, where constitutional rules emphasize the unique status of the Crown in Parliament.[3]

The pages that follow test the applicability to the United Kingdom of alternative models of government by the Mace and the maze. The first section examines the familiar proposition that the Crown in Parliament governs through a simple hierarchy of institutions. The second tests the less familiar but very English view that the Mace operates through a dual polity, segregating "high" from "low" concerns of public policy. Two models of governing by the maze are derived from experience in other countries: government as a complex of interorganizational relationships, or as a system of intergovernmental relations. The concluding section proposes a model of government by oligopoly; this integrates elements of both the Mace and the maze to represent the dispersed inequalities found in the territorial and functional government of the United Kingdom today.

Government as Simple Hierarchy

A simple hierarchy is the extreme representation of the concentration of power by the Mace. A government by hierarchy not only implies a chain of command *within* each government organization but also a chain of command *between* different organizations of government. Inequalities of power are clearly defined in a more or less pyramidal hierarchy, converging upon a single point at the top. Each organization of government is assumed to be an agent of the unitary authority at the top. In a hierarchy the relationships are primarily administrative. The task of governing is to identify the appropriate organizational unit that can most efficiently deliver a particular public policy; the identification of the directing institution is never in doubt.

Even a simple hierarchical government requires both differentiation and decentralization. Differentiation is necessary at the centre of government: A uniform and unitary government must still be divided into a number of functional ministries concerned with the economy, defence, welfare and so forth. In other words, the hierarchical pyramid has a number of sides. Decentralization is necessary for a government to deliver goods and services to subjects throughout its territory. The base of the pyramid, like the territory of a modern state, covers a very wide area; the peak is still a single point. In a simple hierarchy, decentralization proceeds by "pluralization"; more or less identical schools, hospitals, public utilities and the like are created, that are operating according to clearly specified central standards, and reporting directly to their appropriate hierarchical superior "up the line."[4] The centre thus avoids the details of administration, and its superior authority is maintained unchallenged.

At first glance the government of the United Kingdom appears to conform to the model of government as a single hierarchy. The doctrine of the Mace stipulates that there should be a "top" to government. The Cabinet is the custodian of the Mace. Individual ministers have differentiated functional responsibilities, but each holds office as a member of a collective Cabinet. The unique position of Parliament as the sole legislative authority in the United Kingdom gives the Cabinet the power to lay down a statutory framework within which all government organizations act. The centralized revenue raising and allocation responsibilities of the Treasury allow the Cabinet to scrutinize the actions it finances. Government in the United Kingdom ranks high on four of five major criteria of centralized authority: the frequent issuance of directives from the top; central finance; monitoring of and reporting by subordinate organizations, and reference upwards or "calling in" decisions about major issues.[5] It lacks only a unitary personnel system for central government, local government and nationalized industries.

But centralization in form does not necessarily achieve centralization in practice. Any hierarchy of authority will have major difficulties in exercising its *de jure* claims *de facto;* this is particularly true of an organization the size of government in the United Kingdom. Laws and regulations can never be sufficiently specific to cover every contingency faced by individuals delivering public policies. Uncertainties and gaps in legislation are not specially caused by the practice of legislating differently for different territorial parts of the United Kingdom. The problem is intrinsic in the nature of legislation. As Aristotle noted, "Enactments are universal, but actions are concerned with particulars."[6] Laws empower officials to do certain things in certain ways, or prohibit certain actions or procedures. The breadth or narrowness of direction varies from policy area to policy area. It is, for example, easier to control the grant of pensions, because they are determined by readily verified age, than to control the grant of supplementary benefit payments, which are determined by notoriously hard to define individual "needs." Actions taken under the authority of Acts of Parliament by officials at the bottom of an administrative hierarchy need not be illegal to depart from the intent of Parliament, and conformity to legal procedures may at times even lead officials to act contrary to the substantive intent of a policy.

The growing differentiation of government activities reduces the degree of simplicity attainable at the top of an administrative hierarchy. The peak of the pyramid is not a small group of senior ministers concerned with a limited number of problems such as defence and finance. The peak is now a large cluster of fifteen to twenty ministries, each concerned with a major functional set of programmes.[7] Because the peak can handle only a limited number of concerns, more and more responsibilities for decisions are being pushed down the hierarchy, where the pyramid's base is broader and coordination far more difficult. When departments are internally differentiated in terms of their functional responsibilities (cf. table 5.2), as in the United Kingdom, complexity is disproportionately increased. The result can be, according to the Central Policy Review Staff, that "central government departments, in making and implementing policies, still act for most purposes in isolation from each other."[8]

While lines of authority may be hierarchical constitutionally, in no sense is government a single integrated institution. In a simple hierarchy, the organization responsible for delivering a particular public policy would be a subordinate part of a major government department. For example, in education, schools would be provided nationwide, with teachers the employees of the Ministry of Education. Education policies could be laid down at the top of the hierarchy and delivered in every locality. This is done in France. In the United Kingdom, however, it is not the practice for a Whitehall ministry to deliver most major policies for which a minister is ultimately answerable to Parliament.

In the United Kingdom today, the norm is to *distance* the organization delivering a policy from the ministry formally responsible for it to Parliament. Responsibility for delivering public policies is placed in the hands of local government, nationalized industries or other public corporations and the National Health Service. It is very unlikely to be placed in the hands of civil servants working for a Whitehall department; only one-eighth of public employees in the United Kingdom work for Whitehall. The one major welfare state programme that a Whitehall department directly administers is the payment of social security benefits. Ironically, it can do this only because most pension claims are so highly routinized that the principal Whitehall *(sic)* office for social security can be nearly three hundred miles away in Newcastle upon Tyne.

The great bulk of public policies are delivered at a distance from Westminster, and the organizations delivering them are separate from Whitehall departments. Local government, nationalized industries and the health service are subject to oversight by ministers in Whitehall. But immediately each organization has executive power in its own hands and does not have to take orders from Whitehall, except in unusual instances when the force of law is invoked. Moreover, the extent of distancing has been increasing since the 1960s, with the spread of the doctrine of "hiving off," i.e., removing executive tasks such as the post office and employment services from the hands of a ministry.

Where a minister is organizationally distant from the delivery of a service, there is a dual responsibility. The organization delivering the service, typically a local authority or a nationalized industry, is immediately responsible for what is done. These organizations have separate identities and staffs, recruited independently of the civil service. They also have competing claims for accountability. A nationalized industry is immediately accountable to customers for the services it provides, and to the marketplace, which judges value in terms of profit or loss. Local authorities are responsible to their local electorate in the first instance, as well as subject to Parliament for the statutory powers (and much of the money) they receive. The health services are accountable to the needs of their patients for care, and to the professional standards of a medical profession that defines what that care should be.

Whitehall departments are normally supervisory institutions; they are not executive agencies with their hands on the delivery of public policies. This creates the potential for conflict because of partisan or functional differences. This is most obviously the case in the Department of the Environment, which is concerned with major programmes of local government. It is even more the case in the Scottish and Welsh Offices, which are nominally responsible for an even wider range of programmes, yet pass on responsibility for executing policies to distant local authorities and health agencies. It is also true of ministries with important economic responsibilities, such as Industry, Energy, Trade and Transport, which leave the execution of policies in the hands of nationalized industries, other public and even private corporations.

The main types of executive organizations outside the Whitehall hierarchy are these:

1. *Local government.* While local government institutions cover the whole territory of the United Kingdom, in no sense are the 548 different local authorities part of a hierarchy under four different Whitehall ministers. In fact, local government is itself subdivided into two tiers—districts and counties or regions—and their organizational forms differ *within* as well as between nations of the United Kingdom.[9] Local authorities deliver major services of the welfare state—education, housing, personal social services, environmental services and fire and police. Local authorities act under powers conferred by Act of Parliament, and the bulk of their money comes from Treasury grants, but they remain independent organizations, with their hands directly on the delivery of major public services. For example, whereas Whitehall can stipulate conditions for qualifying for housing grants, local authorities design, build and let the houses thus provided for. To argue whether Whitehall departments or local authorities are more important is to misconstrue the important point here: Each is separately important.

Local governments spend more than one-quarter of total public expenditure (27 percent in 1980),[10] and raise nearly half this money by levying local rates, and charges for council housing, bus services and other municipal facilities. With 3 million employees, local government collectively has more than four times the staff of the Whitehall civil service. Local government staff are recruited separately from Whitehall civil servants; and their background, qualifications and career opportunities differ from higher civil servants in Whitehall. Loyalty to local government, not to Whitehall, is their norm. Moreover, wages are determined by local government unions bargaining with associations of local government employers. Last and not least, the authority to direct local government is placed in the hands of locally elected councillors, not Parliament. Even when councillors and ministers belong to the same party, there is no mutuality of interest, for each is accountable to a different electorate. The tendency of Labour to do well in urban areas and Conservatives in the counties ensures that the government of the day, whatever its colour, will face many councils controlled by partisan opponents. The 1980 legislation of the Thatcher government aimed at containing local government expenditure, such as the Local Government, Planning and Land (No. 2) Act and the Scottish Local Government (Miscellaneous Provisions) Act, emphasized the ulti-mate authority of Westminster. But the scope for local authorities to resist central government direction makes this formal superiority much harder to exercise in fact than a simple statement of the law would imply. For example, a previous Conservative government had to resort to extreme legal means to coerce a small Labour-controlled local authority at Clay Cross, which defied that government's 1972 Housing Finance Act.

2. *Nationalized industries and other public corporations.* When Acts of Parliament took major industries into public ownership, the government of the day very carefully distanced from Whitehall the industries thus national-ized. Whitehall departments did *not* wish the executive responsibility of pro-viding energy, transport or other major economic services. Every nationalized industry is in the hands of a public corporation separate from Whitehall. For example, the Department of Energy has oversight responsibility for the Na-tional Coal Board, the Gas Board, and the Central Electricity Generating Board, but it does not produce or sell coal, gas or electricity. Each public cor-poration is directed by a board which is appointed by the minister, but the task of producing its goods and services is not in the hands of a Whitehall ministry but in the hands of employees of the public corporation.

Nationalized industries are owned by the Crown, but most of their reve-nue comes from the marketplace. The rationale of nationalization stipulates that nationalized industries should pursue goals additional to profit, but every nationalized industry, whether making or losing money, derives the bulk of its revenue from selling its products and not from the Treasury. Moreover, some nationalized industries must compete internationally (e.g., British Steel Cor-poration); most are affected by international market forces (e.g., energy prices); and some compete with private institutions (e.g., British Rail with pri-vate motoring) or with each other (e.g., the Coal, Gas and Electricity Boards). Each nationalized industry also recruits, trains and promotes its own employ-ees and conducts its own wage negotiations with unions that are often specific to their industry. With more than 2 million workers dispersed among more than a dozen public corporations, nationalized industries employ almost three times as many people as the home civil service. When an industry loses money or wishes to invest more money, it must turn to the Treasury. The Treasury can influence investment and pricing policy, but it is equally the case that losses give public corporations a *prima facie* claim upon Treasury funds.

3. *The National Health Service.* The National Health Service is a concur-rent set of institutions with separate organizations and accounts for England, Scotland, Wales and Northern Ireland, and separate Scottish and Northern

Ireland legislation. It is subject to oversight by four different Whitehall ministries. Within each nation, hospital services tend to be much more subject to organized direction than do medical services. The scale and nature of hospital services require large-scale capital expenditure authorized from the top, and many organizational procedures of hospitals are amenable to routine monitoring. By contrast, medical services are provided by self-employed professionally qualified doctors. An area health board or ministry is distant from a doctor's consulting room. Professional medical standards and judgments, rather than statutes and bureaucratic rules, are of first importance where doctor meets patient.

Instead of health being provided by an organization, it is better to think of health as the output of a variety of marketplace transactions in which nearly all the bills (amounting to £9.5 billion in 1980, or 12.3 percent of total public expenditure) are paid by the Treasury.[11] The 1.2 million people employed in the health service range from career health service administrators outside the civil service through menial service employees of hospitals to self-employed doctors and dentists practising what in German is described as a "free" (i.e., extraorganizational) profession.

If government in the United Kingdom were a simple hierarchy, then the great bulk of public policies would be provided by Whitehall ministries. In fact, the great bulk of government organizations in the United Kingdom are neither uniform nor are they Whitehall-based. Only one-eighth of nearly 8 million public employees work in Whitehall ministries delivering uniform policies throughout the United Kingdom, providing such collective goods as military defence or collecting taxes. The overwhelming majority of public employees work in organizations distanced from Whitehall territorially (e.g., local government) or functionally (e.g., nationalized industries).

The result of distancing is to create *two* hierarchies of government institutions, a hierarchy between organizations as well as a hierarchy within organizations. Within an organization, lines of authority can run down hierarchically. But between organizations, this is not the case; horizontal distance can be greater than vertical superiority. In a legalistic sense, all organizations directly or indirectly depend upon the Crown in Parliament. But in practice, hands-on responsibility for delivering public policies is vested in organizations outside the Whitehall hierarchy. If the Cabinet wishes to exert its formal power as custodian of the Mace, it must do so by means more complex, subtle and indirect than issuing binding directives to its own officials. Exerting influence between organizations is not as easy as exerting influence within an organization. At the end of a lengthy process, a minister's wish may be followed, but in no sense can the process be described as a chain of command in a simple hierarchy.

The Dual Polity

Dividing the functions of government into categories of "high" and "low" politics results in a very different view of government in the United Kingdom. Jim Bulpitt's model of the dual polity does just this. High and low politics are thus distinguished: "The former were regarded as essentially matters for the executive, and were to be settled, as far as possible, independent of outside, particularly territorial pressures. The latter were seen as part of the wide game of political activity, and could be settled by bargaining between the executive and interests involved."[12] Two types of politics implies two levels of government: the Imperial authority at Westminster and lowly local government.

As in a simple hierarchy, the two levels of the dual polity are unequal. The institutions concerned with high politics are superior, but choose not to interfere in affairs that are deemed beneath them. But the relationship differs from a simple hierarchy, in that both sets of organizations enjoy autonomy. When Stormont governed Northern Ireland quietly, the reciprocal autonomy of Westminster and Stormont exemplified the division of functional responsibilities in a dual polity. In a dual polity, the holders of the Mace do not need to administer what goes on beneath them; within their areas of concern, those involved in lowly affairs also enjoy autonomy.

The dual polity model reached its fullest expression in the exercise of Imperial authority. Imperial colonies were unrepresented at Westminster. Equally, Westminster had very few representatives on the ground in the colonies, nor did communications technology make it easy to issue directives from afar. In any event, Westminster did not wish to become involved in details of governing colonies. Day-to-day affairs of the colonies were matters of low politics, which could be left in the hands of colonial legislatures, district commissioners or political residents. Westminster preferred systems of indirect rule involving collaboration and cooption of indigenous chieftains, maharajahs and other local leaders. In Edmund Burke's words, Westminster could then retain its "imperial character, in which, as from the throne of heaven, she superintends all the several legislatures, and guides and controls them all, without annihilating any."[13] Until electoral reform made Irish and Scottish MPs representative of their populations in the late nineteenth century, Westminster could try to "manage" business in these nations by indirect rule through interlocutors, such as the Scottish Lord Advocate or a Viceroy in Ireland.

The dual polity model catches the class distinctions of British government. It is a sociological rather than constitutional explanation for the territorial and functional division of responsibilities of the Mace. Matters of "high" politics — foreign affairs, defence, the Bank of England, the law, the monarchy and the Church — are meant to be determined by small but not necessarily like-minded collections of "top" people clustered around the sites of the ancient palaces in Westminster and Whitehall.[14] In addition to Cabinet ministers and higher civil servants, the world of high politics includes trusted and knowledgeable experts, with trust as important as knowledge. Issues such as the application for Britain's entry to the European Community, major decisions about defence strategy or the "mysteries" of the international monetary system re meant to be discussed only in the world of "high" politics. Just as Bagehot once said that he would no sooner consult the *demos* than go into the kitchen to reason with his cook, so his latter-day equivalent would no sooner listen to an official of the National Coal Board or a councillor from Clapham than attempt to reason with a dish-washing machine.

Low politics concerns matters that are necessary because they concern everyday affairs: rubbish collection, sewage, bus transportation, planning permissions and all the many services delivered by non-Whitehall agencies of government. In the world of low politics, people become councillors or take a job in local government because they expect to deal with the problems of the community immediately around them. They are and want to be concerned with matters that affect their own area.

As long as politicians in the worlds of high and low politics have few dealings with each other, then the two can coexist as a stratarchy, that is, a political system in which each stratum exercises more or less autonomous powers.[15] The model also has similarities with the continental Catholic doctrine of *subsidiaritaet,* which similarly emphasized the importance of *not* burdening peak institutions with any governmental functions that can be performed at a lower level. The *subsidiaritaet* principle does try to limit claims for action by top politicians, but is vague about which functions should be the responsibility of a given level.[16]

High politics is not determined by the scale of an issue but by traditional status, reflecting origins in government by aristocrats. For example, traditional concerns of government (e.g., the appointment of Anglican bishops) are matters of high politics. Generally, high politics concern all those policies that are by definition responsibilities of a state or a Crown (e.g., the law, defence, money supply). Anything to do with industrialization or the contemporary welfare state is low status.

A half-century ago the Cabinet was still principally concerned with high politics. The Cabinet formed by Stanley Baldwin in 1935 had fourteen ministers in offices of high politics: the Prime Minister, the Lord Chancellor, the Chancellor of the Exchequer, the Home Secretary, the Lord President of the Council, the Lord Privy Seal, the Foreign Secretary, the Indian Secretary, the Colonial Secretary, the Dominions Secretary, a League of Nations minister and ministers for War, the Admiralty and Air. By comparison, only seven members of Baldwin's 1935 Cabinet were concerned with low politics: Agriculture, Education, Health, Labour, the Board of Trade, Scotland and the Ministry of Works.[17]

But the dual polity has not proven durable.[18] The economic weakness of a no longer Imperial United Kingdom has turned the attention of politicians from high affairs to down-to-earth economic issues. Politicians in the Wilson-Heath era felt impelled to intervene increasingly in what they previously had regarded as matters remote from their principal duties. Equally, Mrs. Thatcher's subsequent Conservative government has had to intervene in local government and in industrial problems as part of its long-term ambition of removing government from these mundane concerns. Concern with traditional "high" affairs of state has been eclipsed by concerns with "big" problems measured in money terms.

The balance of the Cabinet is very different today from a half century ago. The Prime Minister remains primarily concerned with high politics; one of the six Downing Street civil service advisers is concerned with the distribution of honours and bishoprics and Regius professorships, another with foreign affairs and a third with the Treasury. Managing traditional concerns of state — foreign affairs, the national economy and Parliament — are the primary concerns of a Prime Minister.[19] But most Cabinet ministers do not have these responsibilities. Of 22 Cabinet ministers appointed to the 1979 Conservative government, 11 were concerned with low politics (Industry, Employment, Agriculture, Environment, Scotland, Wales, Northern Ireland, Social Services, Trade, Energy, Education) and 11 with high politics (the Prime Minister, the Home Secretary, the Lord Chancellor, Foreign Secretary, the Chancellor of the Exchequer, the Chief Secretary of the Treasury, the Minister of Defence, the Leader of the House of Lords, the Leader of the House of Commons, the Lord Privy Seal and the Paymaster General). To some extent, the balance reflects party predispositions: In the 1974 Labour Cabinet, 12 ministers were primarily concerned with low politics and 9 with high politics.

But many ministers in high politics today have little or no involvement in what government does; five are nondepartmental, managing the business of government: the Prime Minister, the Leaders of the Commons and of the Lords, and the Lord Privy Seal and the Paymaster General. Of the eleven ministers involved in low politics, all are concerned with policies that make major claims upon society's resources, and are meant to have a major impact on society. If public expenditure is the criterion for assessing importance, low politics is four times more important than high politics. In 1980, 81 percent of total public expenditure was the responsibility of low-status ministries such as

Health and Social Security, Education and Science, and Environment, as against 19 percent being the responsibility of "high" ministries, principally defence.[20] The bulk of public expenditure is devoted to providing goods, services and cash benefits for ordinary citizens at a very great remove from the traditional concerns of high politics.

If public employment is the criterion for assessing the relative importance of low and high politics, then 90 percent are involved in low politics.[21] The great bulk of public employment—all of local government, nationalized industries and public corporations, and nearly half of the home civil service—is concerned with low politics. The shift has been steady through the generations. In 1851, more than three-quarters of public employees were concerned with high politics because the armed forces were the principal source of public employment. Half of public employees were in high politics as late as 1901.[22] The "armies" of public employees today have a very different status from traditional aristocratic servitors of the Crown. Today the typical public employee is a teacher, hospital orderly or a lorry driver for a nationalized industry, rather than a soldier, a Treasury administrator or a diplomat.

Ironically high politics now has little to do with the activities of government. An Act of Parliament of particular concern in high politics, for example, the Sri Lanka Republic Act of 1972, has far less impact than a measure of low politics, such as the Housing Finance Act of 1972. Nor do MPs, Cabinet ministers or Prime Ministers today have the aristocratic background traditionally deemed appropriate for matters of high politics.

To argue that British politicians should only be concerned with high politics is to imply that they have no interest in the great bulk of the activities of British government. This is not the case. A seemingly simple and lowly matter, like the wage rate of public-sector workers, can have major implications for the Chancellor and the Cabinet. Every time £5 is added to the weekly wages of public employees, an extra £2 billion is added to annual public expenditure. Nor can politicians ignore lowly concerns of voters when the issues decisive at an election are such mundane domestic matters as the cost of living, rather than international diplomacy. Nor is the United Kingdom unique in its contemporary political priorities; these are common to most mixed-economy welfare states. Moreover, the increasing interdependence of economic and international diplomatic issues tends to force low politics into the arena of high politics. This is particularly true in the European Community, where international negotiations may turn out to be about herring fishing rather than *la haute politique.*

The dual polity model, whatever its historical value in accounting for the evolution of the governance of a Crown of indefinite domain, does not describe how the Crown in Parliament governs its domain today. A better description is provided in Weber's words: *"Herrschaft ist im Alltag primaer; Verwaltung"* ("Everyday rule is primarily administration").[23] Low-status departments and officials deliver most of the benefits of public policy and consume most of public expenditure, and low-status policies give most citizens their primary and continuing contact with government. For every time a person may see a member of the Royal Family or a high-status politician, the ordinary citizen will see dozens of postmen, teachers, nurses or other public employees as friends, neighbours or family members, as well as in their normal work.

Interorganizational and Intergovernmental Relations

In the interorganizational model of government, the organization is the central concept. It can be, in Rupert Emerson's sense, the nation, "the largest community which, when the chips are down, effectively commands men's loyalty."[24] Each organization has its own employees and clients sharing a number of more or less common goals and priorities. An organization is both an object of loyalty and a source of political interests. In a complex political system, where organizations are many, an organization can be a terminal community to which people attach themselves, and in whose name they fight battles. Policies can be the outcome—or the by-product—of conflicts between organizations, not the choice of a central authority. As Kenneth Hanf notes,

> Territorial and functional differentiation has produced decision systems in which the problem-solving capacity of governments is disaggregated into a collection of sub-systems with limited tasks, competences and resources, where the relatively independent participants possess different bits of information, represent different interests and pursue separate potentially conflicting courses of action.[25]

The interorganizational model provides an aerial photograph of the maze of territorial and functional institutions that act on behalf of the Crown, concentrating on the relationships between them. The choice of the unit analytically considered as an organization depends upon the problem at hand. The Crown can be disaggregated into Whitehall ministries, local authorities and a host of public corporations and nationalized industries. But each Whitehall ministry can itself be disaggregated into a number of different divisions, the bureaus of bureaucracy. Local authorities can similarly be divided into separate departments, each with its distinctive functions, statutory authority and oversight ministry (e.g., education, housing or social services). A nationalized industry like the British Steel Corporation can be subdivided into factories on different sites and divisions making different types of steel.

The interorganizational model of government is more concerned with the relations between different organizations than with relationships within a single organization; individual organizations are seen as not politically self-sufficient.

The ability of individual decision units to achieve their own objectives will depend not only on their own choices and actions but also on those of others. Actions at any one level of decision-making will be influenced by the relationships that exist between levels as well as across functional boundaries.[26]

The maze of interorganizational relations differs fundamentally from the Mace of government. First, the interorganizational approach sees government as a vast quantity of organizations rather than as a single integrated hierarchy or a complementary dual polity. Second, it emphasizes that each organization has resources guaranteeing it a measure of political autonomy. The emphasis is upon equality between organizations (i.e., each has something that others want) rather than upon inequalities (i.e., some have much more of what is wanted than others). Third, political bargaining rather than hierarchical command is assumed to be the normal method of resolving political differences.

To reduce all interorganizational relations to the level of bargaining between autonomous actors, as in Lindblom's theory of partisan mutual adjustment, is to ignore "the troublesome question of sovereignty."[27] One difficulty with the interorganizational model of government is that it tends to blur or ignore the boundaries between governmental and nongovernmental organizations. From the perspective of a sociologist of organizations, there is no necessary difference between the Department of Industry in Whitehall and a privately owned company. A central government department and a local authority appear as two organizations, just as the Department of Employment and the Trades Union Congress are two organizations. But to ignore differences between public- and private-sector organizations is to ignore the authority of the Crown in Parliament. The distinction is particularly important when nongovernmental organizations challenge the authority of the Crown itself (e.g., Cymdeithas yr Iaith Gymraeg [the Welsh Language Society], the Scottish National Party or the Irish Republican Army).

Interorganizational analysis also blurs institutional differences between different systems of government. Writers describing patterns of interorganizational relations can reduce countries as different in their governments as Germany, France and the United Kingdom to their lowest common denominator, an interorganizational maze. It is also possible to view the Soviet Union in terms of interorganizational conflicts.[28] But even if similarities can be adduced in organizational forms, this is not proof that they are more important than differences in political values and processes.

In international relations there are major differences between governments and nongovernmental organizations. Interorganizational relations between Whitehall and Washington, or a Whitehall department and its functional opposite number in other member countries of the European Community, are not the same as relations within Whitehall. There is a common loyalty between Crown organizations, a loyalty activated in international relations. The dealings of a Whitehall department with a foreign government are not the same as relations between Whitehall departments; and dealings across national and public/private sector boundaries differ yet again, for example, between the Department of Industry and the Ford Motor Company.

An American alternative to interorganizational analysis is to speak of intergovernmental relations. The United States Bureau of the Census defines a governmental unit as "an organized entity which, in addition to having governmental (public) character, has sufficient discretion in the management of its own affairs to distinguish it as separate from the administrative structure of any other governmental unit." The Census then proceeds to enumerate 38,602 general-purpose local, state and federal units of government and 39,666 special-purpose districts for schools, sewers, transportation and other activities.[29]

In America, the intergovernmental relations approach starts from the irreducible minimum of 51 governments, that is, the 50 states that are constituent units within the federal system plus the federal government itself. The existence of tens of thousands of additional units, deriving their status from 50 different state constitutions, further entrenches the autonomous status of governmental organizations, for the federal government cannot abolish or alter the powers of a local authority. The intergovernmental relations model thus starts from a recognition of the importance of organizational autonomy based upon constitutional laws. The multiplicity of governments in America are juridical equals, even if unequal in resources.

The American intergovernmental relations approach includes, as equally relevant for analysis, special-purpose functional units of government such as boards of education, sewer districts and port authorities, as well as general-purpose state and local authorities. The intergovernmental relations approach, however, suffers from its thoroughness, for it counts as equal units with unequal resources. The federal government is counted as only one among the 78,266 "governments" enumerated. Yet this too has meaning, for the picture of government, as seen from the White House, *is* a picture of fragmented institutions.[30]

The fundamental weakness of the intergovernmental and interorganizational models is that they deny that government exists, that is, that there is any organization that can resolve differences between organizations through the exercise of collective authority. Fritz Scharpf argues:

> It is unlikely, if not impossible, that public policy of any significance could result from the choice process of any single unified actor. Policy formation and policy implementation are inevitably the result of interactions among a plurality of separate actors with separate interests, goals and strategies.[31]

Generalizing from research in France, where centralization of authority has tended to be greater than the United Kingdom, Crozier and Thoenig argue that there is no central directing agency in government. They assert that organizations engage in "cross-regulation," that is, a kind of organizational checks and balances, or, to use their mazelike metaphor, a "honeycomb."[32] Such statements are both profound and platitudinous. They are profound in emphasizing the importance of the plurality of organizations within government, as against the philosophical ideal of an undivided national will, a state or, in the British case, a sovereign Crown. Yet the approach is platitudinous insofar as it only asserts that significant actions of the Crown involve a multiplicity of organizations.

In the United Kingdom, the Cabinet is *not* an organization just like any other. The Cabinet is the practical custodian of the powers of the Mace. It is the point at which differences can be resolved between organizations, reflecting conflicting interests within the political system. In the United Kingdom, by contrast with the United States, there is a government as well as a maze of interorganizational subgovernments.[33] The British Cabinet does not meet daily, nor does it need to, because its function is not to deliver the goods and services of government. The Cabinet can act like a high court sitting in judgment of disputes between organizations responsible for specific public policies. It has the power to arbitrate differences between Whitehall organizations and to make decisions binding on them and on the network of subgovernment organizations (and extragovernmental pressure groups) that each represents. The Cabinet is the umpire in the game of interorganizational politics. It has the power to decide which organization has won and which has lost, and what each has won or lost.

The authority of Cabinet, like that of any high court, is more important when it is implicit. The very existence of a Cabinet to resolve conflicts influences interorganizational relations without Cabinet meeting. A Cabinet decision is potentially reversible — but it cannot be treated like a mere bargaining counter between independent organizations. Moreover, a Cabinet decision is a collective decision; the organizations that play in this game cannot avoid being identified as winners or losers.

The American intergovernmental relations approach is a useful foil for understanding the United Kingdom because it highlights differences between a unitary and federal system. In the United States, it is meaningful to talk of a multiplicity of governments. But the United Kingdom is profoundly monotheistic: Thou shalt have no other government but the Crown in Parliament. Her Majesty's Government is *the* government, not *a* government like Strathclyde Region or Kirklees District Council. The Mace is the symbol of this unitary authority, and the Cabinet gives it formal and practical expression.

In a federal system, it is meaningful to talk about the policy process as both interorganizational and intergovernmental. When organizations deal with each other, they must recognize and accept the autonomy of each contractual partner in a federal covenant. The supreme authority is a court; it can resolve disputes when the authority of government is splintered into a multiplicity of juridically equal authorities, as in the American federal system.

By contrast, the United Kingdom is interorganizational but *intra*-governmental. There is only one government holding the authority of the Mace. The government has a multiplicity of organizational instruments that make for intragovernmental divisions, both territorial and functional. Different organizations come into conflict with one another. But there is a unitary authority, typically along functional lines, that charters all these organizations and can (and has) abolished or suspended organizations that prove troublesome, or otherwise appear in need of change. In its collective form, the Cabinet, acting as the agent for the high court of Parliament, can determine the outcome of disputes between organizations.

Oligopolistic Policy Making

To conceive of policy making by oligopoly is to accommodate some of the diversity of the maze within the authority of the Mace. The concept of oligopoly is borrowed from economics, which uses it to describe a market in which the number of organizations selling a given product are relatively few, interdependent and unequal in influence. In place of commercial vendors, we can think of government organizations, for just as the number of firms producing automobiles is relatively few, so too the number of organizations providing education or motorways is relatively few. Like all analogies, economic analogies are imperfect. But oligopoly better describes relations between the organizations that collectively constitute government in the United Kingdom than does the monopoly of power implied by a simple hierarchy or perfect competition in a "free market" of interorganizational or intergovernmental policy making.[34]

The basic idea of oligopoly is indicated by its root term *oligo,* "a few." Like the Mace, this concept emphasizes the relative unity of organizations in government. But the concept differs from oligarchy (rule by the few) because it does not assume domination by a few people; instead, the emphasis is upon a few organizations providing a given policy. In the United Kingdom, there is no free entry to the ranks of government organizations; organizations can be created only under the authority of the Mace. Although in population it is one-quarter the size of the United States, it has something like one-hundredth the number of government organizations. By comparison with continental countries with similar populations, the United Kingdom has about one-sixth the number of government organizations of Italy, one-twentieth the number of Germany and about one-thirty-fifth the number of France.[35]

When attention is concentrated upon organizations specifically relevant to a given policy, the complexity of the maze is reduced to manageable proportions. This is most evident in uniform policies, for the Crown then speaks with one voice. For example, the Foreign Office is not the only ministry concerned with foreign issues; the Ministry of Defence and the Treasury are also internationally oriented. But the number of organizations involved with any one international issue will normally be few enough to be represented in a Cabinet committee. Furthermore, the United Kingdom's membership in the European Community has institutionalized mechanisms for producing a single voice from several different organizations concerned with a given policy. Within the United Kingdom, a concurrent policy by definition involves more than one organization. But in the United Kingdom, the maximum number is 4, compared to 11 German *Länder,* 30 Italian regions or 50 American states. Relations between Whitehall and nationalized industries may involve more than one ministry and more than one nationalized industry; for example, the National Coal Board selling coal delivered by British Rail to the Central Electricity Generating Board to provide electricity to the British Steel Corporation. Yet all the parties can literally be represented around a single table. When policies are delivered by local government, a lecture hall would be required to hold all the organizations involved. For that reason, local authorities are organized into a number of pressure groups representing their distinctive interests, and Whitehall ministries discuss particular issues round a table with representatives from local government pressure groups.

The fact that few government organizations are concerned with a given policy is particularly apparent to an individual citizen. Within a local government area, the local authority has a virtual monopoly of providing many services, such as council housing; this can be challenged, but only by appeal to one place, Westminster. There is little opportunity to play off different levels of government, as in a federal system, or to play off different government agencies with overlapping and competing jurisdictions, as in the American system. While nationalized industries may compete with each other, say, in energy supply or tranportation, there is only one National Coal Board and one body supplying electricity or gas to a given area. Oligopoly is apt to describe this "almost" monopoly of the supply of particular public policies.

The few organizations concerned with a given policy issue are invariably *unequal*. Government appears like a maze if one catalogues the numbers of organizations. But the authority of the Mace keeps government in the United Kingdom from becoming lost in a maze. Decisions usually involve a small number of organizations, or one organization with preponderant influence. Influence differs from situation to situation: Disputes about foreign affairs tend to involve a few Whitehall ministries, each significant in its own right, whereas issues about local government delivery of policies laid down in Whitehall involve large Whitehall ministries and many relatively small local governments.

In oligopolistic policy making, measures are not laid down by command, as in the case of the simple hierarchy, nor can high officials ignore lowly activities, as in the dual polity. Nor are policies bargained between *de facto* or *de jure* autonomous and equal organizations, as in interorganizational and intergovernmental models of policy making. A distinctive feature of oligopolistic policy making is the role of a *lead* organization, the equivalent of a price leader in an oligopolistic market. Within Cabinet, functional ministers are likely to take the lead in promoting legislation and spending programmes, and the Treasury to take the lead in imposing ceilings on public expenditure. A price leader administers prices by taking actions that have such an impact upon other organizations that they must adapt their behaviour in response. In government, a lead organization such as the Treasury can take actions that spending departments, such as the Scottish, Welsh or Northern Ireland Offices, cannot ignore.

Normally, a Whitehall ministry will see itself as the single lead organization in relations with local government; for example, the Department of Environment and the Scottish Office each deal with many local authorities. In relations with nationalized industries, there is likely to be a duopoly, with the public corporation and its sponsoring ministry both important. In the health service, oligopoly works best in hospital policy, because of Westminster's centralized control of capital and current hospital expenditure. Oligopoly works less well in the much more fragmented system of providing health care to individuals by professional doctors and dentists, who are paid in ways that are much harder to control by cash limits.

In dealings with non-Whitehall organizations, the first resource of a Whitehall ministry is *legitimacy*. A Cabinet minister will claim to represent the views of Parliament and to speak with the authority of the Mace. Any other view can be dismissed as unrepresentative because it is held by a nonelected organization. An elected local government's views may be made subordinate to Westminster because the latter has a far wider constituency, as the Conservative government showed by imposing spending cuts on Labour-controlled local councils in 1981. Within Cabinet, the functional minister responsible for England will normally claim to be the legitimate expert on functional matters, and take the lead vis-à-vis functional departments of the Scottish, Welsh and Northern Ireland Offices.

Power to *make or alter laws* is the second major resource of Whitehall ministries. All organizations of government are subject to Acts of Parliament, but Whitehall departments are unique in being able to alter these acts, or under these Acts to lay down regulations by statutory instruments or orders in council. While a ministry cannot change the law every year to suit its immediate convenience, it can threaten to change the law to its own advantage as a means of influencing dealings with other organizations, and even do so retrospectively if overruled by the courts.

Money is a third resource of Whitehall. The great bulk of public revenue in the United Kingdom is collected by the Treasury, and local government is dependent upon central government grants for maintaining its scale of services. Because Whitehall provides money, this does not *ipso facto* mean that it calls the tune in local government. It has no choice but to pay out funds to local government if it wishes to maintain public education and a whole host of services delivered by local government.[36] Nationalized industries may make Whitehall feel "captured" by public corporations that present Whitehall with an eleventh-hour bill to meet operating losses arising from unexpected changes in market conditions. About 90 percent (or more) of the money that the Treasury approves for spending each year goes to programmes that are virtually uncontrollable; that is, they cannot be altered without changing laws or causing controversy within Cabinet. The scale of Whitehall's funding of government organizations is sufficiently large to make it a major influence upon other organizations, but it is not thus made all-powerful.

In addition to being few and unequal, organizations are also *interdependent*. The Mace oversimplifies the practice of government by reducing it to a simple hierarchy of organizations that are all meant to be dependent in practice as well as theory upon the Crown in Parliament. The maze overcomplicates the government of the United Kingdom by emphasizing organizational independence. Oligopoly recognizes the mutual interdependence of the few organizations involved in a given policy area. Moreover, because public organizations are persisting, there is a considerable stability in a given oligopolistic network of organizations.

The interorganizational and intergovernmental models of government are correct in emphasizing the need for different organizations of government to exchange resources with each other, and the importance of bargaining in setting the terms of exchange. The endless process of consultations among Whitehall ministries and between Whitehall and extra-Whitehall institutions of government is evidence of this interdependence. Busy public officials do not parley simply to pass the time; they talk because each wants cooperation from the other.

The most important resource that extra-Whitehall organizations have is *hands-on control* of the delivery of the great bulk of public policies. Whitehall ministries authorize and often pay for policies, but they rarely produce goods and services. The oversight role of Whitehall ministries reflects their distance from where the action is. Education is provided in classrooms under the direction of a local education authority, health care in a doctor's consulting room or in hospitals run by a regional health authority, and the National Coal Board mines coal far from Trafalgar Square. The dual polity model is correct in that Whitehall does not want to become involved in the day-to-day provision of policies, nor can it easily do so when it does not have its hands on the great majority of government activities.

The second major resource of non-Whitehall organizations is expert *knowledge* of how programmes work in practice. Whereas Whitehall is headed by ministers specializing in managing Parliament and civil servants specializing in managing ministers, non-Whitehall organizations are normally headed by functional experts. Unlike Department of Industry staff, leading officials in the British Steel Corporation know how to make steel. Unlike Department of Education administrators, who specialize in laying down policy guidelines for others to carry out, local education officials know how to run schools. The claim to expertise is particularly important for territorial ministries. In dealings with other Whitehall ministries, they can claim to know the context of policies in Scotland, Wales or Northern Ireland in a way that other departments cannot.

A third major resource of non-Whitehall organizations is close *contact with the clients* or beneficiaries of major public policies. Organizations working at the point of delivery are likely to know how policies work, and can judge what works well and what does not. Whitehall ministries depend upon these organizations for reports from the field about the success of policies. This is particularly so in the United Kingdom, given the weakness of Parliament as a channel for communication and the relatively low status of individual MPs vis-à-vis Whitehall. Extra-Whitehall organizations can use their proximity to pressure groups to encourage lobbying of Whitehall in support of the mutual interests of producers and consumers. For example, education officials, teachers and groups representing child welfare press Whitehall for more spending on education. Nationalized industries can ask for cash subsidies as an alternative to increasing prices, knowing this position will be favoured by their customers. In the 1970s territorial ministers could invoke a special pressure group argument: the threat of Nationalist electoral gains if more benefits of public policy were not given.

The models of government by the Mace and the maze differ from each other (see table 7.1). Both models of the Mace emphasize that power is unequally distributed and concentrated. By contrast, the models of the maze see power as dispersed and shared more or less equally among many organizations. In the maze, cooperation within government is a matter of bargaining between autonomous organizations. With the Mace, it involves a hierarchy of superordinate and subordinate institutions.

TABLE 7.1. MODELS OF THE MACE AND THE MAZE COMPARED

	(1) How many organizations?	(2) What formal status?	(3) What relations between organizations?	(4) How is power distributed?
The Mace				
Simple hierarchy	One	Integrated	Hierarchical	Unequal
Dual polity	Two	Autonomy	Stratarchy	Unequal
The Maze				
Interorganizational	Many	Autonomy	Bargaining	Equal
Intergovernmental	Many	Autonomy	Bargaining	Equal
Oligopoly	Few	Interdependent	Leadership	Unequal

Notwithstanding important attributes in common, the two models of the Mace differ significantly from each other. The simple hierarchy assumes that the people on top wish to influence their subordinate agents more or less continuously. By contrast, the dual polity assumes a division of labour in which the top people in government, in order to be free to concentrate upon their distinctive concerns, offload unwanted tasks upon more or less autonomous but inferior institutions.

The two models of governing in a maze both emphasize that a multiplicity of autonomous organizations bargain as equals in the policy process. The distinction between the models is the difference between sociology and politics. The interorganizational model is indiscriminately concerned with relations involving private-sector and public-sector organizations. Nor does it see any difference in conflicts between two public-sector organizations and between a public- and a private-sector organization. The intergovernmental organization model recognizes the distinctive role of government. As is appropriate to its American origin, it then proceeds to derive a mazelike set of relationships between thousands of organizations, each of which can claim to be a government.[37]

Oligopoly provides a model of intragovernmental relations. Starting from the constitutional stipulation of inequalities between organizations, it adds the important empirical point that organizations are also unequal in practice. The Treasury is not to be confused with the Highland and Islands Development Board, nor is the Royal Navy to be confused with the Port of London Authority. The oligopoly model reconciles the conflict between the unitary doctrine of the Mace and the observable maze of public organizations. Within a single policy area, the number of relevant and significant organizations will be few. It is only when the whole range of public policies is scanned at one time that there appears to be a confused maze.

Oligopoly emphasizes interdependence and organizational leadership, attributes particularly important in the formally unitary Constitution of the United Kingdom. In determining policy outcomes, one organization will normally be the leader, taking the initiative in stimulating responses from other organizations. When the stimulus comes from a functional Whitehall ministry, other organizations—including territorial ministries in Whitehall as well as service delivery institutions outside Whitehall—cannot ignore it. But they are free, like any group of followers in a democracy, to respond as they think suitable. Because the sum total of organizations involved are relatively few, differences can be resolved by negotiations. The negotiations involve each participant making concessions in exchange for benefits. But they are not bargaining between buyers and sellers in a perfect market because the ministry carrying out Cabinet policy can dominate by asserting the authority of the Mace.

NOTES

1. Royal Commission on the Constitution, *Report,* chap. 9.
2. Christopher Hood, *The Limits of Administration* (London: John Wiley, 1976), p. 17.
3. Cf. C.E. Lindblom, *The Intelligence of Democracy* (New York: Free Press, 1965), on government by markets, with the limitations noted in Richard Rose, *What Is Governing?* (Englewood Cliffs, N.J.: Prentice-Hall, 1978), pp. 125ff.
4. See Manfred Kochen and Karl W. Deutsch, *Decentralization: Sketches toward a Rational Theory* (Cambridge, Mass.: Oelgeschlager, Gunn and Hain, 1980), pp. 17f, 35ff.
5. Ibid., pp. 28f.

6. Quoted in Hood, *The Limits of Administration,* p. 53.
7. See Richard Rose, "On the Priorities of Government," *European Journal of Political Research* 4, no. 3 (1976): 247-89.
8. Central Policy Review Staff, *Relations Between Central Government and Local Authorities* (London: HMSO, 1977), p. 1.
9. And their organizational forms differ. See Edward C. Page, *Comparing Local Expenditure: Lessons from a Multi-National State* (Glasgow: University of Strathclyde Studies in Public Policy No. 60, 1980).
10. See *Cmnd. 8175* (London: HMSO, 1981), table 1.5.
11. Calculated as current and capital expenditure on health services for 1979-80 in England, Scotland, Wales and Northern Ireland, excluding local authority expenditure on personal social services in Great Britain. See *Cmnd. 8175,* tables 2.11, 2.15-17.
12. Bulpitt, "The Making of the United Kingdom," *Parliamentary Affairs* 31, no. 2 (1978): 180.
13. Quoted in Vernon Bogdanor, *Devolution* (London: Oxford University Press, 1974), p. 13.
14. See, e.g., C.J. Hewitt, "Elites and the Distribution of Power in British Society," in *Elites and Power in British Society,* ed. P. Stanworth and A. Giddens (Cambridge: Cambridge University Press, 1974); and "Policy-making in Postwar Britain," *British Journal of Political Science* 4, no. 2 (1974).
15. See S.J. Eldersveld, *Political Parties: a Behavioral Analysis* (Chicago: Rand McNally, 1964).
16. Cf. Hans von Heppe and Ulrich Becker, "Zweckvorstellungen und Organisationsformen," in *Verwaltung: Eine Einfuehrende Darstellung,* ed. Fritz Morstein Marx (Berlin: Duncker and Humblot, 1965), p. 88.
17. See D.E. Butler and A. Sloman, *British Political Facts 1900-1979* (5th ed.; London: Macmillan, 1980), pp. 22ff.
18. Bulpitt recognizes this in the concluding section of his forthcoming Manchester University Press book, *Territory and Power in the United Kingdom,* but hopes that a new dual polity may be reconstructed.
19. Richard Rose, "British Government—the Job at the Top," in Rose and E. Suleiman, eds., *Presidents and Prime Ministers* (Washington, D.C.: American Enterprise Institute, 1980), tables 1.4, 1.5.
20. Calculated from *Cmnd. 7871* (London: HMSO, 1980), tables 1.8, 2.1-2.15, 4.1-4.4.
21. Calculated from *Civil Service Statistics 1980,* table 1.
22. See Richard Parry, *Changes in United Kingdom Public Employment* (Glasgow: University of Strathclyde Studies in Public Policy No. 62, 1980).
23. Max Weber, *Wirtschaft und Gesellschaft* (5th ed.; Tuebingen: J.C.B. Mohr, 1972), p. 126.
24. Rupert Emerson, *From Empire to Nation* (Boston: Beacon Press, 1960), p. 95.
25. Kenneth Hanf, "Introduction," in *Inter-organizational Policy-Making,* ed. K. Hanf and F.W. Scharpf (London: Sage Publications, 1978), p. 1.

26. Ibid., p. 2. See also J.K. Friend, J.M. Power and C.J.L. Yewlett, *Public Planning: the Inter-Corporate Dimension* (London: Tavistock Publications, 1974).
27. Lindblom, *The Intelligence of Democracy,* p. 12.
28. Cf. Daniel Tarschys, "The Soviet Political System: Three Models," *European Journal of Political Research* 5, no. 3 (1977): 287-320. Jean-Claude Thoenig, "State Bureaucracies and Local Government in France," in Hanf and Scharpf, *Interorganizational Policy Making;* and the United States, as described in Deil S. Wright, *Understanding Intergovernmental Relations* (North Scituate, Mass.: Duxbury Press, 1978).
29. Wright, *Understanding Intergovernmental Relations,* p. 10.
30. See, e.g., Hugh Heclo, "Issue Networks and the Executive Establishment," in *The New American Political System,* ed. Anthony King (Washington, D.C.: American Enterprise Institute, 1978); and A. Grant Jordan, "Iron Triangles, Woolly Corporatism or Elastic Nets: Images of the Policy Process," *Journal of Public Policy* 1, no. 1 (1981): 95-123.
31. Fritz W. Scharpf, "Inter-organizational Policy Studies: Issues, Concepts and Perspectives," in Hanf and Scharpf, *Inter-organizational Policy Making,* p. 347.
32. See the quotations in R.A.W. Rhodes, "Analysing Inter-governmental Relations," *European Journal of Political Research* 8, no. 3 (1980): 305.
33. See Richard Rose, "Government against Sub-Governments: A European Perspective on Washington," in Rose and Suleiman, *Presidents and Prime Ministers,* pp. 284-347.
34. For a succinct definition, see Jesse W. Markham, "Oligopoly," in the *International Encyclopedia of the Social Sciences* (New York: Free Press, 1968), 11: 283-90. All government organizations are viewed here as cooperative producers of policies related to each other. In certain contexts it is possible to view Whitehall ministries as buyers and other organizations as producers of goods and services. The general point about few participants in an imperfect market remains true.
35. For continental data, see L.J. Sharpe, "'Reforming' the Grass Roots: An Alternative Analysis," in D.E. Butler and A.H. Halsey, eds., *Policy and Politics* (London: Macmillan, 1978), p. 95.
36. See Edward C. Page, *Grant Dependence and Changes in Intergovernmental Finance* (Glasgow: University of Strathclyde Studies in Public Policy No. 80, 1981).
37. Note the title of a book about local government in the Greater New York area by Robert C. Wood, *1400 Governments* (New York: Anchor Books, 1964).

8. Cracking the Cake of Custom

The easiest way to maintain political authority is unthinkingly. In a traditional society, neither governors nor governed question how or why government is as it is. Ordinary people do not require a rationale for political allegiance; what Bagehot called the "cake of custom" can suffice to sustain authority.[1] The authority of the Mace has a traditional justification: It is as it is. It did not arise from a rational calculation by an enlightened despot or from a constituent assembly of rational citizens deliberating about the best principles of governance. The authority of the Crown is an historical accident, like an Oxford townscape that congenially juxtaposes buildings in styles 400 years apart, yet withal fitting together. The mystery is normally justified by the practical assertion "It works," even if those who work the Union do not fully understand why it works. An unthinking justification for Union is the strongest possible explanation—as long as it is not challenged.

To question traditional assumptions is to destroy their tacit validity. The past two decades have shown people in the United Kingdom in a questioning mood. The central political question, repeated through every medium, is: What's wrong with Britain?[2] In phrasing, the question implicitly assumes the maintenance of Union. Yet the responses can differ in English and non-English parts of the United Kingdom. In England, the question invites analysis of the problems of government, implying reform under the authority of Westminster. In non-English parts of the United Kingdom, Nationalists can thrust the blame for political ills upon membership in the Union, and prescribe independence as the solution.

In the 1970s Her Majesty's Government itself described as unsatisfactory conventional institutions for the territorial government of the United Kingdom. In a great rush to "modernize" Britain, no part of the United Kingdom was to be left untouched. The attack upon the status quo (even if it was the very recent "tradition" of a Welsh Office established in 1964) reflected a diffuse reaction against established practices of government. Harold Wilson and Edward Heath were both ready to voice a cry for change. In 1972 a Conservative government suspended the Northern Ireland Parliament, and a Labour government in 1976 introduced bills intended to establish new institutions of devolved government for Scotland and Wales. The characteristic outlook of the self-styled reformers was epitomized by the statement of Ted Short, the Labour minister originally in charge of devolution: "The status quo is not an option."

In the 1980s, confidence in reform has been weakened by failure. But the challenge to established institutions has left its mark: the cracking of the cake of custom. The questioning of the government of the United Kingdom—by Privy Councillors sworn to uphold it, as well as by Nationalists—has undermined the traditional rationale for political allegiance. There is confusion about why the United Kingdom exists. And Nationalists question whether the United Kingdom should continue to exist. From the perspective of history, the concept of the United Kingdom can appear transitory. But salutary as such a perspective may be, it does not focus sharply enough upon questions of here and now.

How did the cracking of the cake of custom come about? To understand this, we must first consider the steady-state United Kingdom that prevailed from the 1920s to the 1960s. Next, it is necessary to examine how destabilization occurred in Northern Ireland, following the civil rights demonstrations in 1968. The 1978 Devolution Acts for Scotland and Wales, actions that promised to destabilize government in Great Britain, are considered in the third section.[3] In view of the scale of constitutional change implicit in the Devolution Acts, the chapter concludes by considering what devolution has in fact demonstrated, namely, the strength of the Mace.

The Steady-State United Kingdom

For almost half a century from 1921, the government of the Union was "steady state" government. Unionists held undoubted hegemony everywhere within its territory. During this period the different parts of the United Kingdom were undoubtedly nations, in the sense of having distinctive identities, and also, in very different degrees, distinctive institutions of governance. But even more than that, they were nations in which Unionist political values and institutions were dominant. Accounts can be written of Nationalist or "home rule" groups active at this time, but such accounts inevitably distort reality greatly. Such a focus concentrates upon a very small portion of the politics of a nation in the steady-state United Kingdom. It ignores the overwhelmingly dominant group within each nation, the Unionists.

Northern Ireland, seemingly the most distinctive part of the United Kingdom, paradoxically demonstrates the dominance of Unionism. The existence of a Stormont Parliament was accepted by the majority there *because* the Northern Ireland Parliament in effect had a right to vote upon and reject any proposal to remove Northern Ireland from the Union. Stormont was an exam-

ple of the compatibility of having a devolved Parliament *and* affirming Unionism. The circumstances in which it affirmed Unionism were extreme: the
threat of an armed challenge to its authority by sporadically active units of the
illegal Irish Republican Army and a continuing political challenge from a Nationalist party that refused to be called a loyal Opposition and from the government of the Republic of Ireland. Because of this challenge, Stormont was
permanently controlled by one party, for Protestants voted as a bloc to defend
Union, just as Catholics voted against it. The divisions that affected government at Stormont were within the ranks of Unionists.[4]

In Scotland and Wales, the steady-state United Kingdom was not a period
of nil change but a period in which all changes were within the assumption of
continuing Union. This was most strikingly the case in Wales. Throughout
the interwar depression there was no significant demand for devolution, home
rule or independence, notwithstanding the contrast between Liberal and then
Labour dominance in Wales and Conservative dominance at Westminster.
The postwar campaign for the creation of a Welsh Office was led by the Labour Party in Wales. It was not seen as a step toward distancing the principality from Westminster; it was integrationist. A Welsh Office was reckoned to
have more influence at Westminster. The creation of the Welsh Office in 1964
was implicitly a rejection of demands for a "home rule" Assembly for Wales.[5]

The Scottish Office evolved in an increasingly centralist way during the
steady-state United Kingdom. In the interwar period it gathered into its own
administrative divisions a variety of peculiarly Scottish boards and bodies that
had survived the attention of late-Victorian reformers. In the postwar era it
first expanded the activities of the functional departments into which the Scottish Office was divided. Thence it grew with the growth of government United
Kingdom-wide. It also began to develop a set of central services so that the
Secretary of State for Scotland could exercise greater control and direction of
functional departments. Given the position of the Secretary of State as a Cabinet minister, this inevitably tended to reduce the scope for distinctive national
variations in policy.[6]

During the steady-state United Kingdom, nearly the whole of the popular
vote went to Unionist parties at every general election in Scotland and Wales,
and in Northern Ireland the Unionist Party was even more strongly entrenched
as the electoral majority. Accounts of electoral politics of the period are normally written as accounts of class politics because the parties divided along
class lines. Equally, parties united in upholding the Union. Except in Northern Ireland, the Unionist dimension can be ignored because there is nothing to
differentiate the parties: All the parties winning seats in the Commons were
Unionist parties.

Accounts of Nationalist politics in the steady-state United Kingdom are inevitably blinkered accounts. Vision is restricted to activities undertaken by very small groups of individuals who express Nationalist sentiments. The overwhelming majority, who held to Unionism, are ignored. For example, an account of Plaid Cymru can start from its origins in 1925—but it had only six members then.[7] An account of Scottish Nationalism can go back to the nineteenth century or start with the foundation of the National Party of Scotland in 1928—but it can only record two candidates fighting as Nationalists at the 1929 election, each winning only a few hundred votes.[8]

Unionist parties were overwhelmingly preeminent in Scotland and Wales at every general election in the steady-state United Kingdom. In the interwar period, the Scottish and Welsh Nationalists contested only a handful of seats in their nations; the Unionist parties together took 99 percent of the vote. This hegemony continued after the Second World War, even though the Nationalists began to nominate more candidates. The Unionist parties together continued to take 99 percent of the vote in Scotland at every election through 1959. In Wales Unionists took 99 percent of the vote at every election through 1951 and at least 95 percent of the vote at subsequent elections through 1966. In Northern Ireland there was no question of Unionists losing a Stormont election. At Westminster elections, the only question was whether Unionists would win all 12 seats, or "only" 10 or 11 of the 12.[9]

The preeminence of parties of Union before the Second World War is of particular theoretical importance because of the very real difference in levels of economic distress among the four nations during the interwar depression. Consistently, unemployment was much higher in Scotland, Northern Ireland and Wales than in England. In 1925, unemployment stood at 11 percent in England and 15 percent in Scotland and in Wales. In 1930, unemployment had risen to 15 percent in England, to 17 percent in Scotland and to 25 percent in Wales. By 1938, unemployment had fallen to 13 percent in England, but it remained at 17 percent in Scotland, and 27 percent in Wales. Throughout the interwar period, unemployment in Northern Ireland, albeit calculated on a different basis, was always much higher than in England, though not necessarily higher than in Wales.[10] The interwar period provides a very clear-cut refutation of the thesis that economic disparities give rise to Nationalist parties, because of the weakness of Nationalist parties then. MPs from Scotland and Wales attacked unemployment but they did not attack the Union in which it occurred. Their analysis was functional and Socialist, not territorial and Nationalist.[11]

In the steady-state United Kingdom, unconventional political groups such as Nationalists could gain attention at Westminster only by conventional means. In the mid-1960s, Nationalist groups did succeed in making a break-through by the conventional device of electing representatives to Parliament. Northern Ireland was the first to do so. Gerry Fitt was returned as Republican Labour MP from West Belfast at the 1966 general election. Unlike most of his predecessors elected by the Catholic community of Northern Ireland, Fitt became integrated in Westminster, making friends in the Labour Party, then in the majority, and advocating "British type" economic concerns more than conventional antipartition complaints.

Plaid Cymru made a more important breakthrough, with the party's leader, Gwynfor Evans, becoming its first MP at a by-election at Carmarthen in July 1966, taking the seat from the governing party, Labour. In March 1967, a Plaid candidate finished a strong second to Labour in a Rhondda West by-election on the same day in which a Scottish National Party candidate polled well in a by-election that Labour lost to the Conservatives at Glasgow Pollok. The SNP followed this with a by-election victory over Labour at Hamilton in November 1967, winning a seat the SNP had not even contested at the 1966 general election.

The Labour government had no wish to alter significantly the institutions of territorial governance, but even though it remained secure in its parliamentary majority, there were disturbing implications in Nationalist challenges in parts of Britain that returned one-fifth of Labour's MPs.[12] The initial reaction of the Prime Minister, Harold Wilson, was to do nothing. In reply to a parliamentary question from a Welsh Labour MP asking for the appointment of a Royal Commission on devolution, Wilson, on 11 December 1967, said no.[13] The Cabinet as well as backbench Labour MPs were divided about whether a Royal Commission should be appointed. On the one hand, it could be presented as a positive response to by-election results. If challenged, Labour MPs could dodge substantive issues of principle by treating the matter of devolution or independence as if it were *sub judice*. But this tactic was opposed within the Labour Party by politicians who thought no concessions should be given to Nationalist views, even a concession as limited and dispensable as a Royal Commission.[14]

In the event, the Labour government announced in the Queen's Speech of 30 October 1968 that it would appoint a Royal Commission to investigate "what changes may be needed" in the government of the United Kingdom. The Royal Commission was not appointed until six months later. The terms of reference of the Commission were broad, an inquiry into the government of "the several countries, nations and regions of the United Kingdom," concerning "the interests of the prosperity and good government of Our people under the Crown."[15] The Commission was asked to state *whether* any changes were desirable in government, a shift from the statement in the Queen's Address the previous autumn, referring to "what changes" may be needed. The appointment of the Commission was meant to dismiss the subject of territorial governance until after the next general election. The government announced that it would proceed with local government reorganization in Scotland, Wales and England, notwithstanding the inevitable interaction between changes in local government and the possible devolution of responsibilities to Scotland, Wales or English regions. The Prime Minister coyly noted, "The Commission will inevitably take some time to report."[16]

The extraparliamentary Labour Party was badly divided about how best to maintain the Union. In its evidence to the Royal Commission, the Scottish Council of the Labour Party opposed an elected assembly for Scotland on the traditional ground that "whilst superficially attractive" it would inevitably create an unfavourable environment for realising "the substantial benefits arising from central control of the economy in the best interests of the whole of Great Britain."[17] By contrast, the Welsh Council of Labour recommended an elected Welsh Council with executive, administrative and advisory powers.[18] In its British manifesto for the 1970 general election, Labour endorsed "an elected council for Wales" but opposed a "separate legislative assembly" for Scotland.[19] A declaration by the Conservative Party leader, Edward Heath, at Perth in 1968, initially favoured an elected Scottish assembly. No action was taken to carry out this proposal by the Heath government when it was in office from 1970 to 1974.[20] Conservatives consistently opposed an elected Welsh assembly.

The 1970 general election was unanimously interpreted at Westminster as dispelling the need to alter government in Scotland and Wales, for the Nationalists lost both seats they had gained at by-elections. The Scottish National Party won a single seat, the Western Isles, but a kilted Hebridean politician with a Gaelic accent was not taken as a threat by mainstream mainland politicians. The fact that the Nationalist vote had more than doubled in Scotland and Wales was ignored by Westminster politicians, who regard representation in Parliament as the currency of influence.

When the Royal Commission on the Constitution came to draw up its conclusions, it started from unequivocally Unionist premises. It rejected "the division of the country either into a number of separate sovereign states (separatism) or into states sharing sovereignty with the United Kingdom (federalism)." It declared that there was no great demand for such changes, and considered that "the prosperity and good government of the people of all parts of the United Kingdom" would be best served by maintaining the Union. It was prepared to recommend changes in the institutions of Union. Nothing else would justify more than four years of work. But it did so on the following assumption:

> The transfers of power with which we shall be concerned in this and subsequent parts of our report, therefore, are those which would leave overriding control in the hands of Parliament. The extent of the powers transferred and the conditions under which they were to be exercised would be prescribed by statute and might at any time be changed by Parliament or by Ministers answerable to it. In other words we shall be concerned with devolution, which is the delegation of central government powers without the relinquishment of sovereignty.[21]

Deciding how best to maintain Union was not easy. The seven-inch-high stack of evidence presented to the Commission, primarily from the non-English parts of the United Kingdom, was a jumble of diffuse Unionist loyalties and specific grievances and claims to attention.

The conclusions of the Royal Commission were inconclusive. The Commission split five ways in its principal recommendations. The chief cause of disagreement was whether or not uniform treatment was appropriate for the government of the whole of Great Britain or, at a minimum, whether uniform treatment was required for Scotland and Wales. (No recommendation was made about a troubled Northern Ireland.) These divisions were related to the suitability or unsuitability of devolving executive powers, and legislative as well as executive responsibilities. Ironically, the minority report by Norman (now Lord) Crowther-Hunt and Professor Alan Peacock, recommending uniform devolution for Scotland, Wales and five English regions, was not the principal difficulty. The Commission's report was crippled by the absence of a clear majority view. There was not even a consensus about the number of different forms of devolution that Commission members endorsed. The single most popular alternative was a scheme of legislative devolution for Scotland and Wales and nonelected regional councils for England. The majority recommendation was nonpartisan, in the sense that it was sure to inflame both major parties by recommending proportional representation for Assembly elections. It was logically consistent in recommending reduced representation for Scotland and Wales at Westminster in consequence of devolution, but this invited opposition by Scots and Welsh MPs.[22]

The Commission's report was dismissed by both major parties. The Prime Minister, Edward Heath, declared, "There should be the widest possible public discussion before any decisions are taken on issues which affect so fundamentally the way in which our country is governed." The leader of the Opposition, Harold Wilson, was equally evasive. "It is right that public debate should be allowed and encouraged to continue as thoroughly as possible."[23] Westminster believed that talk could continue indefinitely; no action was needed to alter government in its perceived steady-state condition.

The Destabilization of Northern Ireland

From the perspective of the 1980s, the government of Northern Ireland from the mid-1920s to the mid-1960s appears remarkably stable. It also appears stable if viewed as the aftermath of four decades of agitation that led to the independence of Southern Ireland in 1921. Stability is not a virtue in itself. In an imperfectly legitimate political system, the persistence of an unchanging Stormont was a cause of continuing grievance to the Catholic minority community, just as it was a source of positive allegiance for the Protestant majority.[24] The security forces of Stormont maintained public order confidently and firmly, albeit not in accord with the wishes of Republican opponents of the regime. In the four decades of steady-state Northern Ireland, fewer people were killed in political violence than in an average six months after Westminster became exclusively responsible for public order in 1972.

The 1968 civil rights campaign in Northern Ireland succeeded in destabilizing the province. The civil rights campaign was novel in two respects. First, it ignored the traditional Irish claim to national self-determination; it was neutral about the continuance of the border dividing the United Kingdom from the Republic of Ireland. Second, it challenged the Westminster belief that government by a popularly elected Parliament was inevitably the best and only way to govern a territory. Instead, it argued that every person resident in the United Kingdom deserved "British rights." In the legal sense, the rights were not (and are not today) rights that can be claimed in a court of law anywhere in the United Kingdom.[25] But the more important fact was that the claims advanced—for better political and economic treatment of the Catholic minority in Northern Ireland—were perceived at Westminster as reasonable, and failure to meet them was held against the Stormont regime.

The destabilization of Northern Ireland involved three interacting processes. Support for the Stormont system of government was first undermined at Westminster by organized and vocal attacks upon conditions in the province, attacks that particularly appealed to Labour politicians with no incentive to give the benefit of the doubt to a government allied to Conservatives in England. Allegations of discrimination also made news in the media at a time when civil rights was a worldwide issue. Second, the unity of the Unionists within Northern Ireland was dissipated by internal quarrels, turning partly on personalities and partly on political judgments. These were sufficient to lead to the deposition of three successive Unionist Party leaders—Terence O'Neill, James Chichester-Clark, and Brian Faulkner. Moreover, breakaway alternatives arose proclaiming a "hardline" Unionism, of which the most persistent has been the Democratic Unionist Party, led by the Reverend Dr. Ian K. Paisley. By 1973, the official Unionist Party could no longer claim half the vote for Unionist parties.[26] Third, violent confrontation between civil rights demonstrators and the Royal Ulster Constabulary, Stormont's security forces, captured the attention of the world's media, starting from the civil rights march of 5 October 1968 in Londonderry, held in defiance of a Stormont ban and broken up by RUC water cannons and a baton charge. RUC police tactics brought worldwide sympathy to the demonstrators, further undermining support for Stormont at Westminster.

Disorder in the streets brought about the destabilization of the Stormont system for governing Northern Ireland. British troops were called out to maintain public order in default of Stormont forces in August 1969, following disorder that erupted throughout Northern Ireland after the barricading of the Bogside district of Londonderry during a traditional Protestant march through the town. Seven people were shot dead during the disorder. Calling out British troops effectively meant the end of any pretence of a dual polity. Stormont remained in existence, but Westminster was immediately involved in the province's most contentious concerns, public order and the elected government that its troops were maintaining.

Once a steady-state system is broken, in the neutral language of systems analysis the task becomes one of achieving a new equilibrium, that is, creating a new base for stable government. Politicians would like this to be government by consensus, notwithstanding the fact that the province has a history of governing without consensus. Initially, Labour and Conservative governments sought to "re-equilibriate" the United Kingdom by the reform of Stormont. The Stormont government was the legal power to whose aid the troops had come. Moreover, it was the buffer that insulated Westminster from responsibilities it did not wish to have. In the words of the Home Secretary, James Callaghan, shortly before troops were committed in 1969, "We were debating whether we should intervene but hoping and praying that we would not have to. The advice that came to me from all sides was on no account to get sucked into the Irish bog."[27]

The premises of Westminster's policies were soon revealed to be false. The first was that a Unionist Prime Minister could and would deliver majority support for a reform programme. The second was that Catholic demands could be met by procedural reforms, such as changing methods of allocating council houses, without substantive changes at Stormont. The third assumption was that there was no threat of a revival of the Republican tradition of seeking a united Ireland by physical force.

In response to IRA attacks upon British soldiers, Westminster's policy emphasized defence of a now unstable Stormont. The high point of Westminster's commitment was the use of the full force of the British Army to introduce the internment of suspected Republicans without trial on 9 August 1971. Internment turned what had been sniping between the IRA and the British Army into a full-fledged shooting war. The IRA gained recruits, and Catholic civilians hardened their opposition to Stormont. When British Army paratroopers shot thirteen people dead at a demonstration in Londonderry on 30 January 1972 ("Bloody Sunday"), Westminster felt the full force of worldwide criticism. The Prime Minister, Edward Heath, in the revealing words of his political secretary, decided to treat Northern Ireland as "the most important matter of the moment" and to go "back to first principles on Ireland."[28]

Since reform from within had failed, reconstruction from without was adopted as the alternative to maintain order. In March 1972, Stormont was suspended and Westminster became "temporarily" responsible for the direct rule of the province. Formally, this strengthened Westminster's authority, as it no longer had to work through a separately elected Stormont government. In political terms, the government saw direct rule as placing it in the position of an honest broker between Protestants and Catholics. It hoped to negotiate a new system of government acceptable to both groups, thereby returning peace to the province through a political settlement rather than military victory.

The starting point for reconstruction, in the words of the then Home Secretary, Reginald Maudling, was "that the Westminster pattern of democracy, which suits us so well, is not easily exportable."[29] The reference to "exportability" illustrates Westminster's view that Northern Ireland is an "alien" rather than an integral part of the territory of the United Kingdom. The upshot of the negotiations was the 1973 Northern Ireland Constitution Act, which emphatically differed from the Westminster model of parliamentary government. Differences included election of an Assembly by proportional representation and installation of an Executive only after the Northern Ireland Secretary was satisfied that it had broad support among the Catholic minority as well as the Protestant majority. A power-sharing Executive, consisting of Unionist supporters of Brian Faulkner, the SDLP and the bi-confessional Alliance Party, was launched in January 1974.

The power-sharing Executive collapsed in May 1974 in the face of a general strike called by the Ulster Workers' Council.[30] The Ulster Workers' Council demanded an immediate general election to see whether or not the Executive had the support of a majority of the electorate. The premise of the strikers was that it did not. This premise was shared by the Executive and the Northern Ireland Office; that was why the demand was refused. But the British Army was not used to confront the strikers. When Faulkner saw that Westminster would not defend the government it had created, he resigned and the province returned to direct rule.

The majority rejection of power sharing has been confirmed by subsequent elections. The 1975 Constitutional Convention, elected by a proportional representation ballot, returned a majority of Unionists and loyalists opposed to power sharing. The 78-member Convention approved, 42 to 31, a call for a Westminster-style majority rule Parliament. This was rejected by Westminster. Westminster elections have shown that there is an absolute popular majority voting for Unionist and Loyalist candidates. More than three-quarters of the electorate, including nearly all Protestants, endorse a commitment to maintain the United Kingdom. The Social Democratic and Labour Party is committed to a united Ireland; it has secured the vote of most of the Catholic minority.

Since 1975, Northern Ireland has been governed in a political vacuum.[31] Nominally, the method for governing Northern Ireland approximates that for governing Scotland and Wales; responsibility rests with a British Cabinet minister, the Secretary of State for Northern Ireland, and the major policies of the welfare state are delivered through the institutions of direct rule. In practice, government is fundamentally different because of the vacuum created by the absence of political authority.

The most obvious cause of the vacuum is Westminster's inability to maintain a monopoly of force. Within Northern Ireland, there are at least five different illegal military forces operating against one another, and on the Republican side against Crown forces. Republicans are divided into three armed groups: the Provisional IRA, the Official IRA and the Irish National Liberation Army, which is aligned with the Irish Republican Socialist Party. Protestant paramilitary forces include groups banded together under the aegis of the Ulster Defence Association, and aggressive groups which sometimes act in the name of the Ulster Volunteer Force. Four Crown forces—the British Army and its locally raised auxiliary, the Ulster Defence Regiment, the Royal Ulster Constabulary and the RUC Reserve—together have been unable to stop the violence. In consequence, more than 2200 people have been killed by the political violence in the province since the British Army became responsible for public order in August 1969.

The indefiniteness of Westminster's commitment to defend Northern Ireland against armed attack has been shown repeatedly by British officials negotiating with extralegal or illegal military forces, thus giving *de facto* recognition to them. Backstairs negotiations were initiated by the novel device of sending a Foreign Office official, formerly working in 10 Downing Street, to Northern Ireland in August 1969 as UKREP (the United Kingdom Representative in Northern Ireland). This led to negotiations with both the IRA and Protestant paramilitary organizations, twice producing cease-fires by IRA groups. From spring 1972, the Northern Ireland Office granted "political prisoner" status to Republicans and Loyalists serving long sentences for crimes of violence related to the troubles. This status was withdrawn after 1 March 1976 — but is still sought by Republican prisoners in the H-block at the Maze Prison refusing to wear prison uniform and "going on the blanket." In 1981, protests escalated with IRA hunger strikes in support of a demand for political status, leading to the death by fasting of ten Republican prisoners.

The vacuum is also evidenced by uncertainty about whether, or in what sense, Westminster defends the integrity of that portion of the United Kingdom's border that separates Northern Ireland from the Republic of Ireland. The position of the Republic is clear: Under Article 2 of its Constitution the border is null and void. The whole of the 32 counties of Ireland is claimed by Dublin. In practice, the border is wide open; that is, transit by approved or unapproved roads is easy across the North-South border. There are British Army and RUC patrols, and also patrols by the Irish Gardai, but these are limited in effect. The openness of the border is demonstrated from time to time by IRA groups making cross-border raids, then escaping back to the Republic. If apprehended, IRA suspects can avoid extradition to Northern Ireland for trial for crimes of violence by pleading that the crime is political. The Republic's laws do not allow extradition for political crimes.

In a great variety of ways, Westminster also recognizes the existence of a border between Great Britain and Northern Ireland. This is most evident in the Prevention of Terrorism Act, enacted in 1974 after IRA bombs exploded in Birmingham public houses, killing nineteen people. The Act makes it possible to prevent the entry into Great Britain of British subjects born in Northern Ireland. The political distance between Great Britain and Northern Ireland is also illustrated by the exceptionalist legislation enacted by Westminster for dealing with troubles in Northern Ireland, legislation that is not to be applied within Great Britain. In effect, Westminster seeks to maintain a cordon sanitaire *within* the United Kingdom. In the words of William Whitelaw, speaking in London shortly before becoming Home Secretary in 1979, there is "a determination to prevent violence in this part of the United Kingdom."[32]

Time and again, Westminster has been prepared for the invisible border between Great Britain and Northern Ireland to become a real border. Until 1972, Westminster guaranteed that Northern Ireland would not cease to be a part of the United Kingdom without the consent of the Parliament of Northern Ireland. The abolition of Stormont effectively removed this guarantee from the hands of the Unionist majority. Westminster politicians since have said that Northern Ireland will continue to remain part of the United Kingdom as long as a majority of its people so wish. The 1973 Border Poll gave institutional effect to sounding Ulster opinion.[33] In Wales and Scotland the guarantee of membership in the United Kingdom is unconditional. Throughout the devolution debate nothing was said by the government to imply that it would contemplate the prospect of separation. It rejected a Scottish and Welsh Referendum question on independence, even though confident that the Union would be overwhelmingly endorsed, because such a question would imply that, in the hypothetical event of a positive vote for independence, Scotland or Wales could unilaterally secede from the United Kingdom. By contrast, Westminster offers Northern Ireland a standing right to unilateral secession from the United Kingdom as and when the majority may wish.

Furthermore, Westminster has been ready to engage in a dialogue with the government of the Republic of Ireland about that portion of the United Kingdom that both claim. When the Republic of Ireland left the Commonwealth, Westminster enacted the 1949 Ireland Act, which declared in Section 2: "Notwithstanding that the Republic of Ireland is not part of His Majesty's Dominions, the Republic of Ireland is not a foreign country for the purposes of any law in force in any part of the United Kingdom." The readiness of Westminster to listen to Irish demands for British territory is a continuing source of anxiety to Ulster Protestants. For example, in 1980 and 1981 Mrs. Thatcher preferred joint talks about Northern Ireland with the head of the Irish government rather than with the elected representatives of Northern Ireland.

In office, no British government official has publicly expressed the view that Great Britain should secede from the United Kingdom or that Northern Ireland should be expelled. But memoirs written by politicians soon after leaving office show clearly that many ministers would welcome the break up of the United Kingdom by the departure of Northern Ireland. The case for withdrawal can be made in terms of harsh realism, as when Joe Haines, formerly Press Secretary to Prime Minister Harold Wilson, declared that the deaths in Ulster following withdrawal might be fewer than the "bloodshed and massacre" likely to follow Britain remaining engaged.[34] Normally, the sentiments reflect a general belief that Northern Ireland does not belong under Westminster's authority. It is regarded as an Irish problem and should not be what in fact it is, a United Kingdom problem.

The cracking of the cake of custom took less than four years from the burst of publicity given the civil rights march in Londonderry in 1968 to the replacement of Stormont's authority by temporary direct rule. The evidence of the years since is that it is easier to void a system of government at the behest of an active minority than it is to establish new institutions against the wishes of a majority of the population.

Devolution: The Status Quo Is Not an Option

The devolution debate from 1974 to 1979 was doubly a challenge to the stability of Great Britain. First, it reflected a demand for independence by the Scottish and Welsh Nationalists. While their long-term demands were not new, what was novel was the parliamentary attention given. The Nationalists could claim to hold the balance of power after the February 1974 general election because the governing party, Labour, lacked an overall majority. The prospect of Nationalists exploiting their position, as the Irish Nationalists unsuccessfully did before 1914, was once again present at Westminster.

The devolution policy adopted by the Labour government from 1974 to 1979 was a second source of potential instability. By proposing major change in the constitutional government of Scotland and Wales it raised the *possibility* of unintended consequences, including accelerating progress down the "slippery slope" to independence. Yet proponents of devolution argued that the adaptation of Westminster institutions was needed as a means of preventing a rise in Nationalist support. Doing nothing was said to risk greater disruption than introducing constitutional change.

The breakthrough at Westminster in February 1974 was palpable evidence that something had gone wrong. But what had gone wrong was not so easy to diagnose. Logically, there was no reason to assume that the problems reflected in an increased third-party vote in Scotland and Wales were unique to those two nations, just as there was no reason to assume that the problems reflected in a contemporaneous surge in Liberal votes in England were unique to England.[35] Insofar as the 1974 election results reflected Britain-wide concerns, this implied responding with policies uniform in character throughout Britain. Exceptionalist policies for Scotland and Wales would be justified only by a diagnosis that Nationalist voting arose from problems unique to Scotland or Wales.

The political diagnoses of the 1974 election results can be grouped under six broad headings—nearly all of which implied uniform or concurrent Unionist policies as the most relevant response. Insofar as economic decline was diagnosed as the principal political issue in Scotland and Wales or United Kingdom-wide, then there was no need to frame exceptional policies. To remove this grievance, the Labour government could pursue uniform policies that

TABLE 8.1. ALTERNATIVE DIAGNOSES AND RESPONSES TO NATIONALIST VOTE

Diagnosis of Cause	Relevant Response
1. Economic decline	Restore prosperity to British economy.
2. Loss of confidence	Restore elite and mass confidence in British political system.
3. Institutional weakness	Reform of Parliament, Whitehall, regions, etc., throughout Britain; and/or devolution.
4. Regional economic decline	Specific regional policies from centre and/or restore prosperity to British economy.
5. Cultural differentiation	Use pluralistic political symbols; promote Welsh language in education, broadcasting.
6. Nationalism	Mobilize opposition by Unionist parties—with or without devolution.

would be popular in England as well, where the same concerns were also voiced. Putting the *British* economy and government to rights could provide the government with a secure basis for popularity and restore elite and popular confidence in the effectiveness of Westminster government. In effect, this was the policy pursued by the Heath government from 1970 to 1974. It led to defeat—in England as well as Scotland and Wales—because the Heath government failed in its management of the economy, not because it failed to produce devolution.

There was no shortage of prescriptions to combat what was typically diagnosed in vague, metaphorical terms as a disease or malaise. Most of the measures, such as reform of Parliament, reform of the civil service or reform of the party system, focused upon change at Westminster. It was assumed that if Westminster was properly reformed, then this would restore popular confidence in Scotland and Wales. A few proposals concentrated almost exclusively upon England, such as attacks upon the public school system and the alleged harm its values did.

The Royal Commission on the Constitution diagnosed institutional dissatisfactions as a Britain-wide problem. The Commission majority did not endorse uniform change; it was prepared to argue that national differences permitted national exceptions in devolved government. The minority report was an *omnium gatherum* of reforms. (Lord Crowther-Hunt, a co-author, had also been a moving spirit in the Fulton Committee on the Reform of the Civil Service.) It prescribed devolved regional councils for England as well as devolved Assemblies for Scotland and Wales, changes so great as to involve the destabilization of status quo institutions of government throughout Britain.

In the case of Wales, a case could be made that cultural problems—specifically, the protection of the Welsh language—were the chief stimulus to Nationalist voting. By definition, measures to protect or promote the Welsh language would be exceptionalist measures, inapplicable to England or Scotland.

While controversial within Wales, they would at least be relevant to Wales' distinctive culture in a way that institutional reform was not. By the same token, they would be irrelevant in Scotland, where the SNP eschewed "tartanry"; several of its newly successful MPs were modern mass media communicators.

Accepting the rise of the SNP and Plaid Cymru as evidence of a genuine increase in Nationalist sympathies was difficult, for it meant that Westminster politicians had to admit that their own legitimacy was challenged. The end was clear—mobilizing support for Unionist parties. But the policy prescriptions following from this were ambiguous. It could be argued that only by making exceptional concessions to national (but *not* Nationalist) sentiment in Scotland and Wales could Nationalists be stopped electorally. Alternatively, it could be argued that this would only fan the flames of Nationalism.

In the event, the problem diagnosed by the Labour Prime Minister, Harold Wilson, reflected both a general predisposition to institutional change (he had after all appointed the Fulton Committee on the civil service, endorsed local government reform and approved a bill for House of Lords reform) and an immediate tactical imperative: how to win a parliamentary majority in an autumn 1974 election, Labour having lost four seats to Nationalists in February 1974. This meant avoiding the loss of any more seats in Scotland or Wales to Nationalists. Unpublished polls taken in Scotland by Robert Worcester's MORI firm (Market & Opinion Research International) were interpreted as showing the popularity of a devolution pledge. MORI asked samples of Scottish voters to choose between three alternative forms of government. The two extreme choices—"a completely independent Scottish Parliament" and "no change"—secured support from 19 percent each.[36] This left the third alternative—"a Scottish Parliament as part of Britain but with substantial powers"— endorsed by 54 percent. The evidence was ambiguous. It could be interpreted as showing that four-fifths of Scots were against the status quo, and equally that four-fifths of Scots were against independence. It could also be interpreted as showing that the great majority of Scots would oppose a devolution scheme *without* substantial powers (cf. table 3.2).

Electoral necessity, rather than constitutional argument, produced action.[37] Confidential reports prepared by the Scottish headquarters of the Labour Party warned: "Our strategy on the future government of Scotland is of paramount importance for the future of the British Labour Party."[38] By association, though not by evidence or logic, it was assumed that something would have to be done about Wales as well, not least because the Labour Party in Wales was actively promoting devolution.

For better or worse, the Labour Party had a wide choice of policies. Not only were there controverted recommendations from the Royal Commission, but also different positions held by the Parliamentary Labour Party and the National (i.e., Great Britain) Executive Committee; by the Welsh Council of the Labour Party and by the Scottish Council of the Labour Party. Moreover, both the Welsh and Scottish parties were divided about whether or not to concede a measure of devolution. And any pledge to devolve was almost bound to split the party at Westminster as well.[39] It was these divisions that had led the ..abour Party in its February 1974 British manifesto to adopt a straightforward position: It said nothing about the issue of devolution!

In September 1974, a few days before the announcement of a general election, the Labour government issued a white paper that recommended the creation of directly elected Assemblies in Scotland and Wales. The document was prepared by a group around the Prime Minister, including Lord Crowther-Hunt, author of the minority report to the Royal Commission on the Constitution and specially appointed as a constitutional adviser. The white paper took as its starting point a commitment to Union: The United Kingdom must remain one country and one economy, and constitutional change must be undertaken with the clear objective of strengthening rather than weakening this unity.[40] It carefully rehearsed major objections to change, pointing out that there were "many material aspirations and social objectives which devolution cannot further." It plumped for elected Assemblies for Scotland and Wales, arguing that this would meet the legitimate desire of people there for "democratic accountability."[41] While clear about the principle of devolution, the white paper was full of uncertain and tentative statements about the implications. After the Cabinet approved the final draft of this white paper, the Prime Minister is supposed to have said in an aside, "And God help all who sail in her."[42] Within a few days, the white paper pledge had become embodied in Labour's October 1974 British general election manifesto: "The next Labour government will create elected assemblies in Scotland and Wales."

From the perspective of the Prime Minister, the pledge worked. Labour won the October 1974 election with 319 seats, one more than the number required for an absolute parliamentary majority. Labour did not lose a single seat to the Scottish Nationalists, notwithstanding the 8.5 percent increase in the SNP vote, and the SNP's capture of four seats from the Conservatives. Labour lost one seat to Plaid Cymru, but the Plaid's vote did not rise. Labour's needed gains were not achieved in Scotland but in England, where the party won 18 more seats. In total, Labour had 2 more seats than the Conservatives in England, and a 42-seat advantage over the Conservatives in Parliament. But it had only a 3-seat United Kingdom majority. Each of four disparate groups— 13 Liberals, 11 Scottish Nationals, 3 Plaid Cymru and 12 Ulster MPs—could claim to hold the balance of power.

Labour's election victory faced the government with a new problem: what to do about its commitment to devolution. The pledge had been made without any systematic consultation among ministers in Whitehall or scrutiny by interdepartmental committees of civil servants. It was conceived by party politicians as an election manifesto pledge; it was not the product of an endless series of Cabinet committee meetings. The Deputy Leader, Ted Short, and the Prime Minister's confidant, Lord Crowther-Hunt, were closely concerned with preparing the pledge. However, to turn the pledge into a detailed white paper, a bill, and then an Act of Parliament would require lengthy scrutiny within Whitehall and Parliament. The promoters of devolution were ill-prepared for that. The two white papers issued by the Labour government between the elections of 1974 only emphasized how much had yet to be done.

In seeking to introduce devolution, the Prime Minister faced two major obstacles. The first was the need to run the Whitehall obstacle race. Within Whitehall, devolution had few friends. It was sure to disturb the existing powers and status of the Scottish Office and the Welsh Office. Hence, many leading politicians, including William Ross, the Secretary of State for Scotland, were initially opposed to the very principle. From the perspective of functional ministries, devolution was an irrelevance because it was about territorial administration and not about the major functional problems of government. Insofar as devolution simply involved a reshuffling of tasks between the Scottish Office and a Scottish Assembly, or the Welsh Office and a Welsh Assembly, then ministers and officials in functional ministries tended to ignore the debate. But when devolution proposed changes that would affect their functional interests, then Whitehall departments were quick to defend their functional responsibilities against encroachment.

The Treasury was another powerful and critical participant in Whitehall discussions about devolution. It sought to enforce the strictest interpretation of the principle that nothing should be done to detract from the economic unity of the United Kingdom. To the Treasury, this meant that no revenue-raising powers should be granted to devolved Assemblies. The elected Assemblies might have the responsibility for determining public expenditure priorities, but they were to have far less power to raise money than elected local authorities. The Treasury's concern with constraining expenditure (a policy reinforced by watchful North of England Labour MPs who feared that devolution would give Scotland unwarranted revenue advantages), led it to scrutinize sceptically any measures with implications for public expenditure in Scotland or Wales.

While ministers were prepared to accept devolution as a commitment in principle, they were not prepared to concede anything of importance from their own departments. The mood was captured by the comment of the *Observer's* political correspondent, Alan Watkins:

> I have yet to meet a single minister who actively and positively wants devolution at all. Instead, a variety of justifications or explanations is produced; that the alternative is the complete loss of Scotland to the Labour Party, even to Britain; that it is useless to argue with the inevitable; that the party entered into a rash commitment which cannot now be escaped; that events acquire their own momentum.[43]

Civil servants, as the head of the devolution team, Sir John Garlick, noted, "were closer to the details than busy ministers and more conscious, therefore, of the pitfalls." Lord Crowther-Hunt dismissed the inevitable difficulties raised by civil servants thus: "The hostility of civil servants simply reflected the hostility of most ministers and of Parliament."[44]

The dominant ethos of the Cabinet was revealed in the November 1975 devolution white paper, *Our Changing Democracy,* which embodied in detail what was (and was not) to be devolved to Scotland and Wales, and how devolved Assemblies were meant to operate under Westminster's authority. It started from the assumption that "the fact that our democratic institutions have been admirably stable over a long period does not mean that they are perfect." It proposed to develop and adapt these institutions while also maintaining the "political and economic unity of Great Britain." The anxiety of ministers and Parliament about devolved Assemblies assuming runaway powers was made evident by the number and variety of ways in which Westminster retained the power to veto Assembly measures on policy grounds, to annul them *ex post facto* or to issue overriding directives on policy.[45]

The 1975 devolution white paper was vulnerable to attack on two fronts. Opponents of devolution criticized it because it did not resolve the difficulties that the government's 1974 white paper had identified. Proponents of change such as the SNP, Plaid Cymru and the Liberals argued that little or no power was to be devolved to Scotland or Wales; Westminster was only delegating administrative tasks that it wanted to shed. Moreover, the tone of the white paper was offensive in Scotland and Wales because of the hectoring insistence upon the authority of the Mace. The tone was adopted to offer reassurance to Cabinet ministers afraid that the power of the Mace would be eroded by devolution.

The House of Commons was the second great obstacle to devolution. The very principle of devolution had many enemies in the Palace of Westminster. Devolution challenged the uniqueness of Parliament by giving legislative powers to a Scottish Assembly, and by giving representative status to a Welsh

Assembly. Proposals to strengthen the Assemblies by measures which MPs might regard as trespassing on their prerogatives were sure to meet opposition. MPs were also protective of symbols of the Mace. Representative bodies in Scotland and Wales were to be called Assemblies rather then Parliaments to avoid criticism at Westminster. The title Parliament would have been symbolically more appealing in Scotland and Wales. Scottish and Welsh Labour MPs were also guarded about the prospect of competiton from a national Assembly. The great bulk followed the party line, voting for devolution, but they did not wish to leave Westminster for membership in an "inferior" national Assembly.[46]

Divisions about devolution within the Parliamentary Labour Party further complicated the passage of devolution through the Commons. On paper there was a solid majority for devolution. For a start, the government had an absolute majority of MPs. As that majority was threatened by erosion from by-election defeats, it could reasonably rely upon the votes or support by abstention from 13 Liberals and 14 Nationalist MPs who were confronted with supporting devolution as the only change on offer, even if less than they ideally wanted. Moreover, there was no reason to expect that all 12 Northern Ireland MPs would vote, and vote together against devolution, though most might do so if only to protest the exclusion of Northern Ireland from similar treatment. The 49 seats held by third parties in the 1974 Parliament complicated the parliamentary arithmetic of the opponents of devolution even more than that of the government. In a Commons in which 318 votes constituted a majority, the only party clearly opposed to Labour's devolution proposals, the Conservatives, could muster only 277 MPs — and even the Conservatives had a few "breakaway" supporters of devolution. As long as the Parliamentary Labour Party was united in support of a devolution bill, it was assured passage.

From the first, Labour whips warned the Prime Minister that support for devolution could not be delivered automatically. Divisions within the Labour Party in Scotland and Wales meant that there would be some abstentions or even votes against devolution by Scottish and Welsh Labour MPs. The majority of Labour MPs, representing English constituencies, were at best indifferent to the issue and thought it irrelevant to the major economic problems facing the country. But there were also suspicions that the Scots and the Welsh might be getting away with something. To compel attendance of these MPs at divisions risked stirring some to abstain or vote against this government measure. Abstentions or votes against the bill were costly, for devolution happened to be an unusual issue in which Labour MPs could vote in company with Conservatives against their own government without feeling that they were betraying the party's basic principles, for devolution was *not* a traditional Socialist prin-

ciple. Commitment to the bill was also affected by the fact that the original
proponent of devolution, Harold Wilson, had been succeeded by James Callaghan as Prime Minister. Sitting for a Welsh constituency since 1945, Callaghan
showed no interest in devolving government institutions to Wales.

The parliamentary debate on the Scotland and Wales devolution bill introduced in autumn 1976 moved at a snail's pace. The bill had a majority of
292 to 247 at the second reading debate on principle. More than 1000 amendments were put down to the bill. Antidevolution amendments came not only
from the Conservative opposition but even more from members of the Union
Flag group of Conservative backbenchers staunchly opposed to devolution.
The Liberals, Plaid Cymru and Scottish National parties also tabled large
numbers of amendments intended to increase the scope for devolution. The
government was caught in a crossfire between those who wanted more and
those who wanted less devolution. In response, the government announced
various concessions, including a referendum in Scotland and Wales, a demand
made by opponents of the bill who claimed that devolution was not really desired in Scotland or Wales. After ten days of debate, less than four clauses of
the bill had been dealt with, a rate of progress calculated to require two full
years of parliamentary sittings to secure passage.[47]

Because of the many obstructions to the Scotland and Wales bill, the Labour government moved a guillotine resolution to curtail debate. On 22 February 1977 the guillotine motion failed by 29 votes. The government lost the
bill, notwithstanding the support of 14 Nationalist and 2 Liberal MPs, because
22 Labour MPs voted against the guillotine, and two dozen more did not vote
at all. Except for 3 abstentions, the Conservatives voted solidly against. The
immediate reaction on government benches was a sigh of relief: A bill had
been introduced, and the great bulk of Labour MPs had voted for it. The government could claim that it had tried to introduce devolution legislation.

By a political fluke, devolution was given a new lease of life a month later
as the by-product of a pact between the Labour government and the Liberals,
negotiated at great speed and announced on 23 March 1977 when Labour
faced imminent parliamentary defeat. The Liberals had been in favour of devolution or a federal Britain for years, but had no specific proposals. The chief
document the Liberal leader had at hand was a sharp critique of the initial devolution bill by James Cornford, director of the Outer Circle Policy Unit, sug-
gesting more change than a Labour Cabinet would accept.

The political climate for devolution was transformed by the Lib-Lab pact.
Reintroduction of devolution was an imperative condition of the pact; the
Liberal leader, David Steel, was personally committed, and sat for a Scottish
seat.[48] The Labour government was committed to avoiding a general election

producing a likely Conservative (and Nationalist) landslide. From a constitutional point of view, the difficulties of the devolution bill remained, for "its failings derived not from its drafting, nor from the solutions worked out through hours of toil by skilled civil servants and parliamentary draftsmen, but from the principle of devolution itself."[49] The changes produced by the pact were not so much in the clauses of the bill as in the political impetus behind it. One Cabinet Office official concerned with devolution noted, "It's great to be working with a political imperative behind you." Whips told doubting Labour backbench MPs, "It's devolution or a general election."

In the event, the pact produced *both* Devolution Acts *and* a general election. But it did not produce devolution. Separate bills for Scotland and for Wales were introduced on 4 November 1977, and a guillotine was quickly voted by a majority of 26 for Scotland and 27 for Wales.[50] The government suffered defeat on a number of amendments, both in the Commons and the Lords. The most important was the amendment by George Cunningham, a Scots-born Labour MP sitting for a London constituency, requiring the Act to be referred back to the Commons if 40 percent of eligible electors did not approve it in a referendum. Debates were poorly attended; MPs who did not like the bill avoided the Commons chamber. The government secured their feet to tramp through the division lobby, but not their freely spoken consent. The separate Scotland and Wales bills each received the Royal Assent on 31 July 1978 with many clauses undebated by the Commons.

The devolution referendum in Wales confirmed unambiguously the doubts of ministers, civil servants and many MPs: 80 percent of Welsh votes opposed devolution. The Scottish result was ambiguous, dividing into three almost equal groups—those in favour, those against and the largest group, those not voting. Of those voting, 52 percent favoured devolution. Divisions among Labour voters deprived devolution of a solid majority. Whereas 95 percent of SNP voters cast their ballot for devolution and 79 percent of Conservatives against, only 68 percent of Labour voters favoured devolution.[51] If Labour voters had been as united in voting yes as Conservatives were in voting no, then the yes vote would have been 56 percent. If Labour voters had been as positive about devolution as SNP voters, the yes vote would have been 63 percent.

The government decided the referendum result was inadequate to justify implementing the Scotland Act—nor could it be confident that its own MPs would follow a Labour whip if it asked the Commons to vote for putting devolution into effect in Scotland. Nor did the Labour Party in Scotland, meeting at its annual conference in Perth ten days after the referendum, wish to press hard for devolution before a general election. With time running out—an election had to be held by October 1979 and the pact with the Liberals had expired

— the Prime Minister, James Callaghan, adopted stalling tactics rather than a clear government recommendation to Parliament about Scottish devolution.

Among supporters of devolution the referendum vote was sometimes discounted as simply reflecting the growing unpopularity of the Labour government. But this statement is special pleading by those who themselves favoured devolution. While it is true that devolution would have had more referendum support if Labour had been more popular and the Conservatives less at the time of the ballot, it is even more true that the devolution vote would have been higher if Labour voters, whatever their number, had been as pro-devolution as Conservative voters were anti-devolution. Moreover, the argument assumes that devolution was adopted because a Labour Cabinet wanted it, and Labour voters ought to follow their leaders. In fact, devolution was adopted because (and only because) a Labour Cabinet was told it was what the Scottish and Welsh voters wanted. This claim was supported by interpreting ambiguous opinion polls (cf. table 3.2) as evidence of a desire for the particular position between the status quo and independence taken by Labour's Devolution Acts. The referendum offered voters a single, unambiguous alternative — to vote for or against the only change on offer. Neither the Scottish nor the Welsh electorate showed the broad popular support for change claimed by supporters of devolution.

Appropriately enough, a Labour government sustained so long in office by its devolution pledge fell on a general motion of no confidence initiated by the Scottish National Party on 29 March. In addition to its own supporters, Labour attracted the support of three Welsh Nationalist, two breakaway Scottish Labour and two Ulster Unionist MPs. But the opposition attracted the vote of all the Scottish Nationalists and Liberals, as well as most Ulster MPs. The 3 May 1979 general election result was a clear victory for a Conservative Party that had conspicuously opposed the devolution acts, thus ending a process launched by the lack of a clear victory for Labour in February 1974.

The devolution controversy, for all its confusion, was primarily a controversy among Unionists. The opponents of devolution were traditional defenders of the Mace. The proponents of devolution did not argue against the authority of the Mace; instead, they argued that it was both possible and desirable to be flexible in wielding it. From a Nationalist perspective, devolution did not go far enough. But from the perspective of traditional Unionists it threatened to go too far. Because the Labour government shared with its opponents a desire to maintain the authority of the Mace, at almost every point at which a choice arose, it devolved less rather than more. Yet the little it offered was more than many were prepared to welcome, so strong had been the commitment to the Union as it was.

What Devolution Showed

The collapse of devolution in 1979 makes it very important to understand the significance of a sequence of confused events that were contradictory — Westminster both approved and repealed Devolution Acts within twelve months — and inconclusive about whether or not this collapse means that institutional change in Scotland and Wales will reemerge in the 1980s.

The devolution controversy demonstrated the supremacy of party political considerations in debates about constitutional change. Great principles *may* have been at stake, but more immediately the survival of the government of the day was at stake. Devolution was not on the agenda of Parliament when Labour and Conservative governments were securely in office from 1966 to 1974. Nor is it on the agenda since the Conservatives won a clear-cut victory in the 1979 election. It was on the agenda of Parliament from 1974 to 1979 because the government of the day reckoned that its stand on this issue would determine whether or not it continued in government. This is not necessarily wrong; politicians are meant to pay attention to election results. But it was a very problematic outcome of voting in 635 constituencies that gave the balance of power, albeit temporarily, to the Nationalists. Nor is there anything that the Nationalists (or the Unionists) in Scotland and Wales can do to make English votes so divide that their nation is given the notional balance of power again.

The Labour government's position accurately reflected views within the party; it was divided. The Labour government was prepared to pledge devolution when this was deemed necessary to secure electoral victory in 1974. Equally, the Labour government saw no need to confirm this commitment by strong whipping in the guillotine debate of 22 February 1977, when its future was not in jeopardy. A month later it made devolution first priority, when this was the price of a Liberal pact guaranteeing Labour another year or two in office. Once the devolution referendums were past, the Labour government refused to take a clear stand on Acts that it had pushed through Parliament the year before. Rather than risk asking his own badly divided Labour Party to vote on whether or not to repeal the Scotland Act, the Prime Minister preferred to be defeated in the Commons on a vote of confidence so vague that both Scottish Nationalists and Conservatives could vote together against Labour.

Even though they were not confirmed, the Devolution Acts merit careful scrutiny. They document in great detail what Westminster was willing to devolve consistent with the authority of the Mace, and what it was *not* willing to devolve. The exclusion of responsibilities from the Scottish and Welsh assemblies reveals the priorities of Westminster just as the functions devolved indicate what it could do without.

The devolution controversy showed that Westminster was relatively indifferent to the fate of the Scottish and Welsh Offices. Their concurrent jurisdiction has been accepted in Whitehall — yet their supersession or demise was readily contemplated by Cabinet colleagues as a consequence of devolution. Just as the powers of the Northern Ireland Office were acquired by transfer from Stormont, the great bulk of powers to be devolved to the Assemblies were the responsibility of the Scottish and Welsh Offices. The transferred powers included local government, housing, planning, other environmental services, all education except universities, and health and personal social services. In all, the Scottish Office was likely to lose 91 percent of its public expenditure responsibilities, and the Welsh Office 98 percent.[52]

Equally important, the devolution debate showed that Westminster protected the chief prerogatives of functional ministries. The Scottish and Welsh Assemblies were not meant to have any devolved powers in fields of uniform policy such as defence, foreign affairs or overseas aid. Equally important, they were to have little public expenditure responsibility in nationalized industries, trade, agriculture or the payment of income maintenance grants. Functional ministries did not want to give to the Assemblies responsibilities that had not already been given to the Scottish and Welsh Offices. Most important, the Treasury jealously guarded its near monopoly of taxation against claims to give the Assemblies revenue-raising power.

Ironically, if devolution had come about, the Assemblies would have been relatively *minor* deliverers of public goods and services in Scotland and Wales. The Scottish Assembly would have had less than 10,000 employees, compared to nearly 750,000 in local government, the health service, nationalized industries and other forms of public employment in Scotland. The Welsh Assembly would have had less than 2500 employees, compared to 415,000 in public institutions in Wales but outside the Assembly's direct control.[53] Equally important, the great bulk of money given by the Treasury to the Assemblies would *not* have been spent by the Assemblies. Upwards of 80 percent of Assembly revenue would have been passed on in grants to local authorities and health boards. In other words, the Assemblies were meant to be intermediate institutions between Westminster and major deliverers of public policies. Only by taking funds from the health service and local government could the Assemblies have gained significant scope for new expenditure themselves.

Economists have a catch phrase to describe the decision-making process used to produce the Devolution Acts: It is called a Pareto optimum solution. The defining attribute of a Pareto optimum decision process is that no action is taken unless it will make at least one person better off and leave no one worse off. Westminster was ready to devolve functions to a Scottish or Welsh Assembly — as long as this did not leave any Whitehall ministry feeling worse off.

Since the preparation of devolution legislation involved continuing consultation between Whitehall ministries (and there could be no representative of devolved bodies from Scotland or Wales), the outcome almost invariably protected Whitehall's interests as Whitehall ministers saw them.

In withholding powers from devolved Assemblies, Westminster showed what it regarded as central to maintaining the authority of the Mace. The Devolution Acts are thus important for what they did *not* contain.

1. *No political equality.* Westminster retained final authority over functions nominally transferred to the Assemblies. In the case of Wales, the Assembly was given no authority to enact legislation; like any local authority, it was to act only within the scope of Acts of the Westminster Parliament. In the case of Scotland, the Secretary of State for Scotland, accountable to Westminster rather than the Assembly, was to have "Viceroy" status, with the power, subject to parliamentary approval, to reject any bill, subordinate instrument or act of the Assembly on the grounds that it might affect Westminster negatively and was not in the public interest. Moreover, the Secretary of State was given the power to direct an Assembly to do things that it had not done. The result was to establish what one constitutional lawyer described as "one-way boundaries."

> It is clear that there is an outward limit to what the Scottish Assembly and Scottish Executive can do, without conversely setting an outward limit to what the British Parliament and British ministers can do.[54]

This comment, voiced as a complaint, could equally be regarded as a tribute to Parliament's determination to maintain the supremacy of the Mace over devolved institutions.

2. *No judicial equality.* This absence of any tradition of judicial review of Acts of Parliament made Westminster wary of introducing a court to resolve disputes between Parliament and an Assembly. Consistent with the doctrine of the Mace, it gave the Secretary of State powers to make determinations, *as judge and interested party,* subject only to endorsement by the high court of Parliament, which would not in any normal sense of the term exercise judicial review. There was also provision for the Secretary of State for Scotland to refer Assembly measures prior to enactment to the Judicial Committee of the Privy Council if he believed that they might be *ultra vires.* The Judicial Committee was also allowed to hear post-assent challenges. In effect the government of the day was to be able to ask for judicial nullification of measures and, if dissatisfied with a judicial decision, to use the power of the Mace to nullify an Assembly measure.

3. *No equality of treatment for the parts of Great Britain.* Because the devolution debate was conducted in Parliament, the bulk of the audience consisted of MPs for English constituencies. The great bulk of these MPs made evident by their speeches and actions that there was no demand for positive equality, that is, devolution to an English Assembly, or Assemblies for English regions.[55] Many English MPs were critical of devolution because they believed it would confer special advantages upon Scotland and Wales, including the retention of disproportionate representation at Westminster. The hostility was shown by English Labour MPs refusing to support the guillotine, as well as by the Conservative Party's whipped vote against the guillotine. Ironically, the Lord President of the Council, Michael Foot, told the Commons on 15 November 1977, shortly before introducing the second Devolution bill, that no step would be taken towards regionalism in England, in view of the fact that "a broad consensus of popular support . . . does not exist" — exactly what the referendums later revealed was also lacking for devolution in Scotland and Wales.[56]

4. *No symbolic equality.* Status involves intangible distinctions, and MPs are jealous guardians of status symbols. The elected bodies for Scotland and Wales were to be known as Assemblies, not Parliament; rectification of a mistake apparently made in establishing Stormont in 1921 and corrected by the 1973 Northern Ireland Assembly Act. The responsibility for carrying out government in Scotland was to be vested in a Scottish Executive (not a Cabinet), and its head was to be known as the First Secretary (not the Prime Minister of Scotland). In Wales the responsibility was to be vested in an Executive Committee of the Assembly, consisting of heads of the committees of the Assembly. Its chairman was to be known as the Assembly's leader, with a lowercase *l*.

5. *No grant of general powers.* Whereas the Government of Ireland Act gave Stormont broad grants of legislative authority except for powers reserved to Westminster, the Devolution Acts did not grant such powers to the Assemblies. The only functions they could claim were those explicitly transferred by the Acts. The limit to devolution was most obvious in Wales, which was left to administer Westminster Acts of Parliament. In Scotland, the power to legislate was transferred, but the functions transferred to the Assemblies were for the most part not capable of being administered without regard to the functions retained by Westminster. The resulting distribution of functional responsibilities was described by one reviewer as "the most difficult imaginable to operate."[57]

6. *No effective revenue-raising powers.* Transferring power to administer policies without power to raise money to pay for the policies severely constricts actions. This was specially so in the case of devolution, for the Assemblies were expected to continue financing all the major transferred programmes. The proposed review of expenditure on these programmes, taking need into account, might conceivably have resulted in a reduction in the total sum made available to the Scottish Assembly because of its successful previous use of political muscle (cf. table 6.4). The need to maintain economic unity was defined by the Treasury as the need to control *all* revenue-raising powers in *all* parts of the United Kingdom. The Treasury was unwilling to accept proposals for giving revenue-raising powers to the Assemblies, even though they would have had a very small effect on the United Kingdom economy as a whole. For example, a 10 percent variance in public finance by a Scottish Assembly would have been equal to about one-half of 1 percent of total government finance, and affected aggregate demand in the economy by even less. The proportions for Wales would have been even smaller. Nor did the Treasury want to engage in hypothecating a portion of oil revenue, regarding the potential benefits won by such a symbolic concession as less than the loss involved in departing from uniformity. The Acts opted for a block grant from the Treasury, subject to quadrennial review, and certain to involve continuing Treasury surveillance of Assembly spending.

7. *No control of its own civil service.* Given the preeminence of the civil service in the conduct of central government, it was particularly noteworthy that the Devolution Acts did not follow the Royal Commission recommendation for separate Assembly civil services. The Northern Ireland civil service provided a positive precedent. With close ties with trade unions, especially in Scotland and Wales, the Labour government was in a good position to feel the weight of public-sector unions' opposition to devolution, perceived as a potential threat to British wage standards. The decision to maintain a single civil service meant that senior officials serving Welsh and Scottish Assemblies could have had their promotions determined in Whitehall, or even be transferred to Whitehall. The devolved institutions would thus have had less control over their personnel than local authorities or a nationalized industry.

In promoting devolution, the government invariably referred to its aim as "maintaining the economic and political unity of the United Kingdom." In presentation, devolution was intended to adapt Union, and adapt it within bounds acceptable to Westminster. But MPs were not convinced. The first clause of the 1977 Devolution bill rhetorically asserted that nothing in it was meant to "affect the unity of the United Kingdom or the supreme authority of Parliament." Sceptical MPs threw this clause out by a vote of 199 to 84.[58]

By definition, the institutions of devolution were untested when enacted. The consequences of acts do not always match the professed or latent expectations of their proposers, and the consequences could only have become fully evident after a lengthy period of implementation. The Devolution Acts would only have been the start of a process. The future would reveal what could only be conjectural on enactment.

Because the Devolution Acts were constitutional acts, they laid down rules by which politics should proceed; they could not, however, control the political outcomes under these rules. There were many areas of uncertainty within the rules established by the Devolution Acts. These included the position of the territorial Secretaries of State in Cabinet and their relations with elected heads of the devolved Assemblies; the relationship of Whitehall ministries and civil servants with their functional counterparts working for devolved Assemblies; the relationship between Westminster MPs and English MPs, as well as with Assembly representatives elected by the same constituencies; negotiating the block grant of Assembly finance, and determining grants to the local authorities within the jurisdiction of the Assemblies; and procedures for carrying out policies where responsibility was divided between Whitehall and the Assemblies.[59]

The biggest uncertainty of devolution could not have been solved by legislation: whether and how competing claims of representative legitimacy would be resolved. Devolution would have created Scottish and Welsh institutions with the authority of a national Assembly elected independent of Westminster. An Assembly would not have been the legal spokesman for the Scottish or Welsh nation, but it could have claimed to be a legitimate spokesman. In a conflict of wills, Westminster would have appealed to loyalty to the *British* government and Nationalists to loyalty to the *Scottish* or *Welsh* government. The outcome of such an appeal could not be determined simply by the Mace. In Bogdanor's phrase, the Assemblies could have been "a weapon in the hands of the Scots and Welsh, and just as one cannot be sure that a weapon will only be used for the specified purposes for which it was given, so also one cannot predict the use which the Scots and Welsh would make of devolution."[60]

Friction could have been avoided only if the same party were in control of Westminster and the Scottish and Welsh Assemblies. The adoption of the first past the post simple plurality electoral system for the Assemblies was intended to protect Labour's chances of securing a majority of Assembly seats, just as adoption of the Devolution Act was intended to secure Labour's majority at Westminster.[61] Only in Wales could Labour have reasonably expected to have won a majority of Assembly seats on a regular basis. (Cf. the Cameron Commission's strictures about the dangers of a "complacent and insensitive" one-party system, made in the course of an investigation of Northern Ireland.[62]) In Scotland the 1974 election results made it uncertain whether any party would have won an Assembly majority, and especially whether Labour could have repeatedly secured a majority or whether the Scottish National Party would sooner or later win an Assembly majority, if only as the electorate reacted against the party in office. The 1979 general election result illustrates the potential for conflict between a Conservative government in Westminster and Labour-controlled Assemblies in Scotland and Wales.

The possible consequences of devolution would have ranged from success as Westminster intended to the break up of Great Britain and national independence for Scotland and/or Wales.[63] Westminster hoped that elected Assemblies would undercut support for the Nationalist parties. The relations between the Assemblies and Westminster were hoped to involve no more conflict than bargaining between central and local government. Given the continual souring of central-local government relations in recent years and the defects of the Devolution Acts, relations between the Assemblies and Westminster could have led to "rancorous stalemate," or even to reactive centralism, with public opinion and MPs attacking the Assemblies as the cause of problems and demanding a return to the status quo ante. Some proponents of devolution hoped that friction would produce structural reform beyond what Westminster intended. Elected Assemblies might have used their legitimacy to claim greater powers than Westminster intended, leading to federalism by trial and error. The "slippery slope" theory saw devolution leading to independence whenever a Nationalist party gained a majority or by the conversion of most Assembly members into *de facto* Nationalists as a consequence of problems of working with Westminster.

The unpredictable and uncontrollable aspects of devolution gave rise to anxieties among both supporters and opponents of the Acts. Some MPs who voted for devolution feared that it *might* at some future date lead to the break-up of Great Britain. Reciprocally, some Nationalists who voted for devolution feared that it might *not* be a staging post to independence. Some supporters and opponents of devolution were bound to have had their hopes or fears contradicted by events had devolution been put into effect. The authority of the Mace is great, but it is not proof against every possible eventuality.

NOTES

1. Walter Bagehot, *Physics and Politics* (London: H.S. King, 1872).
2. See William B. Gwyn, "Jeremiahs and Pragmatists: Perceptions of British Decline" in Gwyn and Richard Rose, eds., *Britain—Progress and Decline* (London: Macmillan, 1980), pp. 1-25.
3. Proponents of devolution usually argued that it involved adaptation to maintain Westminster's overriding authority. But on the scale of unanticipated changes likely to result, see chapter 9.
4. For contrasting views, see J.J. Harbinson, *The Ulster Unionist Party 1882-1973* (Belfast: Blackstaff Press, 1973); Patrick Buckland, *The Factory of Grievances: Devolved Government in Northern Ireland 1921-39* (Dublin: Gill & Macmillan, 1979); and Paul Bew, Peter Gibbon and Henry Patterson, *The State in Northern Ireland, 1921-72* (Manchester: Manchester University Press, 1979).
5. See Ian Thomas, *The Creation of the Welsh Office: Conflicting Purposes in Institutional Change* (Glasgow: University of Strathclyde Studies in Public Policy No. 91, 1981)
6. See J.M. Ross, *The Secretary of State for Scotland and the Scottish Office* (Glasgow: University of Strathclyde Studies in Public Policy No. 87, 1981).
7. Alan Butt Philip, *The Welsh Question* (Cardiff: University of Wales Press, 1975), p. 17.
8. For accounts of Scottish nationalism when it was weak, see H.J. Hanham, *Scottish Nationalism* (London: Faber & Faber, 1969), chaps. 6-8; and Jack Brand, *The National Movement in Scotland* (London: Routledge & Kegan Paul, 1978), chaps. 11-13.
9. On vote totals, see F.W.S. Craig, *Minor Parties at British General Elections, 1885-1974* (London: Macmillan, 1975); and Richard Rose and Ian McAllister, *United Kingdom Facts* (London: Macmillan, 1982), chap. 4.
10. *British Labour Statistics: Historical Abstract, 1886-1968* (London: HMSO, 1971), tables 110, 162.
11. See, especially, House of Commons, *Debates,* vol. 257, col. 1053 (6 October 1931) for the views of Clydesiders, and vol. 293, col. 1987 (14 November 1934) for Welsh MPs.
12. See Harold Wilson, *The Labour Government 1964-70* (Harmondsworth: Penguin, 1974), p. 485.
13. House of Commons, *Debates* (Written Answer), vol. 756, col. 49.
14. For discussions that are not reliable as fact but indicative of the mood of a minister, see R.H.S. Crossman, *The Diaries of a Cabinet Minister* (London: Hamish Hamilton & Jonathan Cape), vol. 2 (1976), vol. 3 (1977), passim. For an opponent, see Tam Dalyell, *Devolution: The End of Britain* (London: Jonathan Cape, 1977), pp. 8ff.
15. See Royal Commission on the Constitution, *Report,* p. vi.
16. House of Commons, *Debates,* vol. 772, col. 36 (30 October 1968).
17. See *The Government of Scotland* (Glasgow: The Labour Party, Scottish Council, 1970), p. 1; and Royal Commission on the Constitution, *Min-*

utes of Evidence IV: Scotland (London: HMSO, 4 May 1970), p. 28, a statement by J.D. Pollock.

18. Royal Commission on the Constitution, *Minutes of Evidence V: Wales* (London: HMSO, 26 January 1970), p. 12.

19. F.W.S. Craig, *British General Election Manifestos 1900-1974* (London: Macmillan, 1975), p. 360.

20. For background, see Geoffrey Smith's articles "The Conservative Commitment to Devolution" and "Devolution and Not Saying What You Mean," *The Spectator,* 19 February 1977 and 26 February 1977.

21. Royal Commission on the Constitution, *Report,* p. 165.

22. Ibid., p. 8.

23. House of Commons, *Debates,* vol. 863, col. 164 (31 October 1973).

24. For an overview, see Richard Rose, *Governing without Consensus* (London: Faber & Faber, 1971). For contrasting assessments, see Thomas Wilson, ed., *Ulster Under Home Rule* (London: Oxford University Press, 1955); and Michael Farrell, *Northern Ireland the Orange State* (London: Pluto Press, 1976).

25. See Richard Rose, "On the Priorities of Citizenship in the Deep South and Northern Ireland," *Journal of Politics* 36, no. 2 (1976): 247-91.

26. See Rose and McAllister, *United Kingdom Facts,* table 4.13.

27. James Callaghan, *A House Divided* (London: Collins, 1973), p. 15.

28. Douglas Hurd, *An End to Promises* (London: Collins, 1979), p. 102.

29. Reginald Maudling, *Memoirs* (London: Sidgwick and Jackson, 1978), p. 185.

30. See the revealing account by Robert Fisk, *The Point of No Return: The Strike Which Broke the British in Ulster* (London: Andre Deutsch, 1975).

31. For full documentation of the following paragraphs, see the source from which it is drawn, Richard Rose, "Is the United Kingdom a State? Northern Ireland as a Test Case," in Peter Madgwick and Richard Rose, eds., *The Territorial Dimension in United Kingdom Politics* (London: Macmillan, 1982). On noncontroversial policies, see Derek Birrell and Alan Murie, *Policy and Government in Northern Ireland* (Dublin: Gill & Macmillan, 1980).

32. Whitelaw's comments to a preelection press conference held at Conservative Central Office are taken from the author's shorthand notes.

33. The poll *may* be held every decade. It will be revealing to see what Westminster does in 1983 when once again the time comes to allow the Ulster Unionists to register their commitment to maintaining the United Kingdom.

34. Joe Haines, *The Politics of Power* (London: Jonathan Cape, 1977), p. 116.

35. Cf. W.L. Miller et al., "The Connection between SNP Voting and the Demand for Scottish Self-Government," *European Journal of Political Research* 5, no. 1 (1977): 83-102.

36. Figures from a February 1974 MORI survey. For a trend report, see Rose and McAllister, *United Kingdom Facts,* p. 117.

37. This is not unusual. The same is true of debates about electoral reform. See D.E. Butler, "Modifying Electoral Arrangements," in D.E. Butler and

A.H. Halsey, *Policy and Politics* (London: Macmillan, 1978), pp. 13-21. The same is also true about regional changes in France and Italy; see Peter Gourevitch, "Reforming the Napoleonic State," in *Territorial Politics in Industrial Nations,* ed. Sidney Tarrow, Peter J. Katzenstein and Luigi Graziano (New York: Praeger, 1978), p. 54.

38. See Tom James, "Labour Fear Loss of 13 Seats to SNP," *The Scotsman,* 9 July 1974.

39. Cf. Tam Dalyell, *Devolution: The End of Britain* (London: Jonathan Cape, 1977); H.M. Drucker and Gordon Brown, *The Politics of Nationalism and Devolution* (London: Longman, 1980), chaps. 7-8; John Osmond, *Creative Conflict: the Politics of Welsh Devolution* (Llandysul: Gomer, and London: Routledge and Kegan Paul, 1977), chap. 3.

40. *Democracy and Devolution: Proposals for Scotland and Wales* (London: HMSO, Cmnd. 5732, 1974), p. 2.

41. Ibid., pp. 11, 8.

42. Barbara Castle, *The Castle Diaries, 1974-76* (London: Weidenfeld and Nicolson, 1980), entry for 12 September 1974 at p. 179.

43. Quoted in Dalyell, *Devolution,* p. 41.

44. Cf. Peter Hennessy's interview with Sir John Garlick, "The Devolution Effort 'was all worthwhile,'" *The Times,* 16 May 1981; Peter Kellner and Lord Crowther-Hunt, *The Civil Servants* (London: Macdonald, 1980), p. 235; and, Castle, *The Castle Diaries, 1974-76,* pp. 281-83.

45. *Our Changing Democracy: Devolution to Scotland and Wales* (London: HMSO, Cmnd. 6348, 1975), pp. 13, 16.

46. Ruth Wishart, "It's Make Your Mind Up Time," *Sunday Mail* (Glasgow), 14 January 1979; and William Mishler and Anthony Mughan, "Representing the Celtic Fringe," *Legislative Studies Quarterly* 3, no. 3 (1978): 400.

47. Grant Jordan, *The Committee Stage of the Scotland and Wales Bill, 1976-77* (Edinburgh: University of Edinburgh Waverley Papers No. 1, 1978), p. 17.

48. David Steel, *A House Divided* (London: Weidenfeld and Nicolson, 1980), chap. 8.

49. Alistair Michie and Simon Hoggart, *The Pact: The Inside Story of the Lib-Lab Government, 1977-78* (London: Quartet, 1978), p. 117. The Acts approved by Parliament in 1978 were technically improvements upon proposals outlined in the 1975 white paper, and differed in detail—but not on the points of principle important here.

50. For a discussion of the progress of these Acts, see I. F. Burton and G. Drewry, "Public Legislation: A Survey of the Sessions 1977/78 and 1978/79," *Parliamentary Affairs* 33, no. 2 (1980): 174-86.

51. Calculated from data in J.A. Brand "The 'No' Road from Devolution" (University of Strathclyde, Strathclyde Area Survey, unpublished paper, 1980), table 1, applied to party shares of vote at the May 1979 election.

52. Calculated from Cmnd. 7439 (1979), tables 4.1, 4.2, 4.5.1, 4.3, 4.4, 4.5.2, 12; and House of Commons, *Debates,* vol. 974, col. 515 (26 November 1979).

53. See Richard Parry, *The Territorial Dimension in United Kingdom Public Employment,* (Glasgow: University of Strathclyde Studies in Public Policy No. 62, 1980), table 1.
54. Neil MacCormick, "Constitutional Points," in *Scotland—The Framework for Change,* ed. Donald I. MacKay (Edinburgh: Paul Harris, 1979), p. 56.
55. Bogdanor, *Devolution,* pp. 210ff.
56. House of Commons, *Debates,* vol. 939, col. 108-9 (Written Answer).
57. Carol Craig, "The Powers of the Scottish Assembly and its Executive," in MacKay, *Scotland—The Framework for Change,* p. 26.
58. House of Commons, *Debates,* vol. 939, col. 1397-1402 (22 November 1977).
59. See, e.g. Vernon Bogdanor, *Devolution,* chaps. 7-8; MacKay, *Scotland—The Framework for Change;* and Lewis Gunn, "Devolution: A Scottish View," *Political Quarterly,* 48, no. 2 (1977): 129-39.
60. Bogdanor, *Devolution,* p. 215.
61. The rejection of proportional representation for Scottish and Welsh Assemblies, after this electoral system had been imposed in Northern Ireland, was an indication of the alienation of Westminster from Northern Ireland. An "un-British" electoral system could be imposed in Northern Ireland because whatever was done there is not taken as a precedent for politics in Great Britain.
62. The Cameron Commission, *Disturbances in Northern Ireland* (Belfast: HMSO, Cmnd. 532, 1969), p. 12.
63. See Richard Rose, "The Options for Constitutional Unity in Great Britain Today," in *Conference Papers* (Sunningdale Park, Berks.: Rowntree Devolution Conference, May 1976), pp. 23-24.

9. The Contingency of Concurring Consent

The United Kingdom is held together by contingent and concurring consent. It is contingent because the maintenance of legitimate authority cannot be taken for granted by any government; almost daily there are reports of challenges to authority in some part of the world. Nor can representative Western governments assume that they have a divine right to consent. The history of Ireland under the Crown is a pointed reminder that consent can be effectively withdrawn from institutions of the United Kingdom.

In a multinational Union each nation must continuously and separately affirm its consent if the Crown's territories are to remain intact and entire. It is not enough for the largest nation, England, to be committed to maintaining Union. Scotland, Wales and Northern Ireland must concur. If one partner refuses to concur, then the Union may be maintained—but by coercion, not consent. Nationalists, too, must seek consent for their views. As the Royal Commission on the Constitution noted: "For separation to succeed it must command the general support of the people concerned. If it is not widely supported it is a complete non-starter; if it has that support, then even the most serious economic obstacles will not be allowed to stand in its way."[1]

Consent is a variable, not a constant. The fact that the authority of the Crown is taken for granted—especially by those who exercise it—does not make it secure against all challenges. From a long enough historical perspective, almost any set of political institutions lacks permanence. The point is nicely put by the historian J. G. A. Pocock: "Future historians may find themselves writing of a 'Unionist' or even a 'British' period in the history of the peoples inhabiting the Atlantic archipelago, and locating it between a date in the thirteenth, the seventeenth or the nineteenth century, and a date in the twentieth or the twenty-first."[2]

Elections offer a standing reminder of the potential variability of consent in the United Kingdom. In Scotland and Wales, Nationalist parties campaign for votes with the argument that a vote for their cause will be a peaceful and democratic way of refusing consent to the United Kingdom, thus justifying their nation becoming independent. In Northern Ireland, elections produce a clear majority for Union, but the Nationalist minority can refuse consent by street demonstrations as well as ballots, and the Irish Republican Army by bullets as well.

A customary way to dismiss challenges to consent in Northern Ireland is to deny that Northern Ireland is "really" a part of the United Kingdom. The exceptionalist interpretation of the United Kingdom argues that "except for Northern Ireland" the United Kingdom, or at least Great Britain, has impregnable authority.[3] Northern Ireland is dismissed on the ground that the conditions there are very different from Great Britain. But to argue this is to imply that if conditions were the same in Great Britain as in Northern Ireland, then Westminster's consent would be equally challenged.

Any attempt to examine contingent challenges to consent in Great Britain must be speculative. Yet the speculation is worth indulging in order to demonstrate that the status quo, which seems so palpably stable because it is there, is a decreasingly likely probability the farther ahead one looks.[4] The possible breakthrough of the Scottish National Party or Plaid Cymru is one contingent way in which consent could be withdrawn. Nonterritorial groups can withdraw consent too. For example, in the "hot summer" of 1981 blacks in England turned to street demonstrations and riots. Northern Ireland has shown that when police try to maintain order in such circumstances, they cannot necessarily do so in ways satisfying all groups involved. In Northern Ireland the Catholic minority was said to be unable to trust the Royal Ulster Constabulary because only 11 percent of RUC members were Catholic in a society that was one-third Catholic. If that logic be true, then black distrust of police should be even higher in England and Wales. Whereas Catholics in the RUC were present in one-third their proportion of the population, in England and Wales the black numbers in the police forces have been only 6 percent of their share of the population.

The purpose of this concluding chapter is to identify the *contingent* characteristics sustaining Union. To identify the reasons why Union exists today is also to call attention to conditions in which the Union would be disrupted if these conditions were not sustained tomorrow. The first section examines a curious phenomenon: the unthinking maintenance of Union at Westminster. The second section considers the commitment to Union in Scotland, Wales and Northern Ireland, where Union is actively challenged. When consent is asymmetrical, it is more vulnerable to change.

Unthinking Union

Because words are the stuff of political discourse, it is easy to overlook the importance of ideas that are not verbalized. Yet in a country without a written

Constitution, what Sidney Low called "a system of tacit understandings" is particularly important. It is also true that because understandings are tacit, "the understandings are not always understood."[5] To govern with consent, the understandings must hold, whether explicit or tacit.

The Union is a good example of a tacit understanding of fundamental importance for the government of the United Kingdom. It is part of a shared political "tradition of activity."[6] Whatever the disputes of party politics, there is agreement about *where* disputes are to be resolved. Westminster is understood to be the sole and supreme authority for government in the United Kingdom. The idea of Union is implicit; it is nonetheless effective, given the authority of the Mace.

Nationalists have challenged Unionist politicians to defend explicitly what Unionists normally accept without thinking. In an unthinking Union, almost any action will sustain authority, whatever the degree of understanding. But in a Union under attack, it is not only necessary to act but also to be organized for action, and to understand the consequences of what is being done. When Nationalists challenged the Union in the 1970s, Westminster showed itself deficient in organizing policies on a basis likely to assure concurring consent.

When the challenge to the Union arose, it was very clear that something would have to be done. Yet it was never very clear *who* had the chief responsibility in defence of the United Kingdom. There is no special United Kingdom Office in Westminster. Nor, when challenge arose, did MPs or ministers wish to establish bodies representing the nations so that Scots, Welsh or Ulster people could deliberate about the institutions to which they would most like to give consent. Finding some way to deal with defence of the Union within Westminster was a necessity. Finding ways of consulting with nations within the United Kingdom in order to assure concurring consent was not regarded as necessary.

The evidence of disaffection necessary to catch Westminster's attention undermined the credibility of territorial politicians. As long as things had gone well, they could silently claim the benefit in Westminster of managing their territory well, on the ground that no news is good news. This was particularly the case in Northern Ireland, where Westminster wished for the benefits of autonomy in a dual polity. But once things were perceived as going wrong— whether because of civil rights demonstrations and police disorder or Nationalist victories in by-elections—then territorial ministers, as the responsible politicians, stood convicted of having mismanaged their nation's affairs.

When Westminster's attention is caught by an issue, leading politicians who have not taken an interest in the matter before will invariably show concern. This concern is not based upon prior knowledge or claims to expertise, but upon status. Big issues are what important politicians must attend to. This is particularly the case with the Prime Minister, who ex officio has responsibility for major issues for which there is no obvious ministerial home. But 10 Downing Street is far too small a place to sustain responsibility for day-to-day management of a policy. Novel institutional means may be employed to contain or handle ad hoc challenges.

In Northern Ireland the eruption of civil rights demonstrations in 1968 led to the issue being raised from the level of a part-time concern of one middle-rank Home Office official to the continuing involvement of the Home Secretary and the intermittent involvement of the Prime Minister. In 1972 responsibility was placed in the hands of a newly created Northern Ireland Office. But the Northern Ireland Office had two difficulties. First, it could not claim to represent any of the electorate of Northern Ireland, for neither the Conservative nor Labour parties nominated candidates or gained any votes there. Like a colonial governor, the Secretary of State for Northern Ireland could claim undoubted legal authority, but he could not claim popular consent as well. Second, the Northern Ireland Office could not necessarily rely upon other major ministries which also had interests in the province, such as the Ministry of Defence or the Foreign Office, to support its own position. This was most visibly demonstrated in the 1974 Ulster Workers' Council strike against the power-sharing regime established under NIO tutelage. The Westminster government was not prepared to commit troops in defence of this regime. The Prime Minister, Harold Wilson, became drawn in to the dispute by its magnitude, but he only inflamed matters. As in the 1965 Rhodesian crisis he ruled out the use of coercion, then gratuitously attacked the Unionist majority, thus ruling out conciliation as well.

When the Nationalist challenge came forward in Great Britain in 1974, the Prime Minister took the problem under his immediate responsibility. One reason was positive: Getting Scotland and Wales right—whatever the term was taken to mean—was seen as central to the government's electoral survival. Other reasons were negative. The governing party's own institutions were not trusted to reflect opinion, when they were palpably losing votes; from 1966 to February 1974 Labour's share of the vote in Scotland fell by 13 percent, and by 14 percent in Wales. Secretaries of State for Scotland and Wales were distrusted politically; the upsurge in Nationalist strength was interpreted as reflecting their failure to maintain a steady-state Britain.

Responsibility for preparing and piloting the Devolution bills through the House of Commons was placed in the hands of the Lord President of the Council, leader of the House of Commons, and deputy leader of the Labour Party,

Ted Short, succeeded by Michael Foot. The Lord President's Office used staff seconded to an ad hoc Cabinet Office Constitution Unit, known by the unfortunate acronym of COCU. This placed the making of policy on devolution close to the Prime Minister, who kept a continuing concern because of the tactical importance of devolution as part of the governing party's political strategy. These institutions also distanced control from territorial ministers. When it was suggested to a senior official that a Welsh or Scottish MP might be added to the Lord President's team preparing the Devolution bill, the response was, "That would be wrong. After all, he would be biased."[7]

From a Westminster perspective, devolution was viewed as a conventional Act of Parliament. But from the perspective of a multinational Union, the procedures were deficient because they ignored the need for concurring consent. The Westminster Parliament could claim to represent the whole electorate of the United Kingdom, but it could not equally represent each nation singly or be as well informed about conditions in each nation as a specially elected body for the nation. In a federal system, a central government has no choice but to negotiate with duly elected representatives of its constituent parts, whether these representatives are called Governors, provincial Premiers, or *Landesminister Präsidenten*.

Westminster's claim to deliver the concurring consent of both the whole of the United Kingdom and each national part has most obviously failed in Northern Ireland. From 1968 it proffered advice to successive leaders of the Unionist Party and used its superior status to make elected Ulster politicians follow lines laid down in Whitehall. The result was that each of the leaders — Terence O'Neill, James Chichester-Clark and Brian Faulkner — was in turn repudiated by his party, and by the majority of the Ulster electorate. The adoption of power sharing as Britain's preferred form of government for Northern Ireland was meant to institutionalize a voice for the minority in government. The logic of power sharing is government by a concurring majority. Power sharing failed because this concurrence was lacking; the majority repudiated the doctrine by consistently electing anti-power-sharing representatives from February 1974.

The most extreme expression of the unitary claims of the Mace occurred in Westminster's establishment of a Northern Ireland Constitutional Convention following the collapse in 1974 of power sharing in the face of the Ulster Workers' Council strike. Westminster had two broad choices: to lay down conditions about future government of the province, negotiating with politicians until it found a coalition that would accept Westminster's terms, *or* to call for the election of a representative Northern Ireland body that could fairly claim to give (or withhold) concurring consent, and negotiate with it.

In the event Westminster tried and failed in both. It called for the election of a Constitutional Convention to represent Ulster opinion, but said that it would accept only a report that endorsed what it wanted anyway, namely, power sharing. In the event, the Northern Ireland majority voted for what the majority wished, a return to a Westminster-style majority rule government at Stormont. Westminster then refused to parley with the body that it had created because it did what its electorate wished rather than what Westminster wished.

In Scotland and Wales, the Labour government could claim support by a majority of Members of Parliament from Scotland and Wales, but these MPs were elected to speak on functional not territorial issues. Hence, a vociferous bloc of MPs demanded that the Devolution bill be put to referendum to see whether the whipped votes for devolution at Westminster fairly represented voters' views there. In Wales, where the Labour Party's historic position was specially strong, it turned out to have misunderstood Welsh sentiment completely.[8] Whereas the institutions of the Labour Party in Wales unequivocally supported devolution, the Welsh electorate—including a majority of Labour voters in Wales—rejected devolution. In Scotland, while Labour could claim to be the largest single party in a four-party system, it had never won the support of a majority of voters. In the event, the 1974 Scottish Council of the Labour Party turned out to be very representative of public opinion in Scotland about devolution, for it divided almost equally into proponents and opponents of devolution.[9]

Within the customary conventions of Westminster government, there was no institution by which devolution could be dealt with jointly by Westminster and representatives of Scotland and Wales speaking as Scots or Welsh. It would have been impossible to refer the legislation to committees of Scots or Welsh MPs, given the implications of devolution for Westminster as a whole. Nor could Scottish or Welsh MPs have been asked to assemble as a sounding board, for they were divided by party loyalties into four different groups. Nor was the device adopted of a consultative Constitutional Convention involving the election of Scots or Welsh to deliberate in Edinburgh or Cardiff, as happened with Ulstermen in Belfast.

To think of the devolution debate as if all the participants were relating their actions to a single logical goal is to misunderstand the political process. While individuals may be more or less conscious of some of their motives, it does not follow that the collective consequences of intended *and* unintended actions will reflect any purposeful or coherent understanding of how the Union could or should work. One participant in the preparation of the Devolution Acts described it thus:

Imagine a policy being made like this. There is a group of people standing around in a circle with a large lump of dough in the middle. Each person throws stones at the dough, and hits it a variety of blows. The shape that the dough assumes is not the result of the intention of any one person. The result reflects the cumulative effect of all the blows that are struck by different people.[10]

In a sense, Westminster cannot be said to have handled devolution and changes in the government of Northern Ireland much differently from its handling of other important issues. Accidents of circumstance and personality are important in all forms of political decision making. So, too, is readiness to see short-term political advantages. Muddling through is an economical incremental method of decision making for dealing with ordinary small-scale problems. But revising a Constitution by unthinking means is another matter. Constitutions have consequences far beyond the horizons of everyday politicians, whether the people who make constitutional changes do so with forethought or unthinkingly.[11]

The Asymmetry of Commitment

To be committed to the United Kingdom one must realize that it is there. There is an asymmetry of commitment to the United Kingdom today because most people who live under the Union Jack do not realize what it stands for. Scots, Welsh and people in Northern Ireland are well aware of what the Union is. It is a multinational form of government, and a government to which the majority are loyal.

The bulk of Westminster politicians are English and indifferent Unionists. They are indifferent not because they dislike Union but because they do not think about it, and therefore have no emotional commitment for or against Union as do politicians in Scotland, Wales and Northern Ireland. The devolution debate aroused very little interest or anxiety among English politicians, even though it affected all participants in the Westminster system. MPs for English constituencies voted for or against devolution primarily on party, not national, lines. Moreover, there was no significant protest about England being excluded from a vote on devolution. A Gallup poll in autumn 1978 found that 68 percent of English, if voting in a referendum, would have voted against devolution.[12]

Westminster concentrates upon functional measures that are meant to promote good government throughout the whole territory of the kingdom. The logic of functional politics dictates that measures appropriate for one area should be applied uniformly or concurrently with a minimum of exceptionalist policies. Maintaining Union is meant to occur as an incidental by-product of functional policies.

Party competition is along functional lines. The chief functional concerns — unemployment, inflation and low rates of economic growth — are common to all nations of the United Kingdom. When challenges to the Union are raised, parties tend to interpret these challenges in functional terms, even when they are voiced as Nationalist demands. Economic explanation may not fit comfortably with the character of Nationalist politics, but the very prevalence of economic interpretations emphasized what people would *like* to believe about political activity in the United Kingdom. For example, Scottish and Welsh Nationalist parties tend to be ignored at Westminster because they do not fit into conventional class stereotypes. Yet attempts by Nationalists to encompass class politics by promoting movements or parties that are both Nationalist and Socialist invariably fail to win any significant electoral support.[13] At bottom Nationalism is not about good government or prosperity, although such benefits may incidentally be promised; it is about self-government.

Northern Ireland is the extreme example of the inability of Westminster politicians to conceive of politics along other than functional lines. The civil rights movement readily caught Westminster's attention because it was conceived as being about already familiar issues: unemployment and discrimination. The civil rights organizers took pains to omit any reference to Nationalist issues. The Unionists were thought odd precisely because they made the defence of the Union their overriding concern. Subsequent to the outbreak of armed revolt against the Crown, the conflict within the United Kingdom has been reinterpreted into a "colonial" struggle. The Irish Republican movement, by dividing on Socialist as well as Nationalist demands, has tested the relative appeal of a purely Republican movement (the Provisional IRA) as against a Republican Socialist movement (the Official IRA). The Provisional IRA's appeal, based solely upon traditional Republicanism, is far the stronger. The fewer the basic claims of a party, the wider its potential base for support.

The case for Westminster concentrating upon functional economic problems today is real. Economic difficulties appear chronic, and these are problems that plague all parts of the United Kingdom — and would also plague an independent England.[14] For two decades, successive Conservative and Labour Prime Ministers have unsuccessfully made economic growth their chief aim, and for two decades the economy has failed to grow as desired. In absolute terms, the people of the United Kingdom today enjoy a substantially higher material standard of living than in 1960, and differences between the nations of the United Kingdom are lessening. But the economy is not in as good a condition as the government would wish; secular increases in unemployment and inflation bear witness to this.

Politically, the first priority of any Westminster government is to improve (or at least, arrest the decline in) the economy. Doing this would strengthen popular satisfaction with government in all parts of the United Kingdom. It would not remove the challenge from Nationalists who oppose Westminster on noneconomic grounds. But it would encourage those who are committed to Union and wish to see it prosper economically as well as politically. To fail to arrest chronic economic difficulties need not weaken Union. In times of economic difficulties, relatively depressed areas—and Scotland, Wales and Northern Ireland all qualify under this rubric—can turn to Westminster to claim additional economic aid in the name of territorial justice.

The deterioration in the United Kingdom economy, *particularly the rise in unemployment, has been increasing similarities between the nations of the United Kingdom.* In the interwar period, there were great national differences in levels of unemployment. For example, in 1930, when United Kingdom unemployment overall (100) was 15 percent, the level in Scotland was 117, in Wales 172 and on a slightly different basis, 145 in Northern Ireland. At the height of postwar full employment, national differences were still high. For example, in 1951, when United Kingdom unemployment (100) averaged 1.3 percent, it was 192 in Scotland, 208 in Wales, and 469 in Northern Ireland.

As unemployment has increased greatly in size, cross-national differences have *decreased.* In 1979, when unemployment in the United Kingdom as a whole was 5.7 percent, the index level for Scotland was 138, for Wales 140, and for Northern Ireland, 198. By July 1981, when the overall level of unemployment had doubled to 11.8 percent, unemployment was rising relatively faster in England. In consequence, national differences lessened. Unemployment in Scotland fell to being 125 percent of the United Kingdom figure, in Wales to 119 percent and in Northern Ireland to 159 percent. Moreover in some regions of England, such as the North, unemployment was higher than in Scotland or Wales. Between 1979 and 1981, unemployment in the industrial centres of the West Midlands (120) and the North West (122) has "caught up" with Wales and Scotland.[15]

Another major functional priority at Westminster is restoring confidence in Westminster's institutions of governance. The decline in confidence is as much a concern in England as in other nations of the United Kingdom, and it affects party politics as well as public administration. In the 1970s the Liberals benefited from this loss of English self-confidence, just as Nationalists benefited in Scotland and Wales. In 1981 the Social Democratic Party break from the Labour Party and subsequent alliance with the Liberals shows a rising lack of confidence by those who have been leaders in the past. Putative policies for the United Kingdom of the centre Alliance are speculative in the extreme. Initially, the Social Democrats have talked about decentralization, but have said nothing to indicate that members who served in the Labour government that produced the Devolution Acts could or would produce anything likely to resolve the problems that the Acts did not resolve.

A Social Democratic-Liberal Party advance could have an important incidental impact upon the territorial dimension in politics. Insofar as it reflected a continuing rejection of the two major functional parties, this rejection could be capitalized upon by Nationalists in Scotland and Wales as well as by the centre Alliance. If the centre Alliance were to achieve its goal of proportional representation, this would reduce greatly the chances of Scots, Welsh or Ulster MPs holding the balance of power at Westminster, whether Nationalists or Unionists. In a proportional representation Parliament, instead of a party with a dozen or so seats holding the balance, as in 1974-79, a coalition government would pivot on alliances among four big parties—Conservatives, Liberals, Social Democrats and Labour. Inevitably, each of these parties would be dominated by its MPs from English constituencies, given the scale of representation that England deserves in a proportional representation Parliament.

The challenge to Unionism is asymmetrical. A party only contesting seats in Scotland, Wales or Northern Ireland is bound to appear small at Westminster, even though its influence may be great within one nation of the United Kingdom. Nationalists may simultaneously appear unimportant at Westminster yet important within their own nation. Yet any group that threatens to break the hold of the Union in one nation thereby threatens the United Kingdom as a whole.

Challenges to Union are most evident in Northern Ireland; the challenge today is greater than at any time since the Irish rising of 1916-21. The place of Northern Ireland within the United Kingdom is politically challenged by the Social Democratic and Labour Party, which argues that only "national" (i.e., 32-county) self-determination can end Northern Ireland's troubles by amalgamation in a United Ireland. The SDLP proclaims a willingness to wait for Unionists to give consent to a united Ireland, but it wishes steps in that direction to be taken sooner rather than later. The IRA carries on a guerrilla war against the British Army and Unionist forces with the intent of forcing the Westminster government to withdraw from what the IRA refers to as a part of Ireland, and what Westminster formally recognizes as a part of the United Kingdom. Sustaining this war for a decade has shown both the degree of tacit backing for the IRA among the Catholic minority and the limits of British military force in Ulster.[16] In response, Protestants have mobilized under arms in illegal loyalist defence associations to defend their position by all means necessary.

The novel element in the Ulster problem in the 1980s is the relative indifference of Westminster to the maintenance of the United Kingdom. Since 1972, Westminster has governed the province by a system of temporary direct rule. A constitutional status that rests upon an annually renewable Act of Parliament can hardly be considered the firmest of constitutional guarantees. Nor has Westminster shown any particular liking for this form of government. It has three times sought to end it, by establishing a power-sharing Executive in 1974, by the abortive 1975 Constitutional Convention, and by unilateral action in 1979-82. Direct rule, in the words of the Secretary of State for Northern Ireland, offers "absolutely minimal" opportunities for Ulster people to take responsibility for their own affairs.[17] Moreover, it maximizes the involvement of Westminster in the management of the most difficult to manage part of the United Kingdom.

Westminster is today only contingently committed to maintaining Northern Ireland as part of the United Kingdom. It declares that it will do so as long as the majority of the people of Northern Ireland wish to remain in the United Kingdom. To give a conditional commitment is to imply that the condition could be changed. It is just this that redoubles the commitment of the Protestant majority to forces that are unconditionally loyal to the Crown, but only conditionally ready to accept the authority of the Westminster Parliament. The conditional commitment also sustains proponents of a united Ireland in the belief that with just "one more heave" their ambition will be realized of the withdrawal of Great Britain from that territory which makes it the United Kingdom.

The very intensity of divisions within Northern Ireland sets limits to the extent of political change. The people of Northern Ireland know what the issues are, and their commitments are the commitments of generations, even centuries. Northern Ireland must be governed without consensus as long as these divisions persist. Since there are many different ways to govern without consensus, there is uncertainty about the particular form of institutions to contain conflict within the province. There is also an element of uncertainty about whether Westminster wishes to persist in governing without consensus or let that burden fall, by negotiation or default, to an independent Northern Ireland, which is *not* wanted by the people of Northern Ireland, or to a Dublin government which is not anxious to have a million potentially rebellious Protestants on its hands.

In Wales, language is a cultural difference that sustains union. Four-fifths of the population speak only English, identifying culturally as Welsh but politically as Unionists. The distinctive political trait of people who see themselves as Welsh is voting for the British Labour Party. Equally important, among that fifth of the population speaking Welsh, the majority also vote for Unionist parties. Among the most distinctively Welsh group — those both speaking Welsh and identifying themselves as Welsh — 53 percent were against devolution at the 1979 referendum and 78 percent voted for Unionist parties.[18] There is no more a contradiction between speaking Welsh and being British than there is in speaking English and being British.

There remains a world of difference between speaking Welsh and speaking English, especially in matters involving government. The political implications depend upon the policy adopted. For example, the present Westminster policy is to encourage the maintenance of Welsh or learning Welsh — as long as this does not place English-speakers at a disadvantage or lead to exceptional costs or measures that would not be tolerated by Parliament, such as persistent discrimination against non-Welsh-speakers in employment or compulsory education in Welsh.[19]

For Welsh-speakers who make the language their first political concern, the central question is how to protect the language. The question is particularly pointed in the 1980s, for the decline of Welsh-speaking has reached a point where the critical mass of people needed to keep it a language in daily use has been continuously eroded and now can be found only in rural, remote and underpopulated parts of Wales. Because Welsh is now very much a minority language, any political party that promotes bilingualism risks alienating the majority of Welsh people. Plaid Cymru does make safeguarding the Welsh language and culture one of its principal aims. And it is very much a minority party, polling one-tenth or less of the Welsh vote. Plaid Cymru is itself divided about how to respond to its electoral weakness; there are culturally exclusive "fortress" and "militant cultural" Nationalists, and politically extroverted supporters of a modernizing Welsh nation.[20]

In Wales today the strongest challenge to the authority of the Mace is likely to come from extraconstitutional direct action protests by proponents of the Welsh language. The logic is simple: "To try to do things constitutionally has got them nowhere."[21] Nor does it promise success in future. Direct action takes a variety of forms, particularly violence against property (e.g., burning the holiday homes owned by non-Welsh-speakers in predominantly Welsh-speaking areas) and symbolic violations of the law (e.g., refusing to fill in government forms not printed in Welsh as well as English). The Westminster government's reaction has been to minimize the extent of unlawful challenges to its authority in an attempt to defuse protests. In 1980 the leader of Plaid Cymru (and loser of his Carmarthen seat in the 1979 general election), Gwynfor Evans, threatened a hunger strike to death in protest against the Conservative government's refusal to allocate one television channel in the principality exclusively for Welsh-language programmes. In the face of Gwynfor Evans's hunger strike, the government gave in, reversing a position which was itself a reversal of a May 1979 manifesto pledge. If challenges escalate, the government would not find it easy to meet all the major demands of Welsh language speakers, for some demands would mobilize opposition from the majority of Welsh people (e.g., if promoting compulsory bilingualism was at their expense).

In Scotland there is a much clearer commitment to Union than there is agreement about what is the best way to provide government within the Union. The challenge of the Scottish Nationalists has produced a significant SNP vote — but it has also shown that British parties have the support of upwards of five-sixths of the Scottish electorate. Even though the SNP eschews identification with minority cultural interests, such as the Gaelic language, it is a minority within Scotland — even among persons who identify themselves as Scots. The potentially inclusive character of the SNP appeal has not achieved the "national" majority it seeks. Instead, it has made the SNP a second- or last-choice party for most Scots. Equally important, there is a very strong commitment to constitutional politics among more than 90 percent of Scots, and this support is found in all parties, including the SNP.[22]

Scots divide into three broad groups in their views about how Scotland ought to be governed. One group consists of unalloyed Unionists, who wish to leave things as they are. A second category consists of persons who wish to adapt institutions within the Union, whether along lines of the 1978 Scotland Act, which was acceptable to Westminster, or along federalist lines unacceptable to Westminster but still consistent with Union. The third and smallest group consists of Scots who wish independence. No one group has a clear and persisting majority. The confusion in Scottish politics in the 1970s arose from the sudden emergence of a visible political force pledged to independence — and the limited extent of the support that was mobilized for devolution in the 1979 referendum.

Instability is the most significant characteristic of Scottish opinion. The bulk of postwar general election results offers clear testimony to the readiness of Scots to give exclusive support to functional British parties. Support for the SNP could decline to a very low level in default of the "hard core" commitment available to the SDLP or Plaid Cymru, with their well-defined social bases. On the other hand, the support for the SNP could rise rapidly and unexpectedly. Since it is not identified with a divisive minority within Scottish society, there is no ceiling on possible SNP support. As long as the SNP can remain a middle-of-the-road "catchall" party on all issues except independence, it has the potential to gain from an electoral protest against the established (and British) parties.

The consistent conclusion from any appraisal of challenges to Union is that popular commitment to the Union is much the stronger. The very novelty of the Nationalists gives them a disproportionate amount of attention. This is *a fortiori* true in the media of Scotland, Wales and Northern Ireland, which thus differentiate their reporting from conventional Westminster-oriented reporting. The importance of the Unionist commitment is greatest yet most overlooked in Northern Ireland. The Catholic minority has been the subject of countless journalistic and academic studies; a disproportionate amount of attention has been focused, too, on politically ineffective bi-confessional groups, such as the Peace People. There has been consistent neglect of the political views of people committed to maintaining the United Kingdom, people who hold the preponderance of votes, and of guns, in the province.

The principle of concurring consent rests upon a pair of contingent conditions. The first is that Unionists will continue to be the dominant political force in Scotland, Wales and Northern Ireland. *Unionists are politicians for whom protecting the Union is a first claim upon loyalty.* It is a binding and continuing constraint upon everything they do, and not just an ad hoc position adopted after calculating its utility for the moment. A Unionist is a politician who wants to make the government of the United Kingdom work as well as it can, and *above all,* to make sure that it remains the government of a United Kingdom. The conscious commitment of Scottish, Welsh and most Ulster politicians to Unionism confines disputes about policy to issues that can be accommodated within the Union. In any dispute that arises with territorial implications, Unionists have a prior premise: Any differences should be settled in ways consistent with maintaining the territorial integrity of the United Kingdom.

Unionist politicians are concerned with both functional and territorial interests. Most of their time may be devoted to pursuing functional interests, but this is done in ways consistent with maintaining the United Kingdom. National circumstances may provide a specific argument for national advantage. For example, arguments from need have led to higher public expenditure in Scotland, Wales and Northern Ireland than in England. But at times Unionist politicians must accept decisions taken at Westminster on grounds that they may consider against their particular nation's interest, for example, the decision of Britain to enter the European Community. Whereas at every opportunity a Nationalist promotes conflicts between the nations of the United Kingdom, a Unionist will avoid such issues, even at some cost, if dispute is perceived as leading toward the "slippery slope" ending in independence.

To maintain a concurring majority in support of the United Kingdom is a continuing concern of Unionist politicians. It must be so, for nearly every major issue permits an alternative Nationalist solution. In Northern Ireland opponents of Union have continuously been organized and ready to state the case against Union. In Scotland and Wales, Nationalists have been visible and articulate critics of Union and Unionists for decades. Defending the United Kingdom when it is under attack requires a conscious and articulate commitment; Scots, Welsh and Ulster politicians cannot afford the luxury of unthinking Unionism.

The second condition for concurring consent is that unthinking Unionism at Westminster will not unintentionally lead to actions that undermine the position of Unionists within the nations of the United Kingdom. By definition, unthinking Unionism will not initiate overt challenges to the Union, for the minds of such politicians will not be directed toward it. But unthinking Unionists could unintentionally create trouble for Union. This could arise as the unintended by-product of functional policies adopted in ignorance of their territorial implications. Or it could occur as a consequence of politicians being forced to think about the Union when they had never thought about it before. On past record, Unionists cannot be sure whether Westminster would know how to judge if the Union comes under threat, and whether it would discriminate effectively between Unionist allies and their implacable Nationalist opponents.

The devolution debate at Westminster, like the challenge of Republican violence in Northern Ireland, has shown that Westminster does not put commitment to the Union first. For example, the policy of the 1974-79 Labour government was to maintain the Labour government.[23] It showed this by the way in which it adopted devolution as an electoral policy without regard to its constitutional consequences; by the way in which it backed and filled in the House of Commons in accord with the needs of parliamentary tactics, and by adopting a system of election to the assemblies that gave Nationalist parties the maximum chance of securing a majority in the event of an electoral swing of the pendulum against Labour.

The outbreak of IRA violence in Northern Ireland has also demonstrated that Westminster does not put the Union first. The primary goal at Westminster appears to be the physical security of Great Britain, that is, the avoidance of any actions that would cause the violence in Northern Ireland to spill over into other parts of the United Kingdom. This policy is paralleled by the Irish government not putting Irish unity first, but rather seeking to avoid violence spilling over from the six counties of Northern Ireland to the twenty-six counties of the Republic.

Even if it recognized a challenge to Union, there is no evidence that Westminster would have at hand the institutions or the knowledge to respond. The devolution debate demonstrated how badly organized Westminster is to deal with questions that affect the integrity of Union. This is understandable, given Parliament's conception of itself as the sole representative body in the United Kingdom. But it is ironic that Conservative and Labour politicians and Whitehall civil servants can more easily parley with representatives of an institution pledged to break up the United Kingdom, the Irish Republican Army, than find a means to dialogue with politicians elected specifically to represent Scotland or Wales in a constitutional convention. Without such a dialogue, there can be no assurance that commitments made unilaterally at Westminster would have concurring consent. Such a dialogue is normal in a federal system, but in the singular domain of the Crown, there can be no reciprocity between an entity and a nonentity.

The United Kingdom today is held together by asymmetrical commitments. As long as Westminster has an unthinking awareness of Union, its commitment is bound to be weaker and less informed than that of politicians whose adherence to Union as well as national loyalties are repeatedly tested by the challenge of Nationalists. As long as the majority of people in Scotland, Wales or Northern Ireland wish the United Kingdom to continue and elect representatives expressing these views, the Union can be sustained by asymmetrical commitment. The fight to maintain the United Kingdom is not between Westminster and Nationalist challengers; by definition, consent will be given at Westminster and withheld by Nationalists. The decisive conflict is between Nationalists and people with dual loyalties to their nation *and* to the United Kingdom; the latter face a continuing choice between reaffirming Unionism or endorsing an exclusive Nationalism. The fact that dual loyalties rather than Nationalism has predominated does not make it any less contingent.

Political authority is not to be won once and for all, like a victory in some distant battle of the past. Instead, it must be reaffirmed every day. In the largest part of the United Kingdom, this reaffirmation occurs *faute de mieux* in the absence of any real challenge. In Scotland, Wales and Northern Ireland, consent is active but not inevitable. It requires renewal by the conscious commitment of Unionist politicians and by actions at Westminster that do not undermine the commitment of Unionists to maintaining the United Kingdom.

NOTES

1. Royal Commission on the Constitution, *Report,* p. 151.
2. J.G.A. Pocock, "British History: A Plea for a New Subject," *Journal of Modern History* 47, no. 4 (1975): 603.
3. The following paragraphs draw upon Richard Rose, "Is the United Kingdom a State? Northern Ireland as a Test Case," in *The Territorial Dimension in United Kingdom Politics,* ed. Peter Madgwick and Richard Rose (London: Macmillan, 1982).
4. See Christopher Hood, *The Future of the United Kingdom: a Probabilistic Analysis* (Glasgow: University of Strathclyde Studies in Public Policy No. 90, 1981).
5. Sidney Low, *The Governance of England* (rev. ed.; London: Ernest Benn, 1914), p. 12.
6. Cf. Michael Oakeshott, *Political Education* (Cambridge: Bowes & Bowes, 1951).
7. A Scottish advocate, John Smith, was appointed as Minister of State to the Lord President on 8 April 1976, but this was after the major decisions of principle had been taken and published concerning devolution.
8. There is nothing unusual in Labour politicians misrepresenting the views of a majority of their voters on functional as well as territorial issues; see, e.g., Richard Rose, *The Problem of Party Government* (London: Macmillan, 1974), chap. 11.
9. That is, the Scottish Council of the Labour Party voted 6 to 5 against a Scottish Assembly at a meeting of 22 June 1974; a majority, 18, was not present. Following decisions in London to endorse an Assembly, the Scottish Conference of the Labour Party was called for an extraordinary meeting on 17 August 1974, and the Conference, with union block votes counted, gave an overwhelming endorsement to devolution. This may explain the apparently abrupt shift in views of Labour supporters in Scotland about devolution. Cf. John Smith, "Portrait of a Parliament," *The Bulletin of Scottish Politics,* no. 2 (1981): 242ff. See also *Interim Policy Statement on Devolution* (Glasgow: Labour Party Scottish Council, 1981).
10. When asked whether it might also be the case that some people were not so much wishing to throw stones at the dough but at each other, the speaker replied, "Yes, you have understood my meaning precisely."
11. D. Braybrooke and C.E. Lindblom, *A Strategy of Decision* (New York: Free Press, 1963), p. 78, recognize that such types of decisions can be taken—but they do not discuss at length their causes or consequences. Cf. Richard Rose, "Coping with Urban Change," in Rose, ed., *The Management of Urban Change in Britain and Germany* (London: Sage Publications, 1974), pp. 7ff.
12. See Richard Rose, "Assembly—English No's and Scottish Aye's," *Glasgow Herald,* 26 October 1978.
13. E.g., the Scottish Labour Party founded by Jim Sillars or various Republican Socialist groups in Northern Ireland. A leftwing Welsh Republican Socialist group, or an SNP that veered left on economic issues, could simi-

larly be expected to lose support. Advocating two major philosophies divides support rather than doubling it. People who might back a Nationalist party may be put off by Socialism, or vice versa.

14. Particularly if North Sea Oil revenues were affected. On the Scottish perspective, see W.L. Miller, Jack Brand and Maggie Jordan, *Oil and the Scottish Voter 1974-79* (London: Social Science Research Council North Sea Oil Panel Occasional Paper No. 2, 1980).

15. See *British Labour Statistics: Historical Abstract, 1886-1968* (London: HMSO, 1971), tables 110 and 162; *Employment Gazette,* August 1981, tables 21, 23.

16. See E. Moxon-Browne, "The Water and the Fish: Public Opinion and the Provisional IRA in Northern Ireland," in *British Perspectives on Terrorism,* ed. Paul Wilkinson (London: Allen & Unwin, 1981), pp. 41-72; and Christopher Walker, "Bright Future for the Terrorists," *The Spectator* (London), 14 July 1979.

17. House of Commons, *Debates,* vol. 988, col. 553f (9 July 1980).

18. See Denis Balsom, P.J. Madgwick and Denis Van Mechelen, *The Political Consequences of Welsh Identity* (Glasgow: University of Strathclyde Studies in Public Policy No. 97, 1982).

19. See Phillip M. Rawkins, *The Implementation of Language Policy in the Schools of Wales* (Glasgow: University of Strathclyde Studies in Public Policy No. 40, 1979); and Peter Madgwick and Phillip M. Rawkins, "The Welsh Language in the Policy Process," in Madgwick and Richard Rose, *The Territorial Dimension in United Kingdom Politics* (London: Macmillan, 1982).

20. See Philip M. Rawkins, "An Approach to the Political Sociology of the Welsh Nationalist Movement," *Political Studies* 27, no. 3 (1979): 440-57.

21. A statement by the chairman of Cymdeithas, Rhodri Williams, quoted in David Hughes, "Cymdeithas at the Crossroads," *Western Mail,* 27 March 1979. For background, see Colin H. Williams, "Non-Violence and the Devlopment of the Welsh Language Society," *Welsh History Review* 8, no. 4 (1977): 425-55. Note also David Hughes' interview with Jim Callaghan, "There Is Loose Talk by Leaders of Opinion Who Should Know Better," *Western Mail,* 9 December 1980; and Oliver John Thomas, "The Bounds of Militancy," *Welsh Nation* 53, no. 3 (1981).

22. See the absence of support for violence against persons and property in pursuit of political aims, as reported in W.L. Miller, "Support for Direct Action in Scotland" (University of Strathclyde Sixth Annual Conference of PSA Work Group on United Kingdom Politics, Glasgow, 14-16 September 1981).

23. A Labour Party member who read this passage in draft sought to challenge this view, but only confirmed it, writing: "Labour does not put maintenance of Union first; it comes after maintenance of the Labour Party and that is why devolution took the peculiar form it did."

Index